Dhow Chasing in Zanzibar Waters and on the Eastern Coast of Africa. Narrative of Five Years' Experiences in the Suppression of the Slave Trade

DHOW CHASING

IN ZANZIBAR WATERS.

LONDON:
GILBERT AND RIVINGTON, PRINTERS,
ST. JOHN'S SQUARE.

Frontispiece.] CROSSING THE BAR IN THE "WHALER" TO RESCUE NEGROES FROM A WRECKED DHOW.

DHOW CHASING
IN ZANZIBAR WATERS

AND ON THE

EASTERN COAST OF AFRICA.

By CAPTAIN G. L. SULIVAN, R.N.
LATE COMMANDER OF H.M.S. "DAPHNE."

London:
SAMPSON LOW, MARSTON, LOW, & SEARLE,
CROWN BUILDINGS, 188, FLEET STREET.

DHOW CHASING
IN ZANZIBAR WATERS

AND ON THE

EASTERN COAST OF AFRICA.

NARRATIVE OF FIVE YEARS' EXPERIENCES IN THE SUPPRESSION
OF THE SLAVE TRADE.

By CAPTAIN G. L. SULIVAN, R.N.
LATE COMMANDER OF H M S. "DAPHNE"

*WITH MAP AND ILLUSTRATIONS FROM PHOTOGRAPHS AND SKETCHES
TAKEN ON THE SPOT BY THE AUTHOR.*

SECOND EDITION

London:
SAMPSON LOW, MARSTON, LOW, & SEARLE,
CROWN BUILDINGS, 188, FLEET STREET.
1873.

[All rights reserved.]

HT1327
S8

CONTENTS.

	PAGE
INTRODUCTION	1

THE CRUISE OF THE "CASTOR."

CHAPTER I.

The "Castor" leaves England—Arrives at the Cape—Her Boats detached—The "Dee"—St. Augustine's Bay—Natives of Madagascar—Angoxa—Slave-trade in 1850—Boat Attack on the Forts of Angoxa—Blockade of the River—Rendezvous on Mafamale Island—Encampment on Island—Routine—A Man up a Tree 11

CHAPTER II.

Cruise of Boats—Quizungo River and Natives—Brilliant Phenomena—Casuarena Island—Provisions stolen by Natives—Short allowance—Arrival of barge—Alexander's grave—Catching a Turtle—Return to Mafamale—A grand Dinner—Foster's Illness—Bleeding a puppy—Foster's Death—Mozambique Graveyard—Mozambique Harbour—Capsized in a Canoe—Cruise among the Querimba Islands—An exciting Chase—Friendly Natives—Fittings of Dhows 31

CHAPTER III.

Method of conducting the Slave-trade—The "Legal Trader's Slave-trade"—Difficulty of distinguishing the Slavers—Escape of Slave Vessels in consequence—Arab Interpreters—Chase of a Dhow—Disguise of Negroes—Negoda's surprise at not being detained—South-West Monsoon—Stormy Weather—False Information—Overboard to avoid the rain—Beam-ends in a Squall—"The fellow wants me"—Return to the "Castor" . . . 57

CHAPTER IV.

The "Castor" at Zanzibar—A Farm-yard on Board—Efforts against the Slave-trade—Expedition against the Keonga Slave Barracoons—Native Violence towards Officers—Punishment of the Natives—Illness of the Crew—The Commodore ill—Put the helm up—The Commodore will put the helm down—An exciting Chase, "That's her"—Disappointment—Portuguese Man of War—Disappears—Return to the Cape 73

THE CRUISE OF THE "PANTALOON."

CHAPTER V.

Passage to Aden—Cairo—Suez Hotel—Passengers—The "Pantaloon"—Aden—Seychelles—Coco-de-Mer—Latham Island—Zanzibar, Agreeable Society there—Limits of Legal Slave-trade—Slave-trade is Piracy—Miserable Condition of the Slaves—Illegal Extension of Slave-trade—Jumah's Information—Dhow passes full of Slaves—Her Crew laugh at us   93

CHAPTER VI.

Visit to the Sultan—Pemba Island—A Licensed Slave Dhow—Negro Infant—Island of Mohilla—Visit to the Queen—Reception—Trincomalee—Return to England 119

THE CRUISE OF THE "DAPHNE."

CHAPTER VII.

The "Daphne" commissioned—Outward Bound—Loss of an Officer—Abyssinian Expedition—Annesley Bay—Arrival at Seychelles—Port Victoria, its Unsuitability as a Depôt—Madagascar—Slave-trade in the Vicinity—Commoro Islands—Mayotte—Tour of the Island—Roman Catholic Schools—Johanna—Mohilla—Changes since former Visit—Proceedings of a Frenchman—Visit to the young King — Mozambique — Kiswara River — Shooting Excursion, Appearance of the Country—Interview with Natives—Return to Zanzibar . . . 131

CHAPTER VIII.

Slave Dhows in Zanzibar Harbour—Important Information — Departure from Zanzibar — Domestic Slaves—Chase of a Dhow—Capture of a Dhow—Chase of another Dhow—Dhow stranded—Slaves in the Water—Rescue of Children in Life-boat—Another Slave Dhow stranded—Perilous Position of the Cutter—Capture of more Dhows—Another wrecked—Dreadful Condition of Slaves—Cruel Treatment on Board the Dhows—Arrival of "Star"—Departure from the Coast—Slaves on Board—Becalmed and drifting 153

CHAPTER IX.

Negro Tribes—Gallas—Naming the Negroes—Marlborough—Negroes feeding—Several die—Small-pox breaks out—Examination of Negroes—Their Stories—Mary Carcesey—First Lieutenant's Employment and Patience—Peggy—Native Languages—Arrival at Seychelles—Put in Quarantine—Negroes Landed—Several marry—Arrival at Bombay 173

CHAPTER X.

Number of Captures in 1868—Departure from Bombay—Cruise on Arabian Coast—Chase of Dhows—A Slave Dhow slips away—Maculla—Visit to the Sheik—Capture of two Dhows—Stories of Slaves on Board—Aden—Condemnation of Dhows—Departure for Seychelles—Capture of Slaver with fifty-two Slaves—Arrival at Seychelles—Visit to old Acquaintance 197

CHAPTER XI.

Zanzibar—French Charlie's Shop, his Promptness—Trip to Darra Salaam—Our Party—The Town—Shooting Hippopotami—Mafamale Strangers—Fish Hawks—Mayotta—Marguerite . . . 207

PORTUGUESE POSSESSIONS.

CHAPTER XII.

Portuguese Possessions, their Claims—Population of Mozambique—Full of Slaves—Ibo—Cape Delgado—Quillimane—No other Portuguese Settlements—The Arabs in real Possession—Conducia—The Portuguese Slave-trade—Free Negroes—A Portuguese Schooner with Slaves in her—Defeat of Portuguese Forces—Their Power confined to one Island 219

CHAPTER XIII.

Condition of Slaves in Portuguese Territory—Cruelty—A Slave flogged to Death—Slaves escape to "Daphne"—Slaves or "Free Negroes"—Refusal to give them up—Correspondence with the Governor—The "Star" in sight—My Promotion—Fernando Veloso Bay—An Interview with the Natives—Their Curiosity—A Mystery—The Rivers of Africa 235

CHAPTER XIV.

Jumah's Death—Visit to his Widow—Arab Mourners—Time of Mourning—Prospect of being married again—The Slave-market—Wretched Scenes—Disgusting Conduct of Dealers—A Farewell to Zanzibar and its various Inhabitants, &c. . . . 247

CHAPTER XV.

Immense Number of Slaves released—Misconception of the term "Domestic Slaves"—Many Slaves conveyed under that Name—Distinction quite clear—What are Domestic Slaves and what are not—What has become of liberated Africans—Tariff of Wages—Efforts to improve their Condition—Missions—The Jesuits 257

CHAPTER XVI.

Aden—Negroes worse off—Somallic Boys at Aden—A good Field for Missionaries—Bombay a worse Place for them—Duty of England to instruct them—Depôt necessary on Mainland—Placing them on Islands an Injustice—Zanzibar the worst Place for them—Johanna preferable, but Mainland only suitable—Possibility of returning to their own Country 269

CHAPTER XVII.

A Bulwark on the Coast necessary—British Stations—Abolition of existing Treaties—Basis of future Treaty—Future Treatment of liberated Africans—Darra Salaam—Indian Garrison—Road to Interior—Intrenched Stations—Instruction, &c., of Negroes—Cost of undertaking a Company—Practicability of Scheme 281

APPENDIX.

	PAGE
EXTRACTS FROM EVIDENCE taken before the Select Committee of the House of Commons	297

MADAGASCAR.

The Chief Secretary of State to Consul Pakenham	381
Extract of Annual Report from Commodore Heath to Secretary of the Admiralty, Jan. 22, 1870	382
La Traité des Nègres de l'Afrique Centrale	384
Translation of the annexed Extract from the *Moniteur Universel*, of Paris, of the 10th December, 1872	385

GERMANY.

Mr. Gordon to the Earl of Clarendon	387
Mr. Cope to Mr. Gordon	388
Baron Von Freydorf to Mr. Cope	389
Memorandum by Dr. W. Schimpfer relative to East African Slave-trade	391
The Earl of Clarendon to Mr. Gordon	414

INTERIOR OF AFRICA.

Dr. Livingstone to the Earl of Clarendon	414
Extract of Letter from Dr. Livingstone to Dr. Kirk	428
The Slave-trade on the East Coast of Africa	429
REPORT OF THE SELECT COMMITTEE of the House of Commons, appointed to inquire into the whole question of the Slave-trade on the East Coast of Africa, &c.	431

LIST OF ILLUSTRATIONS.

	PAGE
Map of the East Coast of Africa.	
Crossing the Bar in the Whaler to rescue Negroes from a wrecked Dhow . . . . . (p. 159) *Frontispiece*	
Badane of the Arabian Coast	102
Bugala, or Dhow	ib.
Matapa Boat of the Northern Rivers	ib.
The Island of Mahe	105
Section of the Dhow alluded to at page 168, showing the manner of stowing Slaves on board	114
A Street in Seychelles	135
Zanzibar Harbour, and Fleet of Dhows	153
Fac-simile of the Condition of one of the Slaves taken out of a Dhow captured by the "Daphne"	161
Group of Negro Men and Boys taken out of captured Dhow in a state of Starvation	168
Group of 322 liberated Africans on the Deck of the "Daphne"	171
Group of Galla Women liberated by H.M.S. "Daphne"	175
Group of Negro Women of different Tribes	176
Lumpy Keboko	178
Group of Slave Children on board the "Daphne"	180
Panoramic View of Darra Salaam	286

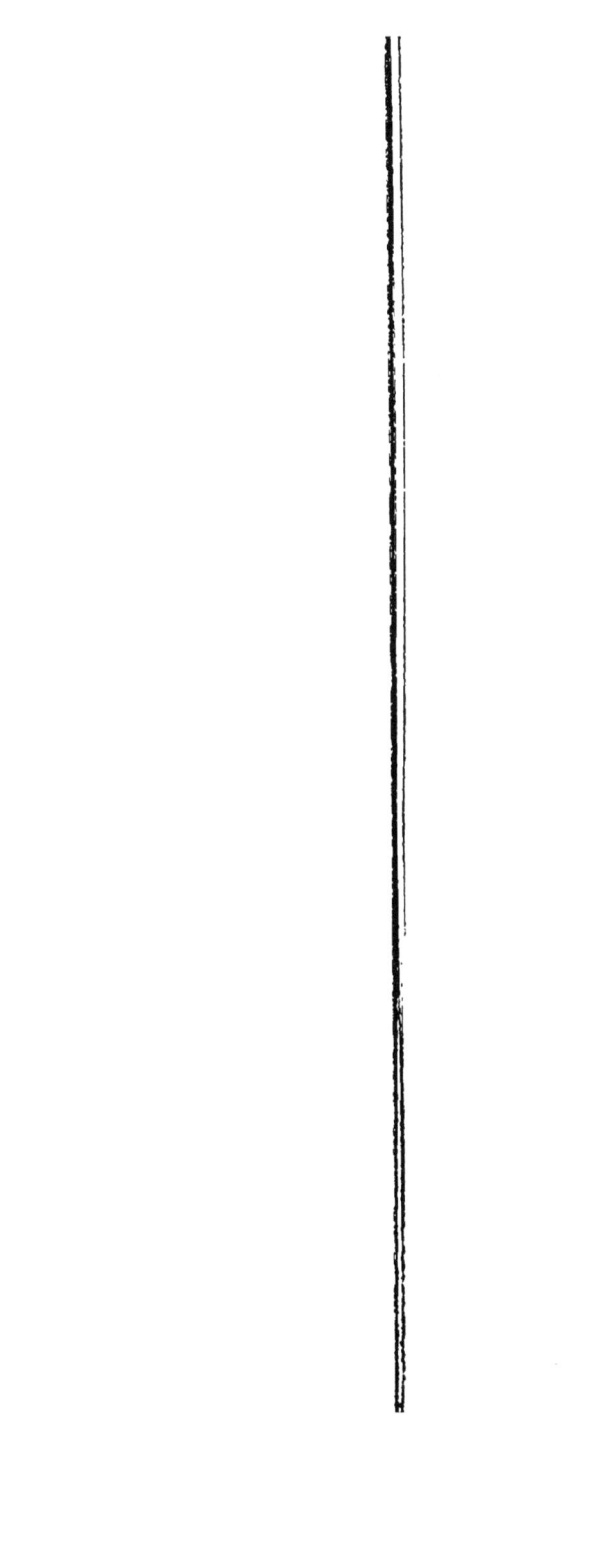

DHOW-CHASING.

INTRODUCTION.

AFTER a few years' lull in the anti-slavery storm, "the old fever," as the Bishop of Winchester calls it, has broken out again: not that it had ever entirely subsided, for there have always been solitary spots where the English flag has prevailed, and this so-called fever has existed, just as there are solitary spots or unfrequented localities where typhoid or other zymotic diseases lurk, and which only become epidemic by some unexpected or sudden meteorological disturbance or atmospheric change. The immediate cause of the appearance of the fever in this case was, as often happens in such outbreaks, local, and may be attributed in no small degree to the renewed efforts of officers employed in the suppression of the slave-trade on the east coast of Africa. They, being eye-witnesses of what was going on, could only conclude that the trade, instead of being diminished by all the costly efforts of England, was rapidly increasing, and that those efforts were indirectly aiding the traffic by enhancing the value of the slaves, and thus making the trade more lucrative. A flame is extinguished by a violent puff of wind, but a slight draught will only make it burn fiercer. It became well-known to many officers on the east coast that those fine points in the treaties with the petty sultans and puny potentates, acknowledging a "legal slave-trade" and "domestic slavery," have acted as an impassable barrier against the abolition of this iniquitous trade; they were aware of the fact that from want of acquaintance with the actual condition of things England had become drowsy and unconcerned, and they could but view with alarm the tendency that appeared in India to allow those clauses in the treaties to be stretched almost to any extent in interpretation. Further, they learnt, with astonishment, that this trade was being openly carried on by British subjects (of India), and, moreover, that in case of any interference with their interests these people possessed the power of arousing dangerous agitation in public opinion in India. These officers found that by giving offence to any of the petty local sovereigns, by increased firmness and decision on their part in drawing the line as distinctly as it is portrayed in the treaties, that they were regarded as affecting the political interests of India and endangering the relations between that country and the parasites surrounding it. As an instance of this, I may mention that an officer connected with one of our Admiralty Courts in India once said to me, at a dinner-table, "If we go on condemning these vessels for having only a few slaves on board, we shall be having our supplies cut off again from the interior."

The result of this state of things has been

that, instead of the horrible traffic being reduced or suppressed, there are at this present time in Zanzibar alone nearly three times the number of slaves imported and exported than there were twenty years ago, and England, though she might have justly expected by this time to reduce her fleets and expenditure, has now, after all her previous costly efforts, to begin again. Yes, whilst these vile cesspools remained undisturbed, though they might have increased in size and number, the fever was only local; now they have been disturbed the fever has extended, and it is with no little pleasure that I say that the clearing out and exposure of these hidden spots by legal sanitary measures, zealously and ably conducted by the officers employed in that service, have in no small degree contributed to the fresh outbreak of this anti-slavery fever. Under the circumstances above stated, I have been induced to publish a brief narrative of my own experience when employed on the east coast of Africa, first as a midshipman, twenty-three years ago, in order to point out how little really was known at that time of the slave-trade as it then existed, and how small the means were for suppressing it; and subsequently and recently, when, in command of H.M. ships the "Pantaloon" and "Daphne," I was enabled to judge of the vast increase of the trade during the interval, and when, in the years 1868 and 1869, I was fortunate enough, with other commanders, to assist in liberating no less than 2179 negroes.

Among the great difficulties which officers meet with in the execution of this duty at first, is the want of personal experience and the absence of any document or record of the experience of others who have preceded them; and it is partly to meet this want, so much dwelt on in the evidence given before a Select Committee of the House of Commons, that I have been induced thus to record my own experience; in doing which I have, in the first place, confined myself as much as possible to a simple narrative of facts, subsequently dwelling more fully on the slave-trade as it now exists on that coast, and especially on that part of it claimed by the

Portuguese. A vast branch of this nefarious trade (that in so-called "free negroes")—which has been almost lost sight of through the apparently sincere profession of the Portuguese Government to abolish it, and through the absence of any European Consul to watch it—is still going on, though in a far more subtle way, to as great an extent as ever, and with greater cruelties than any practised by the Arabs.

I have also endeavoured to point out, that whilst little benefit has hitherto accrued to the trifling percentage of negroes liberated and placed on small islands for the rest of their lives, still less has fallen to the lot of those who have been thrown into the midst of the Hindoos of India with a doubtful liberty and, to some, certain bondage of a worse kind than slavery— uncared for and unthought of afterwards. I have also ventured to suggest a remedy for such a state of things in acknowledging our duty and responsibility to do more for these negroes, and, if possible, to open up their own country and enable them to return to it.

The accompanying engravings, with one or

two exceptions, are from photographs which I was enabled to take at various times when employed on the coast, but not with any idea then of their appearing before the public in their present form.

G. L. S.

February, 1873.

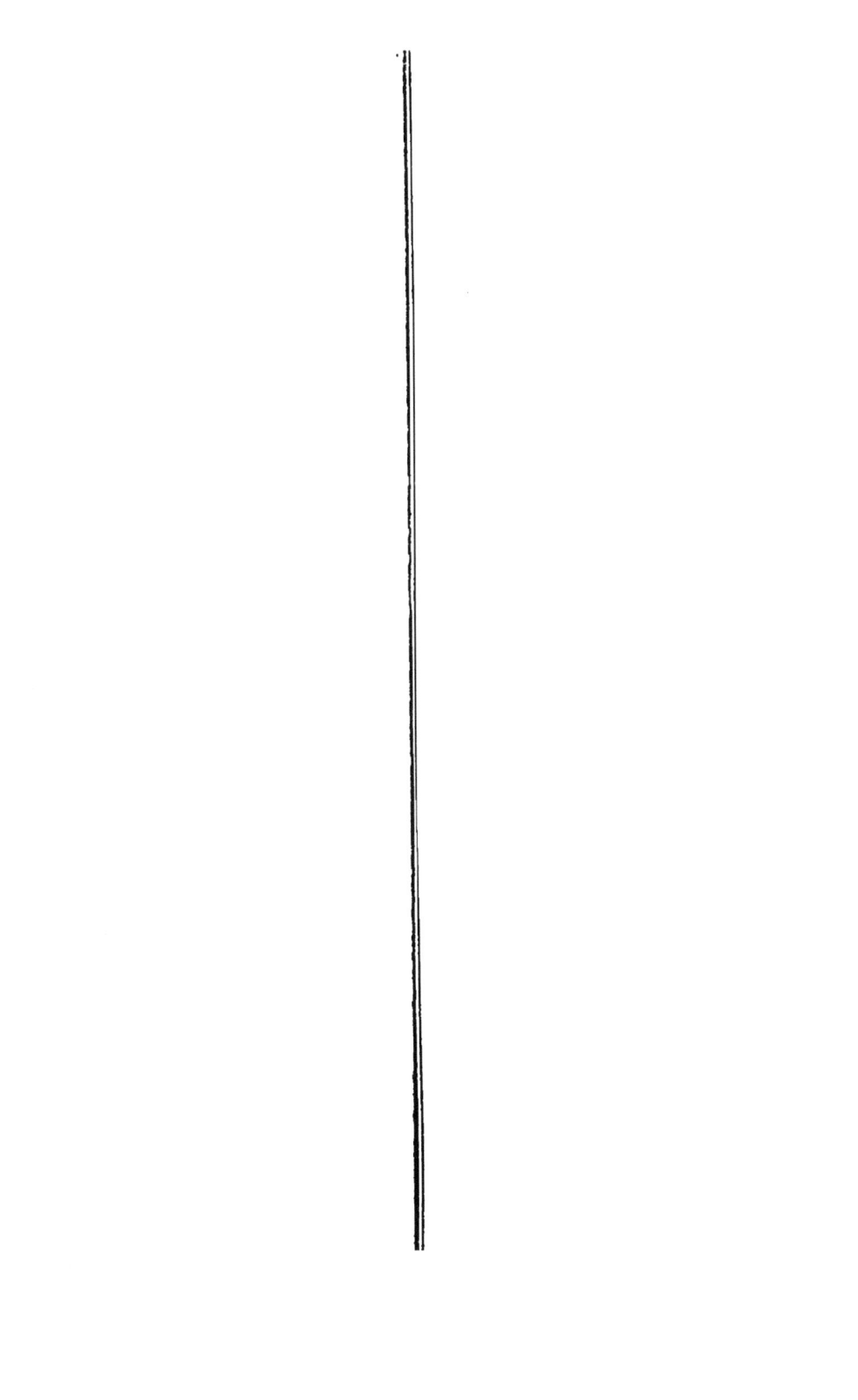

THE CRUISE OF THE "CASTOR."

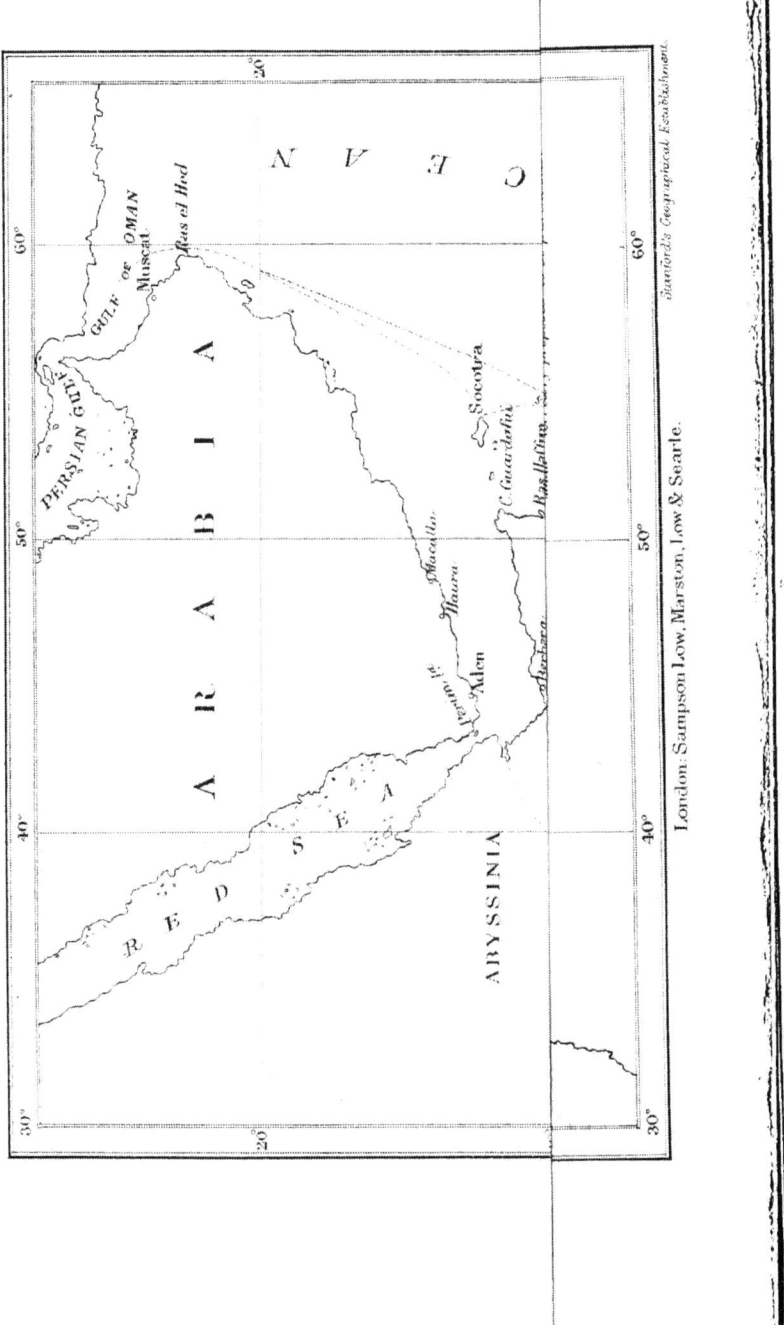

UNIV. OF
CALIFORNIA

THE CRUISE OF THE "CLASIO"

PREFACE

IN May, 1849, I joined H.M.S. "Clasio," commanded by the late Captain ———, the celebrated author of the Discoveries of the ———. [illegible] the cruise of the ship was to [illegible] in regard to [illegible] the supposed [illegible] that was the report has at length ceased to exist. [illegible] actually, it originated probably about that time when Queen Elizabeth, with the view of getting a reserve

THE CRUISE OF THE "CASTOR."

CHAPTER I.

The "Castor" leaves England—Arrives at the Cape—Her boats detached—The "Dee"—St. Augustine's Bay—Natives of Madagascar—Angoxa—Slave-trade in 1850—Boat Attack on the Forts of Angoxa—Blockade of the River—Rendezvous on Mafamale Island—Encampment on Island—Routine—A Man up a Tree.

IN May, 1849, I joined H.M.S. "Castor," commissioned by the late Admiral Wyvil, then a captain, appointed as Commodore of the Cape of Good Hope and East Coast of Africa as far as the fourth parallel of south latitude.

On Friday, the 15th June of the same year, we sailed from Sheerness, the superstition attached to that day by sailors having long ceased to exist. If it ever really existed, it originated probably about the time when Queen Elizabeth, with the view of creating a reserve for her navy and of increasing the number of fishermen in her dominions for that purpose, directed that fish should be eaten on all fast days, or, at any rate, at a time when Mr. Forster's Education Bill would have been treated as sacrilege by a superstitious people who would have trembled at the sight of a magpie and turned pale if the salt-cellar had been overturned.

Towed by the "Sampson" steamer, we reached Plymouth on Sunday, the 17th, and finally sailed for the Cape of Good Hope on Saturday, 23rd June, where we arrived on the 29th August, 1849.

The "Castor" being detained at the Cape on account of the convict dispute in that colony, her boats were detached, under escort of H.M.S. "Dee," to cruise in the Mozambique Channel for the suppression of the slave-trade.

The boats consisted of the ship's pinnace and a barge, a private boat of the commodore, given him by the Imaum of Muscat, when previously on that station in command of the "Cleopatra." With these boats hoisted inboard, the "Dee," under the temporary command of Lieut. Crowder, sailed from Simons Bay, on the 1st October, for the Mozambique Channel and east coast of Africa.

We arrived, after a fortnight's passage, at St. Augustine's Bay, remaining there for two days for the purpose of watering the ship.

It may not be out of place here to give some description of the inhabitants of this part of Madagascar, situated in the south-west of the island, which is, in round numbers, about 700 miles long by 300 broad; St. Augustine's Bay is about 250 miles from the capital. It can hardly be said that it is under the laws or government of the king, for the natives of the villages within a few miles of each other are continually fighting amongst themselves upon the smallest provocation, or to obtain plunder; and so warlike is this copper-coloured race that it has been found too dangerous, indeed almost impossible, to make slaves of them. Intellectually, they are as far superior to the ordinary African negro as are the Somaulies or Gallas in the north of Africa, neither of whom are classed as negroes by the Arabs and so dangerously treacherous are they, that whenever the ship visited this place for provisions or water, in the boats, we could not enter the river without being armed, the arms being, however, concealed under the thwarts, lest the sight of them should provoke the natives to hostilities. On two occasions I witnessed the readiness to refer their disputes to their spears. The first was when visiting it on this occasion, and being at one of their villages in the pinnace, at a place where the river was very narrow, not more than a few yards across, and very deep. As Campbell was skylarking with them, and practising at throwing the assagi or spear, it accidentally went into the river: this enraged the owner, who, by his angry tones, collected a crowd round him that seemed almost equally annoyed; and in vain Campbell offered to pay for the lost weapon. At last matters became so serious that one of our party dived into the river and recovered it, to the astonishment of the natives, who, though expert swimmers themselves, as a rule, looked unusually serious, and their exclamations of astonishment were so great that we could not understand the cause, until told by a French merchant resident there that the river was so full of alligators at that part that no one ever ventured into it, and that only a few days previously a child had been taken off the bank by one of these reptiles.

Another instance was when subsequently there in the "Castor." The boats were stationed off the beach, as a guard over a party from the ship which was employed filling casks with water, to protect the men against any attempt to attack them on the part of the natives. A negro in a canoe came alongside the boat I was in, and offered some fruit and calavancies for sale in a small grass or reed basket: these, together with the basket, were purchased by some one in the boat, who received it out of the canoe. He then shoved off, but returned soon after and demanded the basket back, saying it was not part of the bargain; when, on its being refused him, he shoved the canoe off a few yards, exclaiming, "Then me fight for it!" at the same time lifting his spear, which, had it been thrown, would have been a signal to the rest of the native canoes for a general attack on the white men, and we should have had a similar occurrence to that which took place two years previously a few miles to the north of this bay, when a boat's crew belonging to the "Cleopatra," commanded at the time by our commodore, and consisting of Lieut. Molesworth and ten or twelve men, were attacked and massacred within a few yards of the ship, while laying out an anchor, the whole of the canoes escaping to the shore before the "Cleopatra" could get a gun to bear or fire a single shot at them. This occurred at a place on the west coast of this island that has since been known by the name of Murderers' Bay; and, seeing the serious consequences that must have ensued, the basket was returned to the man, who appeared to be greatly pleased at having got what I suppose he thought the best of the bargain.

We sailed from St. Augustine's Bay for Angoxa (pronounced Angoza) on the 9th November, and anchored off that river on the morning of the 15th, when the boats were hoisted out, manned, and armed, in preparation for exploring the river the next day.

It will be remembered that at this time slavery had not been abolished in the United States, South America, Portugal, or the Spanish settlements, therefore there was a large trade going on with these countries from the east coast of Africa, which, being considered safer than the west coast for the slavers, owing to the number of cruisers on the latter station, although the distance was greater, was for a long time the favourite coast for shipping the slaves, both with the Spanish and American traders. These vessels were generally disguised as whalers until a fitting opportunity presented itself, and when they thought the road was clear they would anchor at the entrance of a river and, aided by the dhows, in one night would take in cargoes of several hundreds of slaves, and be far off the coast the next morning. At that time there were so few cruisers in this part, and the slavers were kept so well informed as to their movements, that capture was impro-

c

bable. It was usual for the men-of-war to remain on the south part of the coast, and in doing so it was impossible to keep a check on the vast coasting-trade then, and still, going on from Quillimane to Mozambique, from Mozambique to Zanzibar, from Zanzibar to the Persian Gulf, &c. The Portuguese settlement, Quillimane, is about the most southern slave depôt, and at Mozambique, their principal fortress on the coast, the largest slave-market was held, not even excepting that of Zanzibar, which is another source of that great human "Nile" which continually increases in magnitude as it runs north and empties itself into the slave oceans of Persia, Arabia, and Egypt; but with this difference in the case of the two rivers, that whereas the sources of the great liquid river are replenished and supplied again from the ocean, the sources of this human stream are being exhausted and dried up from the want of fresh supplies; for the children, being considered of even greater value than the adults, are kidnapped from the country in great numbers, and the population is thus being reduced at the rate of upwards of 180,000 a-year, not more than a third of which, however, reach the chief markets on the coast, as numbers are either killed or die of disease before their march of three or four hundred miles from the interior is over. To give some idea of the number of negroes that are shipped or exported from the coast annually, the lowest estimate from Zanzibar territory alone has been 20,000 a-year, allowing the tax to be 1*l*. per head; giving the Sultan an income of 20,000*l*. a-year derived from this trade. That this estimate is far below the actual number exported is, however, proved by the fact that the highest tax on any slaves amounts only to sixteen shillings per head (four dollars); therefore the Sultan's income of 20,000*l*., said to be derived from this tax, would represent 25,000 slaves; but his income in 1867-68 amounted to about 56,000*l*., or 270,000 dollars (see the Hon. C. Vivian's evidence before the Select Committee, q. 23). If the former sum of 20,000*l*. may be taken as representing the number of slaves exported in 1860 (Major-

General Rigby, in his evidence before the Select Committee, gives 19,000*l.* for that year) the latter sum of 56,000*l.* may be fairly taken as the Sultan's income from the same source in 1870, and will enable us to form a just estimate of the increase in the trade to Zanzibar since that year. But these figures do not represent more than one-half of the trade in slaves on the east coast, for they do not include either that great branch of this human traffic carried on by the Portuguese to the Commoro Islands and Madagascar—and sometimes, too, under the French flag—nor does it represent that portion of it that passes the Zanzibar dominions as it proceeds north by the coast to Arabia, the Persian Gulf, and the Red Sea, without touching at these markets or paying any tax to the Sultan. But, in addition to all this, on the east coast there is an extensive slave-trade being carried on from Abyssinia, through the Red Sea, to Egypt, for an account of which we refer the reader to the memorandum of Dr. W. Schimpfer relative to the East African slave-trade, in the Appendix. What country in the world could stand such a constant drain on its population? and must not the evil of thus rendering that great continent agriculturally barren, checking all trade and produce, be felt throughout the world, perhaps for centuries? The immense wealth of Africa which now lies buried and dormant is yet, I believe, destined to be brought to the surface, when its trade will take the place of the present iniquitous slave traffic and be a benefit to all the other nations of the world, while that which at present is carried on only feeds the lust and avarice of a few uncivilized Arabs, and is a curse to mankind.

On the morning of the 16th November the boats of the "Castor" and "Dee" were manned and armed and proceeded up the river Angoxa. It was known that for several years this river had been entirely in possession of the Arabs, who had a large fortified town of the same name which was a great slave depôt on this part of the coast. The strength of the Arabs on the coast, and the utter inability of the Portuguese to cope with them, may be judged by the fact that although some years previously one or two Portuguese regiments, assisted by the boats' crews of the "President" and "Eurydice," endeavoured to take the place, they were repulsed with heavy loss, the "President" and "Eurydice" having several men killed and wounded, and, notwithstanding the lapse of time, this so-called Portuguese territory was still in the hands of the Arabs, who, as was subsequently proved, would have been willing to enter into a treaty with England which at that time would have been considered an advantage, and, although they would not have consented to suppress the slave-trade entirely, such a treaty would have gone far to curtail it in that locality and have facilitated the operations of the cruisers on that part of the coast.

Our little fleet consisted of the following boats:—"Castor's" pinnace, Lieut. Campbell, myself, mid., and twenty men, with one 12lb. gun; barge, second-master C. Albert, Patterson, mid., and fifteen men, with one 3lb. gun; "Dees'" first paddle-box boat, J. T. Jones, second master, a mid., and about eighteen men, with one 18 pounder; "Dees'" second paddle-box boat, Dyer, master's assistant, and about eighteen men, with one 18 pounder; gig, Lieut. Crowder, commanding expedition; cutter, Dr. Evans.

We proceeded up the river to ascertain if any slavers were in it or under the piratical slave fort of Angoxa, where the barracoons were continually kept full of slaves ready for shipment. We never thought of landing to destroy these barracoons, as was sometimes done on other parts of the coast, for it would have been out of the question with so small a force. Some of the boats grounded on a sandbank at the entrance, where we remained until the tide floated us again, when we proceeded up the river in line and anchored inside Monkey Island. In the evening, after spreading the awnings for the night, the boats being anchored close together, songs were sung alternately by each crew, "the mainbrace was spliced"—that is to say, an extra allowance of spirits was served out, in which quinine was mixed, the spirits compensating for the disagreeable taste of the tonic—" Sweethearts and wives " were toasted, and merry-making kept up until a late hour.

Early the next morning, November 17th, we proceeded farther up the river towards the town, but our approach had already become known to the Arabs, who were able to collect an immense force from the neighbourhood, besides that in the town, which has a population of about 1000 inhabitants; the Sultan of Angoxa lives five or six miles from the town. The fort, at the time of the attack made on it by the Portuguese, already alluded to, had six large guns mounted in it and a force of about 2000 men, Arabs and negroes: its strength had been increased since then. At one o'clock we opened the bend of the river, and to our great satisfaction observed a vessel hauled close underneath the fort—to the right of it; as we appeared in sight a red flag was hoisted on shore and an incessant beating of "tom-toms" and drums commenced and continued until, advancing with the rising tide, we approached near enough to the fort, when, at four o'clock, as we rounded the point within 200 yards, the stockade opened fire, with round shot and grape, wounding two men severely. The boats now advanced towards the fort in line, abreast, returning its now well-sustained fire with shell, grape, and canister, grounding occasionally, for we were still advancing with the rising tide, and there was scarcely water enough at the highest to get close to the stockade. Our object was either to cut out this vessel—a large dhow of about 100 tons hauled close on to the beach with her bows high and dry—or to destroy her. Some of the Arabs were firing musketry from her at one of the "Dees'" boats on the right, which was sufficient to justify us in destroying her without examination. In less than a quarter of an hour the fort was silenced, the spherical case-shot fired from our boat—the only one that could fire shell—bursting so accurately within the stockade that it soon drove the Arabs into the wood on the right or behind the vessel, from which they kept up a fire of musketry; but the grape and canister from the "Dees'" paddle-box boats were too much for them there, and about five o'clock poor Dyer,[1] in one of these boats, was able to get under the stern of the dhow, boarded, and set her on fire. While he was doing this the Arabs came out of the woods and opened fire of musketry on his boat's crew, wounding two of the men severely. At 5.30, the vessel being destroyed and the stockade and woods silenced, we retreated to our previous anchorage for the night, just in time to prevent our being left high and dry by the now receding tide, in which case we should probably have been surrounded and had a more serious tale to tell; as it was we had several men seriously wounded, and one who was reported mortally so, his ribs being smashed by a grape-shot, but, to the astonishment of the doctor and himself, he eventually recovered, after being more than two months in his cot.

Off the mouth of this river Angoxa, and about seven miles from it, there is a low, sandy island about three quarters of a mile long, called Mafamale, having its centre and highest

[1] Dyer, a few months after this, was drowned on Quillimane Bar, his boat being capsized.

part, probably about four or five acres in extent, covered with casuarine-trees and thin grass: round the outside of it is a coral reef, extending from N.E. by S.E. to S.W. It is one of the Premeira group of uninhabited islands, inside which there is a good channel, varying from six to eleven fathoms in depth, with good anchorage near them. On this island two "four-ton" tanks were landed from the "Dee" and two months' provisions for the "Castor's" boats, pinnace, and barge, or "Imaum," which were now to be stationed off this part of the coast, having Mafamale as their rendezvous and head-quarters, to blockade the river and suppress the slave-trade on the south of it between these islands and the mainland. A camp was pitched on the island, where the boats remained alternately.

On the 20th we took up our quarters on the island, and the "Dee" sailed on the following day for another part of the coast. Our encampment consisted of four tents for officers and men, one for provisions and stores, and another at the extreme end of the little wood, for ammunition.

The south and south-east of the island, protected by the reef, proved an admirable harbour for the boats, while at the head of the beach a blacksmith's forge and a carpenter's bench, under tents, constituted our dockyard establishment.

Our usual routine was to bathe at six and breakfast immediately, then, after cleaning arms and inspection, to wander about the island collecting oysters—which adhere plentifully to the rocks, but require a hammer or tomahawk to break them off—and occupy ourselves in various ways until dinner at 1 p.m.

In the evening we generally, after bathing again, hauled the seine on the west of the island, when we invariably got more fish in the first haul than was sufficient for ourselves, and what we did not use was salted for the ships on their visiting the island, so long as we had empty casks and salt sufficient for the purpose. Our dinners had very little variety in them, they generally consisted, for officers and men alike, of what was known amongst us by the name of "kettler," and was by far the most popular dish at our command. It consisted of everything that was to be cooked, excepting fish, being put into the same boiler, beef or pork cut up, fowls, peas, biscuit, flour, and fresh or preserved vegetables, with various seasonings, according to the taste and fancy of the cook of the day; this was supplied, alike to officers and men, in the good old-fashioned willow-pattern basin, and when served out it was of that consistency that no one would have disputed the expression whether you said that you had eaten or drunk it; it resembled Scotch hodge-podge, and was always devoured with a relish and an appetite that many an alderman would have envied; and he would perhaps have gladly exchanged even his turtle soup for the "kettle" beverage if he had tasted it.

I need scarcely add that the officers had a stock of beer with them, and the empty bottles were piled like shot on the island, having rather a formidable appearance, and proved in a pecuniary point of view of as much value empty as full, being used when the boats entered the rivers in bartering with the natives for fresh provisions, eggs, &c. There was a good look-out kept from the island, and at noon it was regularly recorded in the log, in a more literal sense than is usually understood by the expression, that there was—

"A Man up a Tree."

CHAPTER II.

Cruise of boats—Quizungo river and natives—Brilliant phenomena — Casuarena Island — Provisions stolen by natives — Short allowance — Arrival of barge — Alexander's grave — Catching a turtle — Return to Mafamale — A grand dinner — Foster's illness — Bleeding a puppy — Foster's death — Mozambique Graveyard — Mozambique Harbour — Capsized in a canoe — Cruise among the Querimba Islands — An exciting chase — Friendly natives — Fittings of dhows.

ON the 23rd of November, leaving the barge with Albert and Patterson at Mafamale, we proceeded in the pinnace to the south, anchoring under shelter of Hurd Island, another of the wooded banks in the Primeira group. The following morning we continued our course south, cruising between the islands and the main-land until the 29th November, when we entered Quizungo river in search of water. Crossing the bar, we anchored off a village a short distance up the river. The natives, who at first seemed to view us with suspicion, would not come near us, but at last, on our making signs to them that we were friends, and throwing them some empty bottles, they approached us in their canoes, and, after receiving tobacco, &c., for what they had to sell in the way of fruit and eggs, they showed us where we could obtain water and helped us to fill our casks. Leaving the river again before dark, we stood along the coast to the northward for the night, keeping a look-out for dhows.

Sailing along the coast during the night, with scarcely a ripple on the water and just enough wind to fill the sails, one of the grandest scenes I ever witnessed, and of which nothing but familiarity could lessen the charm, presented itself to our eyes. The starlight was so brilliant that every object was as clearly visible as in a bright moonlight night in England. The low coast lay outstretched before us from north to south;

the men were all asleep, and the silence was only broken at intervals by the flapping of the sail or an extra ripple against the bows of the boat, caused by a "cat's paw" of a breeze, but beyond and over that long extent of coast, only a mile or two from us, was one almost incessant sheet of lightning illuminating the distant hills and broad extent of sea with the brilliancy of daylight and bringing the outline of the whole country into full relief. The flashes of lightning succeeded each other at intervals never exceeding five seconds, and their duration was at least twice that period. This brilliant phenomenon lasted half the night, but the lightning was too far off for the thunder to reach us. The scene became familiar to us afterwards, losing much of the charm of novelty, but never shall I forget that first night when we remained under-weigh in the boat and I watched that supernatural light, with almost rapturous awe, till nearly blinded by the sight, and, in the absence of any accompanying noise of storm, was reminded of the "still small voice" in the sacred writings.

On the 1st December we anchored under Casuarena Island, and on the 3rd we returned to Mafamale, having seen nothing in the shape of a vessel of any kind since our departure.

We found the "Dee" had returned to the island, completed us with provisions, and left again.

This was the sort of service in which for several months we were engaged with these boats. On one occasion we met with anything but an agreeable adventure. We had left Mafamale in the pinnace with a month's provisions, and, finding so large a quantity stowed in the boat very inconvenient, as it left little room for our crew of twenty-one men to lie down, on arrival at Casuarena Island we buried three weeks' stock of it on the beach. This consisted of a large pork cask, several tins of preserved meat, some bags of biscuit, a bag of tobacco, some kegs of rum, and one magazine of reserved ammunition. The pork cask, unfortunately, was only just covered by the sand.

The island is thickly covered with trees and dense bushes, dried grass, &c., and we were just about to leave it for a few days when a spark from one of the men's pipes fell on the grass, which instantly caught fire, like tinder, and commenced smouldering rapidly. We thought, with a few buckets of water, we had extinguished it, so we left the island for the southward, where we remained cruizing for about a week; but on our return we observed the smoke ascending in dense columns and the whole of one side of the island apparently in a blaze. There had been, fortunately, a great down-pour of rain that morning, which must have put out the fire; but on landing we found that our provisions were gone. They had evidently been dug up, and, as if those who had done so expected more might be buried, there were a great number of pits dug round the spot. There was not even a remnant of anything to be found. The trees for a circle of about fifty yards' radius were burnt down to the roots and were lying on the ground in ashes, with the outlines of the trunks, branches, and even leaves, as beautifully defined as if they had been traced with a pencil.

In vain we searched for tin cases or staves of

the casks; so, coming to the conclusion that the natives were hidden on the island among some of the bushes, we marched through it in skirmishing order—not at all easy work, as the ground was thickly covered with thorny bushes, making a perfect jungle. But on arriving at the other side, a much cooler locality, for the remains of the fire gave out immense heat, there we saw enough to tell us what had become of our lost goods and that the culprits had escaped to the mainland.

We arrived at a pretty accurate conclusion as to the cause of all this from the appearance of the beach and the manner in which the sand covered the side of the island where the fire had taken place. It was evident that the intense heat had produced such a whirlwind in that part of the island as to draw up the fine dry sand from the beach around it in such quantities as to uncover and expose our provisions. The natives from the mainland, about eight miles off, must have been attracted to the island by seeing the fire, and on landing discovered the provisions, and had also dug in the several places mentioned, but, finding that part of the island too hot, had withdrawn with their prize to the other side, where we found the remains of a bonfire at which their feast had evidently been cooked, some of the staves of the pork cask, several empty preserved-meat tins, and the backs or shells of two or three turtles, that had probably also landed on the island to ascertain what the illumination was, but were not so fortunate in their adventure as the other animals. Nothing more, however, was to be found, and no doubt the provisions which were not used at this grand "blow out" had been carried off to the mainland before our return. Nor could we trace anything about the place to lead us to believe that the expressed wish of one of the crew had been realized, namely, that the natives, after walking off with the rum and tobacco, might take enough of the former to cause them when puzzled, as they would be, to open the powder-magazine, to try and do it with a red-hot poker.

The result of this loss was that for a few days we had to go on very short allowance until we could return to Mafamale. We sailed from these islands in the evening, but, owing to a light wind and strong current against us, were compelled to return to Casuarena; and, wishing before we started again to clear out and thoroughly clean the boat, we erected tents on shore with the boat-sails and rain-awning, Campbell and I having ours pitched round a small mound, which served as a table by day and a pillow by night. We were at our breakfast the next morning when the barge was reported in sight, coming round the point, and a few minutes after Albert walked into the tent. "Well," said he, "we had almost given you up, and thought you must have been lost; but I certainly never expected to find you where you are—what a melancholy position! Do you know you have pitched your tent on poor Alexander's grave?" He was a lieutenant who had died on board the "Cleopatra." We certainly had thought little of what the mound might be, but, from some cause or other—probably of the inconvenience of moving everything under the tent, or possibly from not wishing to be thought superstitious—we did not remove our tent until we struck it a day or two afterwards and left the island in company with the barge. Albert and Patterson had a great laugh at us for losing our provisions, when we suggested to them that they would have had more cause to laugh if they had not joined us with the barge, for in that case they would not have had, as now, to divide their provisions with us; and so we turned the laugh against them.

We were still, however, even now on short allowance to make the provisions hold out, but no one seemed to care so much for that as for the loss of the tobacco, which was sorely felt by those who smoked; moreover, there was no reserve of that at Mafamale, and we did not know when the ship would return to provision us. But necessity is the mother of invention, and a substitute was found by drying our tea-leaves, which were smoked and declared, by one or two who tried to put the best face on their misfortunes, to be preferable to tobacco, though they did not, I am bound to say, adhere to their opinion when tobacco was forthcoming again.

On the morning after leaving Casuarena, with a light breeze and scarcely a ripple on the water, we observed a turtle asleep on the surface within a few yards of the boat. Waiting till we had passed it, fearing the pinnace would make too much noise, we launched a canoe we had on board, and into this Albert and one of the crew got, with a rope, and, paddling quietly up to it, slipped a running bowline over the fin of the turtle, which instantly dived, but, being caught, towed the canoe at some rate after it. All would have gone well had not Albert jumped to the end of the canoe to assist the man to haul in, when down she went and, being made of the bark of a tree, sank like a stone, leaving her late inmates on the surface looking exceedingly foolish. We were, however, soon on the spot, and they got on board again with no further inconvenience than a good wetting.

We returned to Mafamale and had the satisfaction of seeing the "Pantaloon" brig,

Captain H. Parker, arrive on the 5th January, to supply us with provisions. It was resolved to invite Captain Parker and the officers to dinner, and an invitation was sent in the following terms:—" The governor and officers of the island request the pleasure of the company of Captain Parker and officers of H.M.S. 'Pantaloon' at dinner at five o'clock."

The invitation was accepted, and at the appointed hour the boat of the "Pantaloon" brought the guests on shore. A guard of honour was drawn up to receive them, and a substitute for a band was supplied by two or three fifes, with a tin pot for a drum.

The officers having first walked round the island to inspect it, were much pleased and interested with the arrangements of our camp. When dinner was announced, we proceeded to the tent. The banquet consisted of "kettler soup," a variety of fish, " kettler entrées," fowls, salt junk, pressed vegetables, and yam, with plum-pudding *à la* lower deck, and an ample supply of beer and rum.

After dinner the party left the tents to

witness a game of "rounders" played by the boats' crews, and then adjourned to the beach to haul the seine, by which a large supply of fish was secured and sent off to the ships' company of the brig; a very jovial evening was then passed, every one of us being compelled to sing, whether he could or not, the rule adopted being "That he who could not sing should be made to sing, or else to drink a pint of salt and water." The toasts were various:—"The Queen," "The captain and officers of the 'Pantaloon,'" "The boats' crews," "Sweethearts and wives," and "An end to slavery," concluding with "God save the Queen." After which Captain Parker and the officers re-embarked, with the same guard of honour, and with the addition to the band of ALL the pots and pans that we possessed.

Poor Parker, little did I think on that pleasant evening that in less than four years I should see you bravely fall in an engagement with the Russians at Soulina!

Hitherto the health of the crew had been

very good, in spite of much to try it, and this was probably owing to a strict compliance with the three rules contained in the orders received by Campbell—namely, never to remain in the rivers at night or sleep on shore on the mainland; never to allow the men to sleep without being under the rain-awning, with their blanket, frocks, and trousers on; and last, though not least, to insist upon the extra allowance of spirits, which was to be served daily in the boats, having in it a due proportion of quinine, or bark, which indeed was the condition of their receiving it at all. But we had now been two months away in the boats, and bodies of men under a governing head are very often like children, who, realizing no individual responsibility, leave all the thinking and acting to their superiors, and become careless of themselves and sometimes pig-like under restraint. It was probably some carelessness among the crew in not keeping under the awnings at night when they found it oppressively hot inside, and probably the loss of strength, owing to the climate and to the discomforts of the boats, as we were sometimes several days without sleeping out of them for an hour, that were beginning to tell on some of the crew, for a boat thirty-two feet long stowed with provisions for a week or two is not a convenient resting-place for twenty or more men, though we all thought it a most delightful kind of life. But a gloom was cast over our Christmas by the fact that two of the crew were seriously ill with fever; these men were J. Foster, A.B., and a coloured man, known by no less a name than "Robinson Crusoe," a native of the west coast, who had been in our service from a boy; we had no medical man with us, but had been supplied with medicines, the knowledge of which on the part of our acting doctor, Albert, was decidedly limited.

"What's to be done, Albert?" said Campbell; "Foster is dangerously ill."

"I don't know," said Albert; "but I think he ought to be bled."

"Have you no more medicine?"

"No; I have given him all the emetics."

"All the emetics! why that's enough to kill him."

"Well, then, he ought to be bled."

There was a consultation of officers and men on this proposition; all thought he ought to be bled, but who could do it? No one was sufficiently confident in his skill to be willing to attempt it. It was at last decided that Campbell and Albert should practise on "Castor." Now Castor was a young dog of four or five months old who never could be in better health than he was at that time, and besides, when referred to on the subject, he expressed, in the most decided terms he was master of, his objection to be operated on; but might was right, and Master Castor, being secured in spite of all his struggling and entreaties, was first examined to ascertain if he had any veins, and if so, where they were to be found. But, after being punctured here and there with a penknife with a questionable point, he was pronounced "veinless." It was found, however, that a little blood could be obtained from the paws, but as poor Foster's paws were differently constructed it was deemed unadvisable to try the experiment, so it was at last decided to take the man to the Portuguese settlement of Mozambique, where they were probably more practised surgeons than at Mafamale.

On the 27th December he was placed in the pinnace for conveyance there—but a hundred miles in an open boat against wind and current is not the best remedy for a patient with the fever at its height, and we leave the reader to estimate the chances of his recovery. The pinnace returned in about a week with the intelligence that, after a three days' passage, they had landed poor Foster and placed him in what was called a hospital at Mozambique—and the next we heard of him was that he was dead.

We do not know if the Portuguese doctors were in possession of diplomas or not, but one thing is certain, that, even if they were, an English subject for dissection was as rare to them as the anatomy of the canine species was to a sailor. I have visited Mozambique several times since, but, though Foster is not the only Englishman I have known to be buried there (we buried one from the "Dee" after this), I have never been able to trace a grave there of any kind in what is called the graveyard for Protestants and foreign heretics, except one in which Commander Dacres and another officer of his ship are buried, the relations of whom sent out a stone and iron rails to be placed round the same, which has had the effect of at least keeping it more sacred than the rest of the unprotected ground of irregular mounds and pits, that give one the idea of the ant-hills of the East more than anything else, and where may be seen loitering, quarrelling, squabbling, gaming, fighting, selling cattle, &c., those half-caste Portuguese, a species of human nature that goes far to confirm the truth of the Darwinian theory.

We continued cruising on this part of the coast until we proceeded to Mozambique, of which, together with other parts of the Portuguese possessions on this coast, I shall give some description hereafter.

Early in the month of February we left the island of Mafamale for Mozambique, where we remained with the "Dee" for some days.

While the "Dee" was anchored in this harbour it was our custom to bathe within the paddle-wheels, for the harbour is so full of sharks at all times that it is not an uncommon occurrence for negroes at work on the beach, when wading to the boats to clear them, where the water is not more than two or three feet deep, to be attacked and taken away by these voracious creatures that may constantly be seen around the ship. Within the paddle-wheels of the vessel, however, we could bathe in safety. On one occasion when Jones the second-master and I were so engaged, some natives made their canoe fast to the wheel and left it to go on board the ship; we both got into the canoe and paddled away from the side, imitating the native action and manner, but with a little too much vigour, until we overturned the canoe, which immediately filled with water and sank under us. We were then at some distance from the ship and struck out most eagerly towards it, feeling almost certain every moment that we should become food for the voracious sharks; indeed, once or twice I fancied one of these rascals was touching me with his nose, taking a preliminary sniff as one does with a glass of exquisite wine before carrying it to one's lips, this, however, only made me redouble my efforts of propulsion towards a boat which was made fast to the boom of the ship. Jones, however, was wiser than I, and had made direct for the paddle-wheel again, and was safely arrived there at about the time I had reached the boat. I had intended to get on board from the boom and then to walk along the deck to the wheel, but, to my horror, on reaching the boom I found the deck covered not only with the crew, but with about a hundred ladies and gentlemen, who, though all of them as naked as myself, were black, so it did not signify to them; but a naked white man would have looked singular and made a very conspicuous figure amongst them. The question was whether to face them or the sharks again, and of the two evils I chose the lesser; so looking into the water as far as I could, to see that there were none of the rascals close at hand, I dived from the boom, and, with my eyes all round me while under water and thinking every flash of light was a hungry enemy, I came up underneath the wheel, and was laughed at unmercifully by Jones for not striking out for it at first.

From Mozambique we proceeded in company with the "Dee" to the Portuguese settlement of Ibo, which was now to form the chief rendezvous for the boats; and from thence we were to cruise northward between the Querimba Islands and the main so far as Tongy Bay or Cape Delgado— from ninety to a hundred miles of coast; but as these islands were not considered so healthy as the little sand-banks to the southward, we had no head-quarters on shore, but were strictly confined to the boats.

Before speaking more fully of the slave-trade itself, I think it may be well to give some further account of the cruise of the boats, and also of the ships, so far as my own experience is concerned, which I think presents a fair representation of the usual life on the coast.

We were about to have a very different experience now for upwards of two months more. The rainy season was shortly coming on and we had no camp on shore to retreat to, though owing to the weather, we needed it more than when to the southward—but we never once slept out of the boats. Our ship was still at the Cape, though she had been expected for some time, and we had received no fresh orders in reference to the boats' proceedings. Campbell had been ordered away in charge of a Spanish prize captured by the "Pantaloon," with, I think, four hundred slaves in her, and called by the misplaced name of "The Philanthropy."

Our pinnace was now under the command of Mr. Jones, second master of the "Dee," whose cheery disposition and good temper made him well suited to take the place of Campbell, who, with a similarly cheerful spirit, had succeeded in rendering every one happy in the boats, and in making the service a most agreeable one.

Starting from Ibo at daylight on the 15th of February, with a fair wind, in company with the "Dee's" cutter, we steered to the northward, inside the islands, and anchored at noon under the lee of Maheto Island. From the top of a ruin on this island, we observed what appeared to be a large vessel steering north, and immediately proceeded in chase of her. We had received some information relative to an armed American vessel in the neighbourhood waiting for an opportunity to escape with a cargo of slaves, and as we neared the chase, it was soon pronounced to be a barque; for two hours with a light wind and oars did we pull to the northward and westward after her, now apparently gaining, now losing.

"It's a barque," said Jones; "she has just set her royals, and hauled up more."

"Well, she's inside, out of the current, and we are in the heart of it, and that's how she's gaining."

"If it's the Yankee she'll fight for it."

"Mount the gun."

This done, we gave way again with the oars. The cutter was not far astern of us now.

"It's a Yankee," said the coxswain, looking at her through the glass; "I'd swear to it by her sails."

"She's bore up to run for it," said another, and various were the opinions of those who were not pulling. The gun was loaded, and pointed with extreme elevation, with a view of "letting her have it when near enough;" but a breeze sprang up, and cleared the haze away. The goddess was turned into a laurel, that she might be saved from Apollo :—

IT WAS A TREE!

Occasionally we landed at some of the villages, and were received generally in a friendly manner. However, this was dangerous, as the natives have often proved treacherous, after being on the most friendly terms. On one occasion we landed at the village of Tongy, and were received with some ceremony, and much hospitality; the first being exhibited by numerous negroes singing, or rather howling, in wild, plaintive tones, accompanying their voices with the monotonous beat of the tom-toms. Walking up to the hut of the chief, we were presented with some fowls and rice, and were assured by him that he never had anything to do with the slave-trade,—a statement which we knew how far to give credence to.

We boarded several dhows on this coast; and it may be asked, If the slave-trade is so extensive, why none were captured? some of these dhows must surely have been slavers, or had slaves in them? And so they had, no doubt; but no one in the boat had had any experience in the service before, and we had no interpreter with us, so that we could find out little or nothing about those we boarded, excepting the name of the place they sailed from and whither bound; nor had we any instructions or documents relating especially to the East Coast trade, or the experience of any officers who had been engaged in that service previously, to give us information as to the numerous dodges practised by these Arabs. We expected to find "fittings," "tanks," planks, shackles, rice, if not fettered negroes[1] doubled up in them, according to the experience gained by some of those who had seen the captures of American and European vessels, or which we had learnt to look for from the wording of the official instructions on the subject. There were, however, no such fittings or preparations necessary in these dhows, though in some of the northern vessels, and in a few of those that are employed in carrying on the legal slave-trade under Zanzibar colours and papers, extemporized bamboo decks are used, to enable them to stow their slaves in "layers."

[1] I have never seen a fettered negro in any of the dhows on the East Coast, and I doubt if any one else has, though many are to be seen on shore, in Portuguese territory.

CHAPTER III.

Method of conducting the Slave-trade—The "Legal Trader's Slave-trade"—Difficulty of distinguishing the Slavers—Escape of Slave Vessels in consequence—Arab Interpreters—Chase of a Dhow—Disguise of Negroes—Negoda's surprise at not being detained—South-West Monsoon—Stormy Weather—False Information—Overboard to avoid the rain—Beam-ends in a Squall—"The fellow wants me"—Return to the "Castor."

THERE are three distinct forms of this trade, which may be classed under the following heads:—

1. The illegal slave-trade;
2. The legal slave-trade; and
3. The *so-called* "LEGAL TRADER'S" slave-trade.

Of the two former we shall speak hereafter. It was the last we had most to do with here, because we were south of Cape Delgado, which is the southern limit of the dominions of the Sultan of Zanzibar (or of the Imaum of Muscat as he was then), and therefore no slave-trade was legal where we were.

The "legal trader's slave-trade" sounds paradoxical, but though it always appears to have existed, it is only latterly that there has been any attempt to recognize it, within certain limits, as a legal proceeding, and yet it is by far the most extensive of the three. As regards the two former there can never be any dispute.

By "legal trader's slave-trade" is meant that trade carried on in the coasting dhows which are engaged legally in conveying the produce of the country: ivory, copal, hides, rice, and corn, and in illegally smuggling a few slaves on board, or as many as they can stow conveniently with the least possible risk, but which have no licence or authority for conveying them even in Zanzibar territory, where it is possible to obtain such licences. The negoda (i. e. captain), whether he be owner or not, purchases a few slaves at the first port he puts into, and increases their number at each port as he proceeds north, until, as the dhow nears the destination it is finally bound for, where the inconvenience will be felt but for a short time longer and the risk of capture is almost "nil," she has become filled with slaves stowed in all manner of ways, and unless the cargo is such as they can be fed from, they are in a starving condition.

A common practice exists amongst Arab passengers in these dhows to pay the negoda for their voyage by bringing a slave with them from the shore, the proceeds of whose sale at a northern market yields the passage-money; it is just such cases as this that have been made use of by some persons to prove that dhows have been captured with only domestic slaves on board, and such cases are the most difficult of proof, because the Arabs, who know full well the English view and meaning of "domestic slaves," will swear that they are such. Such a case was that, no doubt, brought before the Select Committee,—I allude to the case of the "Petrel," which captured a dhow with Arab passengers on board, and six wretched creatures, whom the Arabs declared were "domestic slaves," as they will say and swear anything to deceive the authorities and gain their point.

Knowing, as I do from experience, what a few slaves on board a dhow really means, knowing also what the term "domestic slaves" signifies on the East Coast, I can only regret that the question of the slave-trade on the East Coast of Africa has not earlier fixed the attention of the British public, that its true character might be understood; and I cannot suppress a feeling of pride that our determined efforts at its suppression, although they have raised the ire of the petty chiefs on the coast (who, being subjects of our Indian Empire, managed to obtain the sympathy and interference of the Indian authorities, by whom, through being misinformed, the matter was misjudged), have at last had the effect of bringing the whole subject before the world.

By taking in at each port two or three slaves in a tolerably healthy condition, they can pass a considerable number off as part of the crew; and, without an interpreter who can read the ship's papers, ascertain the number allowed for the crew, number of passengers, &c., and cross-question the negroes themselves, detection is almost impossible.

When, however, the number reaches, as it often does in such vessels, to a hundred or more, it is necessary to adopt some other plan. Twenty or thirty, perhaps, are told off to represent part of the crew; the half-dozen Arabs, who are generally on board and concerned in the matter, dress up some of the women slaves, each representing one as his wife, and sometimes he is fortunate enough to have two; the remainder of the negroes, or as many as possible, are dressed up in Arab costumes, turbans, &c., and called passengers, and they too sometimes have their wives sitting by them, if the women are too plentiful to pass off in any other way. All these are usually arranged round the ship in dumb silence, which is sufficient alone to create suspicion in the experienced; and it is in this way, by taking in addition to their cargo as many negroes as they can possibly have a chance of passing through that these so-called "Legal traders" convey, perhaps, one third of the slaves to the more northern market. This plan, however, is generally frustrated, if there be on board the cruiser, a native interpreter who can detect a slave in a moment, however attired, as officers who have had any experience sometimes can, for a few questions to one or two of the poor creatures through the interpreter,—such as, where they came from, and how they got there? —are sufficient. But we, having no interpreter, were unable to put such questions, and how many vessels escaped us in consequence it is impossible to say; but we boarded on this part of the coast sometimes two or three dhows in a day, and, recollecting how full many of them were of Arabs and negroes, I feel convinced from subsequent experience that hundreds of slaves must have so run the gauntlet and passed us, through our then ignorance of this so-called "legal trader's" method of carrying slave cargoes.

It must not be lost sight of, however, that the interpreters are Arabs, who until they have associated for years with Europeans, can never understand why a successful "sharp trick," by fraud, or lie, is not a commendable achievement. It is not, therefore, to be wondered at that one of these should have been discovered—even though engaged in one of our cruisers, and receiving pay and prize-money—giving false information to his captain in order to get the ship out of the way of a slave dhow in which he had a pecuniary interest. And while speaking of interpreters, I will add, that unless they are allowed some advantage in the shape of prize-money for captured vessels, their information will be unreliable; they make so many enemies among their own countrymen by acting as spies and informants against the slave-dealers, that they endanger their lives, even to hair-breadth escapes. If they receive pay only, there is nothing for them to gain by the taking of a slaver, and they will run no such risk, but will play into the hands of the Arabs.

On the morning of the 15th March, we had an exciting chase after a dhow, which there would have been no chance of overtaking had it not been that the wind fell to a calm which enabled us to use our oars, and on our going on board we found a numerous and grotesque crowd arranged round the vessel much in the manner described above. There were about twenty or thirty negroes pretending to be very busy accomplishing wonders in unstowing or stowing some cargo, rolling up sails, hauling taut ropes that ought to be let go, and letting go ropes that ought to be hauled taut; they had no doubt been frightened into this vigorous and deceptive action by the usual Arab story that—"white man eat black man if he get him."

About twenty more black men were dressed up in Arab costume, having a few negresses by their sides, who never before were so rolled up in cotton, lashed up like hammocks, with nothing but their eyes appearing; and half a dozen genuine Arab brutes, one of whom appeared to be "monarch of all he surveyed." By the unaccountable faith of an Englishman, that all languages are so far inferior to his own that bad English most resembles an unknown tongue, and therefore of course ought to be understood, we thus cross-questioned these anxious looking nigger-drivers, who made themselves equally understood to us in their Arabic as we probably did to them in our mutilated English. "How you do?" (shaking hands with every one who chose). "Where you come?" "Where you go?" when as if they understood what they were asked, or the signs accompanying the question, they moved their hands first to the south, then to the north, and spoke the words "Mozambique" with the first, and "Zanzibar" with the second wave of the hand. "What dem nigger der?" They point to the sails, and make a motion with their hand like that of hoisting it, "Oh, dem crew men." "Who dese?" Another wave of the hand from south to north, and a good deal of jargon in which the words "Mozambique" and "Zanzibar" again occur. "Oh! suppose dem passengers." "Where am papers?" This we make them understand by writing with the forefinger of the right hand on the palm of the left. The papers are produced; they might have

F

been for all we knew, Bills of Sale for the niggers on board, or warrants for their execution; or, more probably, directions as to where our boat was, how to avoid it, or to cut the throats of every Englishman if they could get the chance. We could do no more, we had no proof of her being a slaver, or that what they had given us to understand was not true, and we knew so little of this trade, and had no conception of its being carried on in that way; indeed, the efforts of the cruisers were directed at that time chiefly against American and European vessels, which were supposed to be carrying on the most extensive trade. We left the vessel, with the astonished Arabs in ecstasies of delight, and by way of expressing their overflowing gratitude, and surprise too, perhaps, at our not taking their vessel, they passed two or three fowls and several cocoa-nuts into the boat: a gift which boat-cruisers were not likely to refuse, seeing that we were on salt provisions, and what was worse at that time, preserved meats, for it was just then that the contractor for supplying these meats thought it necessary to reside in America, to avoid apprehension, it having been ascertained that he was actually supplying the Navy with offal under the name of preserved meats.

The south-west monsoon was beginning to make its way north, and was felt now in this latitude for two or three days. I find in the log a force of 5 recorded, with rain. The 17th was the first day we had any really bad weather. On this day it commenced blowing very hard, and the wind increased until it was necessary to keep the boat under weigh, the island not affording shelter enough; the seas were washing over the bows and flying deck,[2] keeping us pretty well employed baling out, with now and then a heavy squall of wind and rain—such a downpour as is only known in those latitudes. It was necessary to shorten all sail, and impossible to spread the rain-awning. This and the following day were the worst we ever experienced in the boat. We had sometimes a

[2] A temporary deck, about eighteen inches broad round the gunwale, extending as far as the after-thwart, and made to ship and unship.

foot of water in her before the rain was over; and we were unable to light the fire for nearly two days, and therefore feasted on raw salt pork and biscuit. On the afternoon of the 18th, the gale was at its height, and the wind reached a force of about 8; we were enabled to anchor for a few hours the first night, the wind having fallen light for a short time, and the evening of the second day found us safe under the lee of Caiamimo Island. Can it be wondered at that on that night, wet and miserably uncomfortable, I smoked my first pipe—and enjoyed it!

The next day the weather cleared, and on boarding a dhow we received information of a three-masted vessel off Pengany Point. We had yet to learn that it was a common practice among the Arabs if they wished to get the cruisers out of their way with the object of making a run, to give false information; it is more than probable that the nagoda (captain) of this dhow knew that there was a slaver to the southward of him, bound for the river he was entering, and wished to get us to the northward before she hove in sight. We innocently took the bait, weighed and ran to the northward to chase this phantom, one of many such "Flying Dutchmen," but of course we never found her, and were agreeably surprised to find the old "Imaum" barge there, which had been some time at Mozambique undergoing repairs. We were not long in company with her, however, as she was ordered to cruise in a different part of the coast.

We were now experiencing anything but agreeable weather; at one time the sun was fiercely hot, and again hidden by a storm-cloud which brought down such squalls and showers of rain, that literally we found it necessary to jump overboard to keep ourselves dry. The fact was, we were limited in our costume to one day and one night suit of clothes, and spreading the rain-awning in the daytime, in such squalls of wind, was not always practicable. The plan we adopted was to leave two men in the boat when under weigh, put our clothes under the tarpaulin to keep them dry, and jump overboard until the rain ceased. This we have done as many as ten or twelve times a day; therefore it was not to be wondered at that by the time we had been a fortnight from the ship, we found it necessary to send the cutter back with several sick men, there being two or three cases of dysentery, and one or two of fever, including those of the cutter, and among them Mayne, the second master, who was in charge of her.

Considering the many times we were in the water, as above described, I have often wondered we never saw a shark outside or a crocodile in the rivers, but then we were never alone in the water—this we made a rule of; possibly the number of outlying islands and reefs may account in some degree for our not seeing sharks; yet I have always felt convinced that sharks are the greatest cowards possible, they will always look twice at their food before touching it, indeed they go backwards and forwards repeatedly before making up their minds to take it, and although it must be confessed they are very dangerous customers when you are alone in the water and the ship gone ahead, yet even in this case, if you keep up your courage and make a good splash in the water with your feet, they will be afraid of you.

On the 5th of April, when entering Revooma River against the current of about three knots, we were taken in the heaviest squall we had yet experienced, which literally threw the boat on her beam-ends. It was the work of but a few seconds; fortunately, every rope, being pretty well worn and almost rotten by that time, the sheets carried away, and the main halyards being let go, she "righted" just in time, the weight of the provisions bringing her up again instantly, but with the water in her nearly up to her thwarts; had she sunk, not one of us could have been saved, for the shore was a mile off, the current running out, and the cutter not in company with us; for we had lost sight of her two days before, and were then searching for her.

We had now fifteen officers and men left in the boat, including one of the engineers of the "Dee," Mr. Roberts, who had come with us as an amateur; four more of the crew were now ill with fever, and amongst them Roberts, who one night became so delirious, that on my waking up, I found him just getting into the water.

"Where are you going, Roberts?"

"The fellow wants me," he said, as he swam away from the side; so, going after him, I persuaded him that "the fellow" was in the boat, and induced him to return and get on board again, or, rather, I got him lifted in, for he was too weak to mount the side by himself. We returned to Ibo a day or two later, and discharged the sick to the "Dee;" then, having filled up the vacancies in our crew, left again for the northward.

At noon, on the 19th April, we sighted the "Castor," and at 3 p.m. we returned to the old ship, having been nearly seven months away from her; but notwithstanding this we all felt sorry to give up cruising in the boats.

CHAPTER IV.

The "Castor" at Zanzibar—A Farm-yard on Board—Efforts against the Slave-trade—Expedition against the Keonga Slave Barracoons—Native Violence towards Officers—Punishment of the Natives—Illness of the Crew—The Commodore ill—Put the helm up—The Commodore will put the helm down—An exciting chase, "That's her"—Disappointment—Portuguese Man of War—Disappears—Return to the Cape.

ON the 29th April the "Castor" anchored at Zanzibar. There were no such things as condensers supplied in those days, and ships requiring water had to obtain it from the shore, the chief cause of most of the diseases, I believe, both on the East and West coasts.[1]

[1] And subsequently, when serving out here, diseases (especially dysentery) could be traced to the water drank on shore. We never lost a man in the "Daphne" of disease, and never had a case of dysentery in her that I

Zanzibar has so greatly increased in importance, commercially, since that time, that any description of it would be out of place here: suffice it to say that then, as at present, the water was abominable, and it was that obtained at this and other places on the coast, that subsequently spread dysentery through the ship with fatal results. The Imaum of Muscat, to whom the island belonged, was there at this time. The usual civilities were exchanged, and the undeviating custom among the Arabs of giving and accepting presents gone through, the Commodore receiving a very handsome Arab horse from his Highness, which remained on board for nine months, until the ship returned to the Cape, by which time it could do everything but smoke a pipe, and it is not certain that in another month it would not have done that too, for there were many efforts on

remember, until our return to Bombay, after giving leave to the men. We had been nearly two years in commission, and six months of that was spent in the Red Sea, where, however, nothing but condensed water was used.

the part of the crew to teach it that accomplishment.

The Sultan entertained the Commodore and officers at a dinner, but sat aloof from the table himself, it being against the religion of a Mohammedan to eat with Christians.

Having received some twenty or thirty bullocks, besides sheep, pigs, &c., which made our main deck appear more like a farm-yard than a battery, we sailed from Zanzibar for the southward; in fact, our main deck usually had this appearance, for we were seldom, if ever, without quantities of live-stock in the ship, otherwise we could not have remained on the coast so long as we did. I remember, after sailing from Johanna, once having as many as fifty bullocks between the guns on the main deck, besides sheep, &c. On one occasion, after receiving a number of them on board, the Commodore, who was always astonishing us with something original and inexplicable, came on deck and found one of the men stowing the hay intended for these animals, as he had been directed, under the spanker-boom. Starting back at seeing him, and lifting up his hands as an expression of astonishment, he exclaimed,—

"Captain B——, Captain B——. What's that man doing?"

"Stowing the hay, sir."

"Stowing hay? By G—, Captain B——. What's his rating?"

"Able seaman, sir."

"A. B.?—Not fit for it; send for the clerk, disrate him, he can't make a haystack."

The man was accordingly disrated, and remained so for some time.

From this time to February of the following year we continued to cruise on the coast, leaving it only once during that time to refit at the Mauritius, and never did British man-of-war, since the blockading days of the French war, enter a port needing repair more from truck to keelson.

For several weeks we had been on a reduced allowance of provisions and water; and as far as vessels to eat or drink out of were concerned, in the midshipman's berth, and I believe many lower-deck messes too, we were reduced to cocoa-nut shells to eat out of, cocoa-nut shells to drink out of, and one of my messmates I remember, was reduced to a cocoa-nut shell for washing in; some uncharitable brother officers afterwards asserting, to his annoyance, that the same cocoa-nut shell answered all three purposes with him.

After refitting at the Mauritius, in October we returned to the cruising-grounds on the coast.

It must not be supposed that because we were not capturing vessels that the trade was not an extensive one, but then the efforts were not at that time so much directed against the coast trade in slaves as against the slavery carried on by European and American ships. I do not believe that the extent of the coast trade was then fully known, and we had seldom more than three cruisers off the East Coast, which extended nearly to the Equator.

The Indian Navy was supposed, at that time, to be engaged in the suppression of the trade to the north of this, where it exists in its greatest strength, but we have it in evidence before the Select Committee that it was by no means an enviable position for an Indian officer to place himself in that of the captor of a slaver.[2]

I must now recur to the early part of our cruise; after returning to the ship, in consequence of information received that the barracoons at the town of Keonga were full of slaves which had just arrived from the interior, and were ready for being shipped, the boats were manned and armed, and proceeded under command of Captain Bunce to that town, for the purpose of attacking it, burning the barracoons and liberating the slaves: it was supposed to be well defended. We approached the town in broad daylight, and as the tide was scarcely high enough, anchored and break-

---

[2] The difficulties attending the suppression of the slave-trade with regard to the Indian Navy were so great, that the officers belonging to that service never made any captures. In the Courts of Justice in Bombay, a Captain, after having made a capture, was deprived of his command, in order that the evidence of the officers might not be influenced by him; so that very few captains took the trouble to capture slavers, in fact, I have heard them say they put the helm the other way and went away clear of the dhow whenever they came across one. *Vide* Mr. Churchill's Evidence, Q. 333.

fasted in sight of it, which of course gave the Arabs warning and time to get every slave into the interior, if there were any there. After breakfast we landed on the beach in front of the thickly growing mangroves, and as the boats grounded some distance out, we had to wade on shore. Now, our leader was a very little man, and cared less for the enemy than for getting wet, and moreover it is very doubtful had he tried to wade, how far the water might have gone towards engulfing him, and as this applied also to others, not taller than he, they wisely used the shoulders of the tallest men to mount on, but by some unfortunate accident or other our brave little leader had fixed upon the very tallest of his crew to carry him on shore, who, whether for his own convenience or the commander's, had lifted him in the most unceremonious way possible, and tucked him under his left arm as he had tucked his rifle under his right, the commander's head and shoulders sticking out in front, and his legs drooping down behind with his knees bent to keep his feet clear of the water, in which most undignified position in front of every one he was waving his sword in his usual energetic manner, and in dangerous proximity to his coxswain's nose, exclaiming, "Come on, come on, my lads, skirmishers advance!"—"Fall in on the beach!" &c. After the men were formed, we marched at the double up a little narrow lane or pathway through the mangroves, and on emerging on the other side came in front of the village, which was at the head of a regular slope with a kind of trench and stockade on the summit. At the top of the slope a solitary Arab appeared, waving his hand for us to stop, and asked through the interpreter what we wanted as there were no slaves in the barracoons. He was told we had come to destroy those slave-prisons, and, if resistance were offered, the town itself also. He replied that if we only burnt the barracoons they would not resist us, but if we burnt the village they would fight. It was finally agreed that he should direct us to the former, and that having set fire to them we should return to the boats, and not injure the village. This was done: no slaves were found there, as no doubt they had been marched into the interior on our approach. The best way would have been to have surprised the place just before daylight in the morning, in which case we might have discovered it full.

The inhabitants of one of these villages, after several times receiving the boats' crews in a friendly manner, proved so treacherous on one occasion, that they seized two of our officers on their landing there, Lieut. Campbell, R.N., and Lieut. Reed, R.M., under the plea that they had not paid for the water taken from the neighbourhood; they then lashed them to a tree, and informed them they would be shot at sunset. The boat's crew at this time were in their boat, laying off, and the midshipman, Mr. Staples,[3] on being apprised of what had taken place, mounted the gun and covered it over with a sail, got the men under arms, but wisely refrained from opening fire, as it would have insured their putting their threat into execution immediately. The natives at last

[3] Subsequently lost as Senior Lieutenant in the "Arab" brig.

offered to release the officers for a musket and a piece of cloth; this they received, and then made further demands, which were also granted, and then more still; until at last Campbell said he would give nothing more unless cast off from the tree. This the chief eventually ordered to be done; and Campbell managed to draw him away some distance from his men, and then placing his hand upon him told him through the interpreter that he would shoot him (holding a pistol to his face which he had concealed in his pocket), if he did not walk with him down to the boat, or if any one of his men came near to help him. This was effectual, and between Campbell and Reed the chief was marched to the boat singing out to his men, some hundred or two, not to approach him or he would be killed.

In consequence of this insult the boats of the "Castor," "Orestes," and "Dart" (the frigate's tender), were manned and armed, and sent up to the village to attack and burn it down; they found the village deserted, but, as a lesson to the natives in future, set fire to every hut, and what was more serious to them, for the huts can be built in a few days again, cut some of their cocoa-nut-trees down, which take seven years, after being planted as young trees, to produce fruit. They seldom build the huts excepting where the trees are well grown.

It will not be necessary to dwell longer on the cruise of the "Castor." It would throw no light on, and convey no idea of the present condition of the slave-trade. We were not fortunate in making any captures, the destruction of two slave-dhows by the boats being the only success we had met with. The "Pantaloon" and "Orestes," were more fortunate, however, having taken two or three American or Spanish ships, one or two of which were full of slaves. The monotony of an unsuccessful cruise up and down the coast affords but little to write about, I must not neglect to mention, however, that towards the close of this cruise, the climate, the water, the short allowances of provisions, and the constant boat-work had by that time produced such an effect on the crew, that in December or January, incredible as it may appear, out of our complement of 320 men, from which must be deducted about 50 attached to the "Dart," her tender, we had 113 on the "sick-list," chiefly with diarrhœa and dysentery, from which we lost several men.

But Commodore Wyvill was most energetic and indefatigable in his efforts to what is called "strike a blow" at the slave-trade, the estimate of which expression has been judged rather by what might be expected from such a vast expenditure of lives and money than by the extent of the trade itself; but, on my part, I confess that it reminds me of my early school-days, when I have heard a tiny urchin informed indignantly by some one who wishes to get up a fight that another boy had hit him. "Did he?" says the astonished youngster, as if he was not aware of it; "just let him do it once more." However, no efforts were spared with the means at his disposal, and, notwithstanding the serious condition, physically, of the crew, he would, I believe, have remained much longer on the coast if there had been any reason to suspect a slaver of being there, had it not been for the urgent representation of Dr. Chambers, that unless the ship proceeded to the Cape we should lose many more of the crew.

"Yes! yes! yes! doctor," he said, on one occasion, "but I have information of a large barque in Mazemba river. I am just going up to take her, and then going to the Cape."

That evening there was a violent ring at the bell, and immediately after the "orderly" was chasing over the ship for the doctor and master.

The doctor entered the cabin first, with the master at his heels.

"Doctor, doctor, I am very ill, seized with violent pains here," placing his hands on his stomach. "Master, master, put the helm up and steer for the Cape."

Now, if ever a physician could be justified in not immediately relieving his patient, this would have been a case in point; but our surgeon, whose predecessor had died, had but recently joined, and, therefore, was, perhaps, not well-acquainted with this patient's requirements. It did not surprise us to hear the next morning, what some who had served in the ship from the beginning had predicted, that the master had been sent for at daylight and ordered to steer for the northward again, but that the doctor had not been required since the first visit. It is due, however, to the memory of the Commodore to state that whenever an officer became seriously ill, as some did, he had him brought to his cabin and supplied him with wine and other luxuries, which he alone by that time possessed, and without which these officers could not have recovered.

It was a few days after the above occurrence, about 8 p.m., when off the river Mazemba (all the boats being away, each in charge of one of the lieutenants of the ship), that a vessel was reported to the windward, steering towards us, with studding-sails set. There was no question at the time but that it was the vessel we were in search of, and as soon as she was seen—it was just becoming dark—all sail was shortened and the ship hove to, the topsails lowered on the cap to prevent her seeing us. It was dark soon after, so that we lost sight of her for about an hour, and then we observed her close on the weather-beam, steering straight for us, but evidently not having seen us.

The Commodore, occasionally, as he looked at her through the night-glass, ejaculated, in ecstasies of delight, "That's her! that's her!" It was about 11 p.m. that she had come so close to us we were able to hear the clatter of voices in the confusion that arose on her deck at their discovering us, and the scramble consequent upon having to put the helm over and trim sails to clear us. When just as she came within a few yards the silence in our ship was broken by the stentorian voice of the Commodore hailing her: "What ship is that?" which was replied to in the most squeaking tones imaginable.

"De Portugee man war schooner 'Don ———' What is dat sheep?"

The reply to this question, accompanied by a tremendous stamp of the foot, was a most unearthly sound, produced by the vibration of lips, tongue, and throat. It was something between a roar and a rattle, which must have been utterly unintelligible to the Portuguese Captain, who nevertheless appeared perfectly satisfied, if one may judge by the "Oh! very well," he responded with.

If the Commodore were disappointed, none of us were less so, the difference being that he could give vent to his feelings, which had he not afterwards given us an opportunity we never could have done.

"Make sail and keep her away!" was the order.

Now, with 113 men on the sick-list, fifty in a tender, and half the remainder, nearly, away in boats, this was not likely to be done quickly, and certainly not quick enough for our chief, whose next order was, "Shift top-sails!" but before the men were aloft this was countermanded by the order, "Beat to quarters, man the port guns, and fire four rounds of blank cartridge!" Now, it so happened, that this was the side on which the schooner was nearly becalmed a couple of hundred yards off. The first four or five guns were fired nearly together, and their report was followed by screams from the little ship that were only drowned by the repeated "bang, bang," from our guns, which increased the consternation on board her. Sails were lowered, and voices from terrified men heard hailing us in what appeared to be entreaties for mercy. This ceased with the firing, and when the smoke had cleared slowly away the schooner had disappeared.

Alarming apprehensions prevailed for some time with those who were witnesses of her proximity; for she was never heard of for ten months afterwards, when she was found five miles above the town in Quillimane river, secured to a tree by a hawser, with no one on board her but a nigger; the crew having resolved, I presume, never again to risk the sea while a British frigate was on the coast. A few days after this the boats returned, and the "Castor" proceeded to the Cape, where she arrived on the 5th February, just sixteen months after we had left it in the boats for the Mozambique.

On arriving here we found the Kaffir war had

broken out, and a naval brigade, to which I was attached, was landed from the ship at Buffalo Mouth for service there; but as this does not come within the limits of my subject, I shall now bid adieu to the "Castor."

THE CRUISE OF THE "PANTALOON."

THE CRUISE OF THE "PANTALOON."

CHAPTER V.

Passage to Aden—Cairo—Suez Hotel—Passengers—The "Pantaloon"—Aden—Seychelles—Coco-de-Mer—Latham Island—Zanzibar, Agreeable Society there—Limits of Legal Slave-trade—Slave-trade is Piracy—Miserable Condition of the Slaves—Illegal Extension of Slave-trade—Jumah's Information—Dhow passes full of Slaves—Her Crew laugh at us.

FIFTEEN years later, namely, on the 11th of May, 1866, I left Southampton in the Peninsular and Oriental mail-steamer "Syria," to supersede Captain Purvis in command of H.M. Sloop "Pantaloon," eleven guns, then on the East Indian Station. This was not the

"Pantaloon" previously mentioned, she had long since been broken up.

A passage to India *viâ* Alexandria, in a mail-boat, though so familiar an event to some, has nevertheless many incidents connected with it worth relating, and which to me, at the time, were quite novel. Of course, there was the usual pitching and tossing, and consequent retirement of the passengers for periods varying from twenty-four to seventy-two hours, and their gradual reappearance, one by one, when more accustomed to the motion of the steamer.

If Mr. Bessemer should succeed in his plan of preventing sea-sickness by means of a suspended saloon, he will be a universal benefactor; but there is one motion in a ship which, of all others, I believe to be the most productive of this unpleasant malady, and unless Mr. Bessemer should be able to place his vessel on fixed rails, or Britannia should rule the waves smoother as well as straighter, I fear he will not succeed in counteracting; this occurs when some freakishly disposed vessel, anxious to make herself as disagreeable as possible to strangers, suddenly mounts the crest of a wave,—and we suppose, in such a case, Mr. Bessemer's saloon would accompany her,—as if resolved to pitch those unprepared for such a proceeding into the clouds, and then, even more rapidly, descends into the depths again, as if intending to leave them there; it is just this last act of a vessel determined to make you sea-sick, that is the most effectual, when she appears to sink beneath you, and leave you behind.

Although the passage to India has been so often described, there were one or two points of interest connected with it that may not be thought unworthy of mentioning; the Suez Canal was not at that time finished, so on arriving at Alexandria, the passengers left the mail-boat, and started by train for Cairo, where they remained the night, awaiting the arrival of the passengers *via* Marseilles, who were to go on in the same steamer with us from Suez.

The next morning, however, as they had not arrived, visits were made to the Pyramids,

Turkish Mosque, &c., after which, finding the heat and dust of Cairo almost insufferable, some left for Suez, where they arrived at 8 p.m., and found great relief from the cool sea-breeze, and the delightful refreshment of ices, which could not then be got at Cairo. We had an opportunity also of seeing one of the most interesting sights on the passage out, namely, the hotel at Suez, with its strange concourse of people.

The hotel is built in the form of a square, enclosing a very large open court, covered only by awnings. In this court are several long tables, large enough to accommodate about 300 persons—there must have been nearly that number at the *table d'hôte* on this occasion. Steamers are constantly arriving on both sides of the Isthmus, bringing fresh supplies of passengers, who congregate here on the way. There were people of all nations, chattering away in their various languages, and producing such an amount of discordant sounds, as fully to illustrate the impossibility of building the tower of Babel. Now and then, while dinner was going on, this noise would suddenly cease, and the voices would be hushed to the more agreeable strains of a very good string band; but no sooner was the last note of music struck than chattering commenced, at first like distant thunder, but immediately increasing to a mighty roar; while the clatter of knives and forks added considerably to the effect, till you had to scream to be heard by those sitting next you. There were men and women from Hong-kong, from Shanghai, from Australia, Calcutta, and Bombay; there were Chinese, Japanese, Turks, and Parsees, and representatives of almost every nation, European, Asiatic, African, and American. There were invalid sailors and invalid soldiers; there were fresh-looking Englishmen going abroad, and sallow-faced ones coming home; some there were who had never been home for half their lifetime, and some going out probably never to return; some returning with more than they bargained for when they left home, in the way of small wives and large families, others with nothing but broken constitutions and premature old age; some there were who appeared never to have known a sorrow or anticipated a care, others, more experienced, were silent and sorrowful; some were joyous and some sad, and some were one when they should have been the other. Interesting as it was to us all, this one day was quite enough to impress the scene on the mind indelibly.

The next day, Sunday, 27th, the remainder of our party arrived. We then embarked in the "Carnatic," which sailed early 'the next morning for Aden and Bombay.

I shall briefly allude to the remainder of the passage by quoting from my diary. I remember hearing of a certain elderly lady who departed this life some fifty years ago, who kept a journal, in which constantly occurred the alternate entries: "Peter drunk;" "Peter sober." The following entries are much in the same style:—

"*Monday.*—Heat great. Thermometer 95°. Passengers very silent.

"*Tuesday.*—Heat very great. Passengers who had come so far as Alexandria in the same steamers sociable. Passengers who had come in different steamers, unsociable, reserved, and grumpy.

"*Wednesday.*—Heat greater. "Passengers *viâ* Southampton improved their acquaintance by criticizing passengers *viâ* Marseilles. Passengers *viâ* Marseilles played chess, &c., together, and always looked as if they knew something the other party would like to, but didn't.

"*Thursday.*—Thermometer 98° night and day. Passengers by Southampton steamer laughed and talked together as they had never laughed and talked before the other party joined. The former played croquet on deck, the latter backgammon below.

"*Friday.*—Mr. B——, one of the passengers, died of heat apoplexy. There were four other cases of heat apoplexy among the crew, which, however, were not fatal.

"Anything like the heat I have never experienced, although the thermometer is only 95°; but there is not a breath of air night or day, and the heat is even greater at night, so that there is not a moment's relief. No one should ever attempt to pass down the Red Sea during the months from May to September inclusive, if they can possibly avoid it, unless they have been accustomed to hot climates. The passengers all slept on deck. One lady was so seriously ill, that great fears were entertained for her by the surgeon.

"*Saturday.*—Both parties as sociable as the heat would allow."

On Sunday, June 3rd, we arrived at Aden, and an hour or two afterwards, just as I was anticipating having to proceed to Seychelles in chase of the "Pantaloon" which was supposed to have taken her departure for that place, she rounded the point and anchored. She had captured some dhows about a month previously, and liberated 300 slaves, among whom were fifty Galla women, intended for the harem of the Imaum of Muscat.

I superseded Captain Purvis on the 5th of June, 1866, and on the 8th of the same month we sailed from Aden, quitting our kind and hospitable friends General and Mrs. Reines (late 95th Reg.) with regret,—a regret tempered, however, by the fact that we were leaving the most abominable hole in existence, and which has not inaptly been likened to certain regions that shall be nameless " with the fire just gone out." It is a black lava mountain, with not a green spot to be seen; the thermometer seldom stands below 90°, and generally at 100° at night as well as by day, and this temperature is usually intensified on shore by the addition of the reflected heat from the dark lava rocks with which you are surrounded. Only five weeks before I had driven fifteen miles with snow on the ground! As we steamed down the Gulf the thermometer fell to 85°. Oh, what a relief! and on rounding Cape Guardafui we felt the full force of the south-west monsoon, which we did not get entirely clear of for about fourteen days.

In the Gulf of Aden we passed several dhows, the sight of which, with their huge sails, lofty sterns, and low bows, gives them the appearance of some great sea-monster in the act of diving, or still more do they resemble a vessel going down by the bows; they recalled much of those boat-cruising days long ago, and of many a pleasant incident connected with them, which made me look upon them as if they were old friends, and prompts me to give some description of them. There are four different kinds of coasting dhows, as shown in the engravings, viz. the Bateele, the Badane, Bugala or genuine Dhow, and the Matapa boat. The Bateele and Badane are northern vessels, and are built in the Persian Gulf and Arabian coast, chiefly in the neighbourhood of Muscat; they are by far the largest in size as a class, and being owned by the northern Arabs their appearance is much dreaded at Zanzibar.

The Bugala or dhow is built on all parts of the east coast of Africa; in the rig and shape of their sails they resemble the former craft, the difference consisting chiefly in the hull. They are by far the most numerous class, which has led to the custom, not strictly correct, of the name of "Dhow" being generally used when speaking of any of them; the Matapa is the most remarkable and primitive of these vessels that can be seen anywhere; they are large

BADANE OF THE ARABIAN COAST.   [*Page* 102.

barges, built with the strips of the bark of a tree sewn close together with thongs of hide, and rudely caulked with rags or cotton; they draw only a few inches of water when light, and are purely a native craft built high up the rivers by the negroes, and owned and manned by them alone; they convey ivory and gum down the coast towards the close of the south-west monsoon, when the weather is particularly fine, which enables them to go outside the rivers for some considerable distance along the coast, and return again with the light north-east monsoon; their sail is as primitive as their hull, consisting of a square straw mat, suspended to a pole or yard hoisted to the mast by a rope of the same material; one hand has to be continually employed baling them out, or they would soon fill and sink; for want of this precaution we one night, when at anchor off Brava, in the "Daphne," nearly lost one of them which had been made fast astern, and contained about ten or twelve tons of ivory, cobal, and gum: at daylight she was observed to be half full of water and on the point of sinking, which she must have done in another hour had her condition not been discovered.

On the 27th June we arrived at Seychelles, and anchored in Port Victoria, at the picturesque island of Mahe, the largest of the group.

Hitherto I have not given any description of places visited, preferring to do so later, as, when speaking of subsequent visits, I shall be able to give some account of their present condition and appearance, with a special view to their suitability as depôts or colonies for liberated Africans.

A brief description of Seychelles, however, may not be out of place here. This group of islands was discovered by the French about the middle of the eighteenth century, and taken possession of by them. The largest island was called Mahe, after the name of the then French governor of the Mauritius. They became ours at the same time that the island of Mauritius was secured to us by treaty, and consequently the "Code Napoleon" is still the law by which they are governed.

The islands in this vicinity are of primitive

rock, Mahe being the highest of them; they are situated on a coral bank of soundings, which has so increased and grown within the last half-century that the water has become much shallower in many places, and requires being thoroughly surveyed again. Mahe is an exceedingly picturesque island, being richly covered with verdure, cocoa-nut and other palm-trees. It is celebrated for the "coco-de-mer" tree, which is indigenous to the place and this place only, although it has been transplanted to India, and the Mauritius, where it now grows; this tree received its name originally through a mistake on the part of some French officers, who, picking up one of the huge nuts at sea, never having seen it before, and discovering it to be an unknown fruit, came to the conclusion that it grew in the sea, and gave it the name of " coco-de-mer."

Large quantities of cocoa-nut oil is manufactured here, the cocoa-nuts being collected from the islands around, and from the Amirante Islands, to the southward, where I have seen cotton growing wild, as I have also on the East Coast of Africa: and here the question naturally arises whether the cultivation of cotton in Africa might not do much to put an end to the exportation of negroes from that country.

In 1862 the first hurricane for many years swept over the Island of Mahe, throwing down some of the high cliffs and killing about sixty of the inhabitants. I shall hereafter allude to these islands when considering their suitability as a depôt for liberated Africans.

BUGALA, OR DHOW. [Page 102.

Leaving Seychelles on the 1st July, and touching at Providence Island, one of the Cosmoledo group, to take off some passengers landed there from an abandoned American ship, we proceeded to Zanzibar, where we arrived on the 18th, having narrowly escaped being wrecked on Latham Island, that most dangerous part of this most dangerous, because incompletely surveyed coast of East Africa; where currents are strong and uncertain, and where numerous unknown shoals exist, and are only now and then discovered by the practicable mode of running on them. There have been rumours, not altogether without foundation, we fear, that vessels heavily insured have been sent out there with no very honest intentions of their returning again. There has not, however, be it said in justice to those who have, unfortunately, been concerned where merchant-ships have been lost, a single man-of-war cruiser on this coast for many years that has not left its name attached to some shoal discovered by her, and sometimes by running on it. Great efforts have been made to induce the Sultan to erect a lighthouse on

Latham Island; the necessity for it will be seen by the fact that it lies at the entrance of the Zanzibar Channel, with the current sweeping past at a rate varying from 24 to 100 miles a day, *not into* the channel, where there is little or no current, but outside it, and across the entrance; several ships have been lost on this island, and when we anchored in five fathoms' water just in time to avoid going on it, we supposed the ship (allowing for the usual current) to be thirty-nine miles to windward of it. I should advise ships cruising on this part of the coast to fix a temporary light on it for their own convenience. Trees might possibly grow on the top of the bank, if planted and taken care of for a time, and would be seen at a distance during the clear nights.

On arrival at Zanzibar, I met, for the first time, Dr. Seaward, then acting consul, his wife, and Dr. Kirk, in whose society I have since spent many pleasant hours, and have witnessed, to some extent, his anxious endeavours and indefatigable exertions in all matters relating to the celebrated African explorer Dr. Livingstone.

I have very many pleasant reminiscences, both of this time and when out there a year or two later, of the agreeable entertainments of Mr. and Mrs. Churchill at the British Consulate, the musical parties of Mr. and Mrs. White at the German Consulate, and of the enjoyable hours with Dr. and Mrs. Seaward and their bright little daughter Winny, then about five years of age, whose only playmates consisted of the officers of the ships, who looked upon her as the property of the Navy, and whom she often addressed in her little, wicked, womanly way by their Christian names, with a comic air of authority, and of whom I once heard a mother say, " I always thought my child (whom I have left in Europe) clever, but ever since I have known that child I almost feel disappointed with my own." Nor must I forget to mention our friend Bishop Tozer, who every Sunday, when we were at Zanzibar, made the ship his cathedral, and who was always too good not to remember that, if half his congregation were churchmen, the other half were dissenters;

and here I may add that if it were not for such men as he and Mr. Vaudney, the clergyman at Seychelles, who never failed us, the ships of the squadron out there which have no chaplains would be badly off. In the harbour of Zanzibar may be seen a large fleet of dhows and several European merchant-ships, Germans and English, the former the more numerous of the two, there being a larger German trade than English, a few French ships, and now and then an American; these last invariably created suspicion as to the intention of the captains with respect to the slave-market, but such suspicions have diminished since slavery was abolished in the United States.

It is especially crowded with dhows at the commencement and towards the close of the south-west monsoon; before and after its strength they prepare to leave for the northward, before the calms on the coast, preparatory to the north-east monsoon, take place. At this time of the year they are continually entering the harbour from the southward; and during the months of Septem-

MATAPA BOAT OF THE NORTHERN RIVERS.

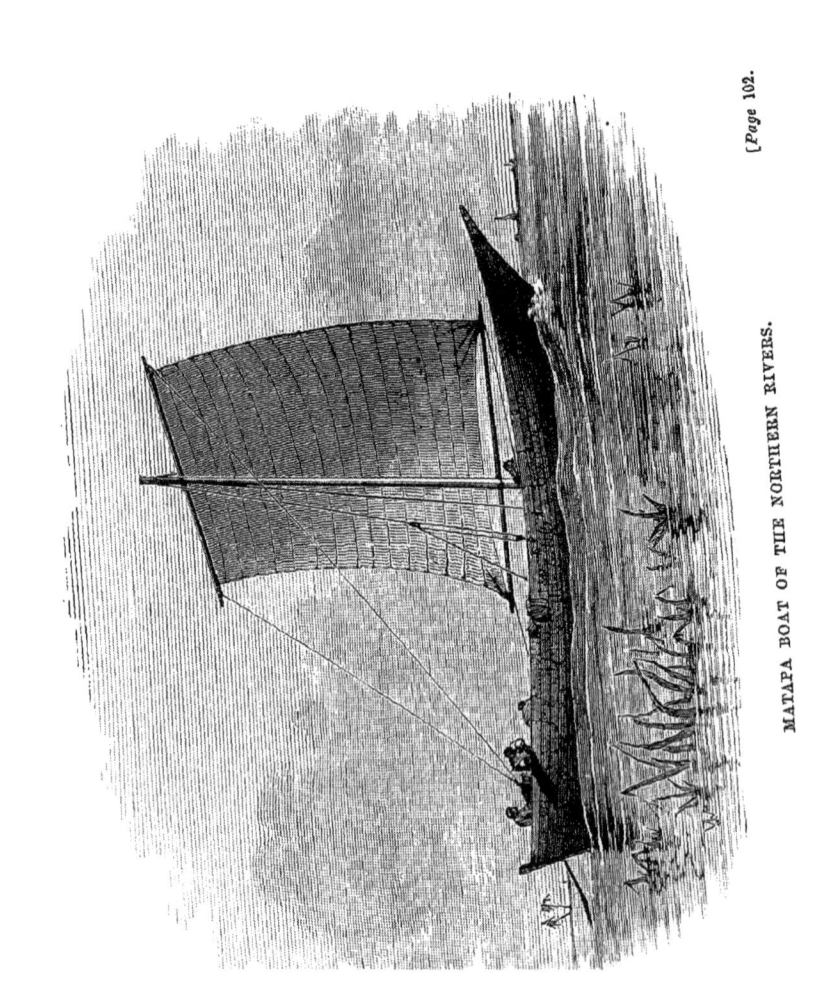

[*Page* 102.

ber, October, and November numbers of them may be seen leaving every day for the northward, bound, some for India, some for the Red Sea, and some for the Arabian Coast and Persian Gulf.

From Quiloa (or Keelwa), 200 miles south of Zanzibar, to Lamoo, 230 miles north, on the East Coast of Africa, the slave-trade is a legal trade; and although the clause in the treaty between Zanzibar and England nominally limits the number of slaves to be carried to that required by the Sultan for agricultural purposes, he alone is the judge of such requirements, and the clause is practically inoperative,[1] for whatever number is required by the traders, they have only to pay the tax and apply for a licence for that number, and they obtain it from the Custom House; and any vessel possessing such licence is exempt from detention and capture on the part of our cruisers; and even supposing

---

[1] The estimate of what is really required for agricultural purposes on Zanzibar territory has been given as 1700 slaves, the number imported into Zanzibar, annually, has been variously estimated from 20,000 to 60,000.

vessels arrived at Zanzibar with the number of slaves on board in excess of those specified in its papers, it is not in the power of a man-of-war to board her without the special permission of the Sultan himself, which he never gives unless to meet his own interests against those of the northern Arabs. Dhows full of slaves may be anchored in Zanzibar harbour in such numbers as to surround the English flag carried by our cruisers, who cannot touch them. In the China seas, should a Chinese junk attack and rob another, we call the crew pirates, attack them, and hand them over to the authorities for execution; yet this infinitely worse piracy is covered by a treaty on the part of a despicable petty Arab chief, who, if we withdrew our protection would be murdered the next day, and his territory transferred to another; unless, indeed, some other European nation than the English should step in, and, without the same sentimental respect for territory possessed and governed by those through whom it is made a curse to all mankind, civilized and uncivilized, take possession of it themselves, and who, perhaps, having no such pure intentions towards the negro as to be any benefit to them, afterwards might simply carry on a limited slave-trade under another name, as is done farther south by the Portuguese and French, who call them "free negroes" and "emigrants," respectively, and acting as the former of these nations has done for centuries in the Mozambique, not only enslave their bodies, but place moral chains and fetters for centuries to come on their whole mental being.

Well was it said of the negroes in the Portuguese territory, on the East Coast of Africa, some few years ago, "Poor degraded beings, how much might their condition be improved! But here they are ground down to the lowest state of human degradation, and it is *frightful to contemplate beings so little raised above the brute creation, in a place which has been in possession of Christians, so called, for hundreds of years.*"[2]

I visited several of these slave dhows in Zanzibar harbour laden with wretched creatures,

[2] Lieut. Barnard's Narrative.

some of them crammed with them, yet compared with those we captured in the "Daphne" two years later, they were comparatively well off; their condition, though thin and emaciated, had not yet, with some exceptions, arrived at that extreme stage of misery and starvation that too plainly indicates certain death to the majority, perhaps to two out of three; for, in the first place, they had only been a few days from Mozambique or Quiloa, before arriving at Zanzibar for food and water; and, secondly, if there had been any bad cases, they would have been landed on arrival, and sent to the slave-market. The poor creatures are stowed sometimes in two, sometimes in three tiers on extemporized bamboo decks, not sufficiently distant from each other to allow them to sit upright. Their licence, as before stated, takes them as far as Lamoo, the limit of the Sultan's territory; I say *limit*, because there has been an inclination of late to induce him to claim—nay! even to help him in claiming also—the territory north of this, which at present is in the hands of a few marauding parties of Arabs, and lately he is

STOWING SLAVES ON BOARD.

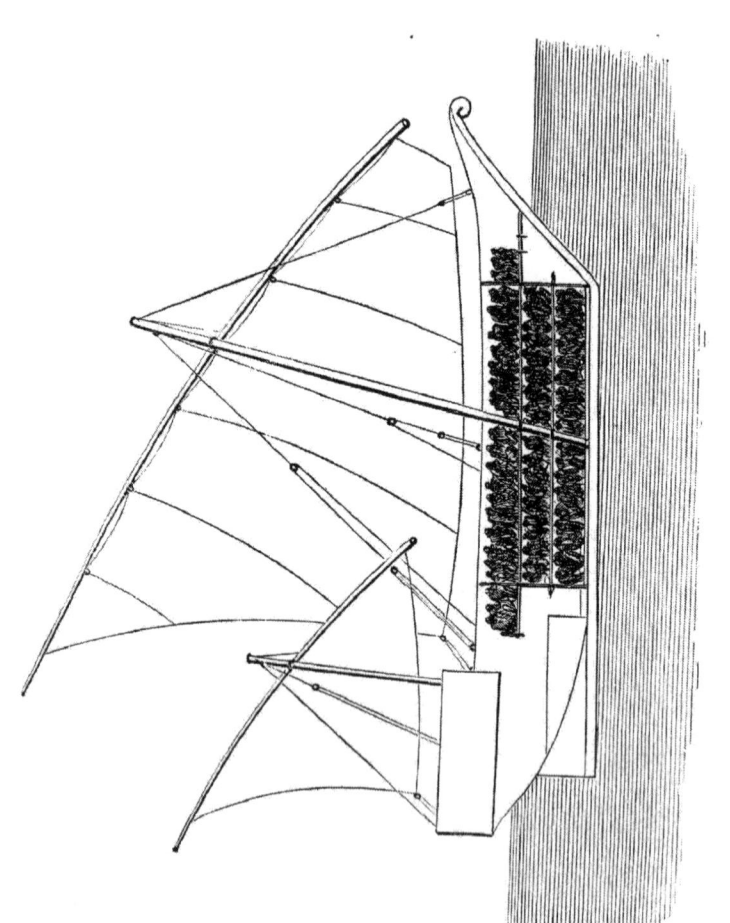

SECTION OF THE DHOW ALLUDED TO AT PAGE 168, SHOWING THE MANNER OF STOWING SLAVES ON BOARD. [*Page* 114.

reported to have erected a fort farther north still. We may possibly obtain, hereafter, some clue to the advantages to be gained by the Sultan being allowed to extend his dominions.

On the arrival of a slave dhow at Lamoo her licence ceases; if she proceeds farther towards the Arabian Coast or Persian Gulf, it is at her own risk, and, acting on the old proverb that "one may as well be hung for a sheep as a lamb," the captains take in as many more slaves as they can possibly carry; and ascertaining first, by messengers sent as far north as the Juba River, the probability of the coast being pretty clear of English cruisers, they start for the northward, keeping close to the land, with the intention of running their vessels on shore if chased, with the chance of saving some of their slaves that are not drowned in the act; and also, if not molested in any way, of touching at the various ports on their way north, to obtain a handful of rice and a cup of water per slave on board, to fill up the gaps in the cargo caused by the death of many of them, and to ascertain if the coast is clear still farther to the northward. This is the illegal extension, and consequent result of a *legal slave-trade in the nineteenth century!* But it must not be supposed that the illegal part of this trade commences at the northern end of the Zanzibar dominions; on the contrary, a vast number of these dhows obtain their cargoes far south of the southern limit Quiloa, from Quillimane, Angoxa, Mozambique, Ibo, the Portuguese possessions on the coast, calling only at Quiloa to obtain the necessary pass for all of them, by possibly paying only a tax to the Custom House there for a few more to be added to their cargo at that place.

Slave-trade abolished in the Portuguese territory! It was never so extensive as it is now, and is aggravated by cruelties that have shocked the Arabs on the coast—cruelties which they are incapable of practising, and which cause an Englishman's flesh to creep at their bare mention, and all this rendered still more revolting by the falsehood and sarcasm contained in the name given the poor wretches— that of "*free negroes!*"

One morning at Zanzibar, Jumah, our interpreter, knocked at my door, and slipping off his sandals, an Arab custom, before entering, exclaimed, "My master," (a term he always addressed me by,) "suppose you come on deck, I show you something."

"What, Jumah?"

"One big dhow commeen in full nigger."

"Well what's the use, Jumah, we can't take her here."

"No, not now, but suppose you meet her yesterday, you take her, for she got more slaves than licence."

"Well, that's not more satisfactory."

However, I went on deck with him, just in time to see a huge dhow pass under our stern; her upper bamboo deck so covered with slaves squatting there, that not a square foot of it was visible. As she passed, every face on board her was turned towards us, and the Arabs from the raised deck or poop abaft, gave a most derisive cheer, followed by laughter, and one of them seeing Jumah, hailed him, which produced more cheers and laughter.

"What does he say, Jumah," I asked.

"He say, ah! ah! why you not come and take us, are you afraid?"

Jumma replied, "We catch you another time."

"I got lots of slaves on board, tell the captain to come and see."

This was followed again by laughter, as she passed inside, lowered her sail, and anchored within pistol-shot of us. In an hour from that time, every slave was doubtless in the market, and the dhow ready to take in another cargo of them for the north.

CHAPTER VI.

Visit to the Sultan—Pemba Island—A Licensed Slave Dhow—Negro Infant—Island of Mohilla—Visit to the Queen — Reception — Trincomalee — Return to England.

THE usual visit being made to the Sultan, Sayed Mejid, then reigning, and a consummate caricature of royal pomp witnessed that would have afforded a glorious subject for poor Tom Hood's pen, we sailed from Zanzibar on the morning of the 30th July, proceeding out of the southern channel, that the slave-dealers might not suspect my intention of visiting Pemba Island, which lies to the northward. We anchored off that island on the following afternoon, and despatched the boats to examine the harbours and creeks, in order to ascertain if there were any vessels with slaves on board without a licence there. Jumah landing at the town in one of them to obtain information from his friends for our guidance.

On the afternoon of the 2nd August, the cutter chased a dhow, and on boarding found a cargo of forty slaves in her. The dhow was brought alongside, and the papers retained until Jumah's return to examine them, which when he did he found her licensed to convey thirty-nine slaves only. Among the forty was a small laughing infant on the back of its mother, and who appeared to be of about that age when, as I have heard in England, they are "beginning to take notice." Through the interpreter, I asked the owner how it was he had one slave more than he ought to have.

" One infant very small," he replied.

" Well, that doesn't exempt it from the tax. Why isn't it included in the papers?"

" It was born since leaving Zanzibar."

" How long since you left?"

" Three days, sir."

"Tell him, Jumah, black baby grow very fast."

"Yes, sir," he says; "nigger woman not know she got baby till she finds it on her back."

"Then tell him God's curse on her is not so heavy as that which man has placed on her since."

There was another question to be considered however; our boat first boarded the dhow inside the ship, and *probably* within three miles of the land, therefore in Zanzibar waters, which exempted her from capture without the Sultan's permission: it was therefore useless to detain her any longer as there would have been no probability of obtaining a condemnation. On returning to Zanzibar, a few weeks later, I found the owner had reported the occurrence in a tone of "injured innocence" to the Sultan, who pretended to be very irate about it. But I gave him to understand that I only regretted not having risked detaining her altogether, and taking her into court, as she had too many slaves on board.

From Pemba we proceeded to the Commoro group, and anchored off the picturesque island of Mohilla. On August 20th some of the officials came on board to convey her Majesty's "welcome to the island," and with an invitation to visit her.

On the afternoon of the same day I landed with Mr. Shapcote, the paymaster, for that purpose; passing through the village, which is chiefly composed of neat huts, we ascended the hill accompanied by our interpreter, and three Arab chiefs whom, whether rightly or wrongly, I set down to be the prime minister, the foreign secretary, and the commander-in-chief of "all the forces." In the last case I was not mistaken, for as we ascended the hill "all the forces" themselves made their appearance, coming down to meet us; they consisted of about twenty-five or thirty men of very different sizes, and of as many shades of colour, and as they approached, the commander-in-chief displayed his authority by exclaiming in a magnificent tone, and to my utter astonishment in plain English, "Halt," "front," "dress," "shoulder arms," which orders were carried out according to the taste and fancy of each individual soldier.

"Hallo! Jumah!" I said in a whisper, "that fellow speaks English and must have heard what we said."

"No, no, my master, that man he no speak more English than that, they always give orders in English, but they only know a few."

The appearance of "all the forces" baffles description, and I would certainly advise those who have not great control over their risible faculties never to venture on a visit to Mohilla, lest they offend the great men of that island, by appearing to ridicule what in all the fulness of their hearts they mean as an honour, and an expression of their pleasure at seeing you.

The military were all dressed in the old scarlet tail-coats, with several different coloured facings, of English soldiers of a date long gone by, fifteen years having elapsed at that time since they were superseded by the tunic. These coats were most probably bought in India from our soldiers at least twenty years before, and how much longer, it is impossible to say, and some of the men wore military hats of a time not in the memory of the present or the past generation, more like bishop's mitres than anything else, while about half a dozen others had those broad brim oilskin caps, that may be seen on the soldiers in all the pictures of Peninsular battles; one or two had comparatively modern shakos, and the remainder wore turbans: all, however, had the red coat over either trousers with the red cord, of as great antiquity as the coats, judging by the patches, or over their Arab garments. Let me add that although the coats had once been scarlet, that was evident, yet the different shades produced by grease, vinegar, or what not, had made them coats of many colours; some of them were too big, and some too small for the wearers—some would have gone round the man's body twice, and some would scarcely reach half-way round. Nothing could be more comic in appearance.

"All the forces" were headed by three or four cracked fifes and several "tom-toms." The men having obeyed the last orders as well as they could, the commander-in-chief of "all the forces" took up a position in front of them, and, after reprimanding about twenty of their number individually and collectively, gave the order, " —sent arms," at which some of them came to the saluting position, and some levelled their old flint-locks at us with dangerous precision, had they been loaded, which they had not been perhaps for many years.

After a great many other ridiculous performances, two men advanced to me with a "bearer," such as I have seen used for taking wounded men off a field, only not so long, and by no means so comfortable, being apparently formed of the bottoms of old chairs secured to two oars with the blades cut off. I was requested to mount, which I at first declined, but being told it would not be etiquette to refuse, I did so; and after getting on and tumbling off once or twice, managed at last to hold on *à la Turc*, in spite of the shaking they gave me as they carried me over the rugged lane. I was thus uncomfortably conveyed the remaining half-mile to the royal country residence. On entering the outer enclosure a number of negroes commenced a dance, or rather walk round in a ring, singing the usual nigger tune, which consists of running up and down half-a-dozen notes over and over again to the perpetual beat of the tom-toms, clapping their hands, and keeping time with their feet.

We were at last ushered into a small room, hung round with coloured calico, where, seated at the farther end on a raised cushion or ottoman placed on a dais, was her Majesty the Queen of Mohilla, the only part of her face visible being her eyes, which were particularly good, but might have belonged to the plainest or the handsomest face. Seated in front at her feet, in a semicircle, were about eight female attendants, ladies of the bedchamber, mistress of the robes, &c., of course. On her right sat the prime minister and foreign secretary, on her left the commander-in-chief of "all the forces," and another gentleman who had made his appearance, probably the lord chamberlain. These all formed a strong guard, outside of which, and on the right, we were seated on chairs. Her Majesty having asked many questions, and expressed her pleasure at seeing an English ship there, I inquired if she desired to see the ship, which she had asked some questions about, to which she appeared inclined to answer in the affirmative; but at this the prime minister became very irate, and probably threatening to throw up his portfolio if she did, made her decline the invitation. We left the place much in the same way we entered, I taking care, when a reasonable distance from it, to tumble off my extraordinary vehicle and not to get on again. "All the forces" went through some dangerous but interesting evolutions by way of a salute I suppose, but I am not sure of that, and in which, fortunately, they had only one man wounded, after which we proceeded to the boats and left the island. Arriving off Cape St. Andrew's, Madagascar, we fell in with the "Lyra" with our orders for Trincomalee, where we arrived on the 7th October, first having returned to Zanzibar and Seychelles.

A few days later Commodore Hillyer arrived

in the "Octavia." On the 14th we sailed for England, calling at the Mauritius, Cape of Good Hope, St. Helena, Ascension, and Sierra Leone, on our homeward passage. At the first-mentioned of these places, I had the pleasure of meeting with Bishop Ryan, whose interest in all subjects relating to the slave-trade is well known.

We arrived at Plymouth in the month of February following, and paid off on March the 6th, 1867.

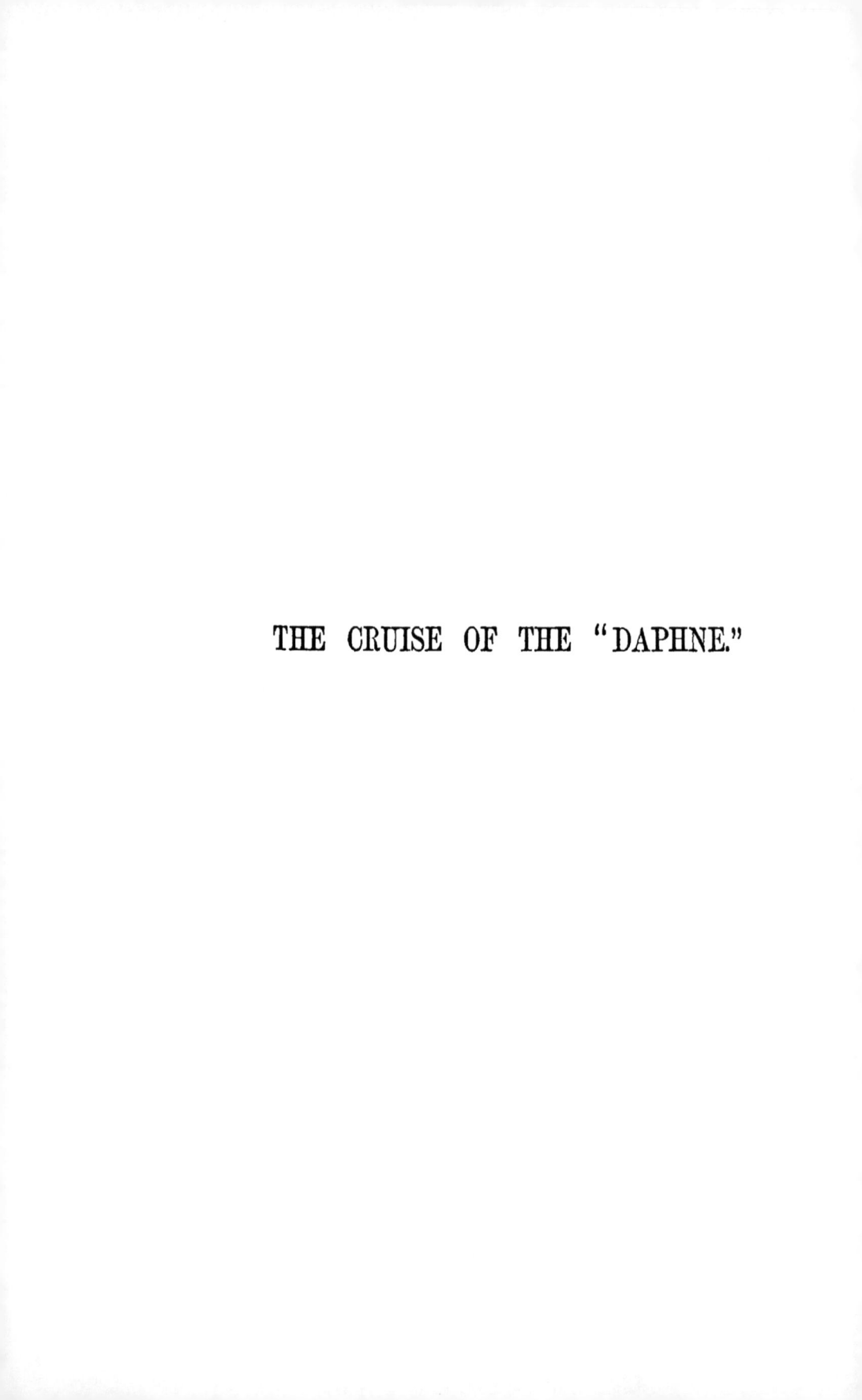

THE CRUISE OF THE "DAPHNE."

THE CRUISE OF THE "DAPHNE."

CHAPTER VII.

The "Daphne" commissioned—Outward Bound—Loss of an Officer—Abyssinian Expedition—Annesley Bay—Arrival at Seychelles—Port Victoria, its Unsuitability as a Depôt—Madagascar—Slave-trade in the Vicinity—Commoro Islands—Mayotte—Tour of the Island—Roman Catholic Schools—Johanna—Mohilla—Changes since former Visit—Proceedings of a Frenchman—Visit to the young King—Mozambique—Kiswara River—Shooting Excursion, Appearance of the Country—Interview with Natives—Return to Zanzibar.

ON the 4th June, 1867, I was appointed to H.M.S. "Daphne," and commissioned her at Plymouth for service on the East Indian station, to which had belonged for some years previously the East Coast of Africa so far south as the twenty-third parallel of latitude, which from lat. 4° south formerly belonged to the Cape of Good Hope.

After the naval review of that year, we sailed finally from Plymouth on the 19th August, calling at Sierra Leone for Kroomen, the Cape of Good Hope, and Mauritius. We arrived at Bombay on the 19th November, when we found that the pioneers of the expedition to Abyssinia had already left, and thither, when we had refitted, we proceeded, having the "Semiramis" factory-ship for Annesley Bay in tow.

In our passage out to India in the "Daphne" a sad event occurred; after leaving the Cape, running to the eastward before a severe gale, the wind on the starboard quarter, under close-reefed main-topsail and reefed foresail, topmast staysail and storm main-trysail, a heavy sea struck the ship on the starboard beam, knocking in the upper-deck iron ports and waist netting, lifting the end of the bridge on which Sub-Lieutenant Orton was standing as officer of the watch, and washed him overboard. The sea had so covered the deck, and poured down the hatchway also, that for a minute or two no one missed him. He who should have been on the alert for such an occurrence, and have acted in the event of such an accident, was himself the victim.

Two minutes, or perhaps more, elapsed before those on board missed the officer of the watch from the bridge, or suspected its cause—a lapse of time that may be estimated by the fact that the first lieutenant had just reached my cabin to report that the lower deck was covered with water, and to ask if he should batten down, when the boatswain's mate ran aft to report the officer of the watch overboard. The ship was brought to the wind, and life-buoys let go, but poor Orton could be seen swimming half a mile astern. It was already late in the evening, and dusk; the fires were lighted with the view of using steam if possible, but it could not be up for nearly two hours. It was a question of minutes with the poor fellow, and it blew too hard to allow of the boats being lowered.

I know of no more painful position to be placed in than that of the commander of a ship under such circumstances,—with volunteers around him begging to be allowed to go away in the life-boat to rescue a shipmate, perhaps a messmate, and who, though they do not see it, are ready to leave the responsibility of their lives in their commander's hands, without considering the consequences,—to be compelled to come to the decision that the powerful swimmer must sink, knowing that to lower a boat would be certain death to many more. It was the second time that I had been so painfully situated, once in the "Pantaloon," and now again in the "Daphne." It was now dark, and blowing harder than ever, and with sadder feelings than I can express, I left the deck, giving orders that the ship should be steered her course again. Thus the career of one who promised to be one of the best of officers was prematurely and most painfully ended.

We remained at Annesley Bay the greater part of the time, entering the Red Sea on the night of the 31st December, 1867; we did not leave it again until the 18th June, 1868, when the expedition was ended, and the troops had been re-embarked.

A STREET IN SEYCHELLES.

(*From a Photograph by the Author.*)

[*Page* 135.

It was not, therefore, till after this date that we proceeded to cruise for the suppression of the slave-trade on the coast of Africa.

We arrived at Aden, from Amsterdam Bay, on the 21st June, and sailed thence to Seychelles on the 28th July, and, after experiencing the south-east monsoon in all its strength, reached there without the loss of one main-yard.

Here, fortunately, we found anchored the "Oberon," Commodore Heath, as there is neither dockyard nor stores of any kind on the island for our consort, though it is admirably situated for keeping a supply for the ships, which generally come to this island to refit, and also for giving the men leave, it being the only place on the coast where it is safe to do so; for it is an extremely healthy island, which cannot be said of any part of the coast or the islands close to it, unless it is the Comoro Islands — Johanna — but those are filth and consequently disease during the rainy season. It did, however, well for us now.

Maize, th[...] Seychelles to keep in the healthy [...]

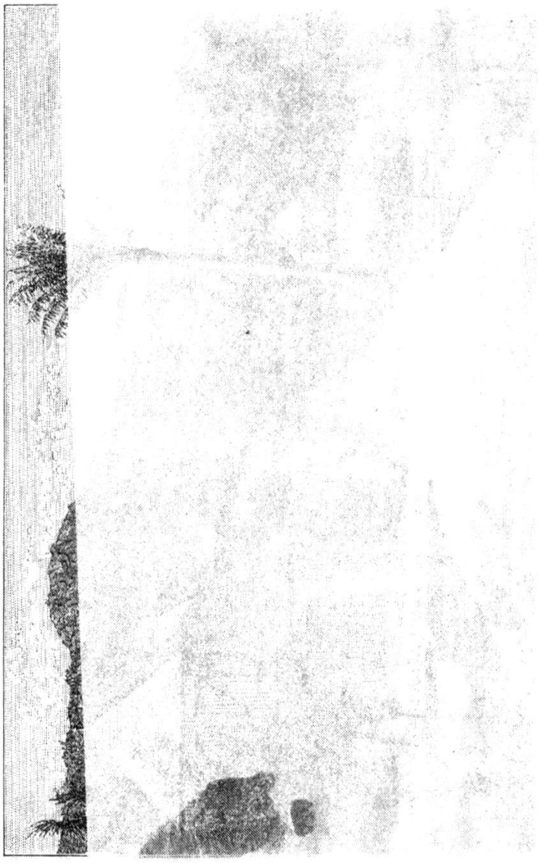

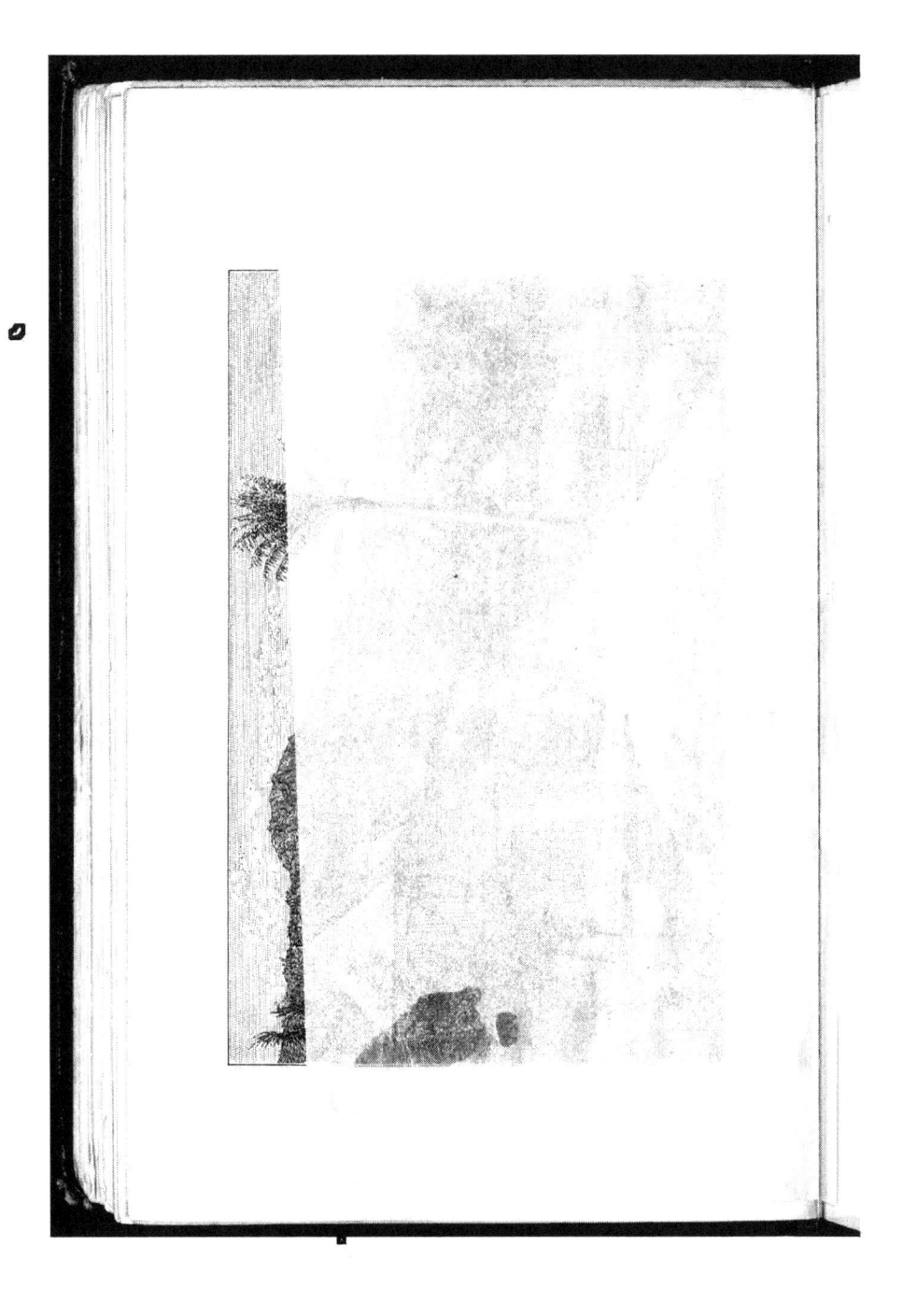

It was not, therefore, till after this date that we proceeded to cruise for the suppression of the slave-trade on the coast of Africa.

We arrived at Aden, from Annesley Bay, on the 21st June, and sailed thence to Seychelles on the 18th July, and, after experiencing the south-west monsoon in all its strength, reached Mahe with the loss of our main-yard.

Here, fortunately, we found anchored the "Octavia," Commodore Heath, as there is neither dockyard nor stores of any kind on the island for our cruisers, though it is admirably situated for keeping a supply for the ships, which generally come to this island to refit, and also for giving the men leave, it being the only place on the coast where it is safe to do so; for it is an exceedingly healthy island, which cannot be said of any part of the coast or the islands near to it, unless it is the Commoro Island, "Johanna," but there the filth and consequent diseases among the natives render it dangerous to give leave to crews.

Mahe, the largest of the Seychelles group, is the healthiest spot of the East Coast, as

Ascension is of the west; but unlike this barren burnt-up pile of cinders in appearance, with its solitary little green tuft on the mountain crest, where Ascensionians resort to cool their tempers and to try and forget the petty quarrels, social broils, and scandals at its sandy base, that used formerly to exist there, it is one of the prettiest islands in the Indian Seas, covered as it is almost with varying shades of green from its summit to its base, from north to south, here and there relieved by a bit of its brown cliff peeping through.

Port Victoria is well protected by coral banks, and the prevailing winds are on the opposite side of the island. One of our old wooden hulks moored here as a store-ship and hospital, would be a great boon to the station; another as a coal depôt, would produce such a saving in the cost of coals[1] as would almost pay for both vessels; while some of the captured dhows would make capital coal-lighters, and

---

[1] Coals in 1868 were about 4*l.* a ton here, purchased from the shore; what the price is now I do not know, but probably double.

save the enormous cost now incurred in the hire of lighters there; and a number of the liberated Africans might be retained on board these hulks for a certain time, at the very small cost at which they are now hired as labourers on the island, and thus save expense in coaling our ships, for which large wages are paid at present (I speak of as late a period as 1869). The only stores for men-of-war on the coast are now kept in a room lent for that purpose by Bishop Tozer at Zanzibar, being a part of the mission-house, where large quantities of what is not eaten by weevils, is generally destroyed by ants.

Fortunately we obtained a new main-yard from H.M.S. "Octavia," her main-topsail yard being the length required, and having re-fitted, and given four days' leave to each watch, we sailed again on the 24th of August, for Tamatave, where we arrived on the 4th of September.

Mr. T. C. Pakenham is the British Consul here, and from him I gained much information in reference to the slave-trade with Madagascar, and whose indefatigable exertions have done so much to suppress it on the island.

By a treaty with the Queen of Madagascar, the traffic in slaves to that country has been abolished, but slavery still exists as a legal institution within the island.

Whenever it has been discovered that slaves have been landed, the Consul has been enabled to compel the authorities to the fulfilment of the treaty, the punishment of the delinquent, and the surrender of the slaves to the British: and we may congratulate ourselves that we have in the position of Consul at Madagascar, one who fearlessly acts up to both the spirit and letter of the treaty and instructions respecting the suppression of so nefarious a trade; but, notwithstanding this, detection is rare, and the trade is very extensive, carried on chiefly from the Portuguese territory, sometimes direct, and sometimes through the Commoro Islands; and it must be added that very often slaves are taken to these islands, and through the French settlement at Nos Beh, under the French flag, and with the designation of "passengers" or "*engagés.*" On one occasion I received information at Mozambique that two dhows under French colours were taking in cargoes of slaves at Sofalo, and although we did not arrive off that port in time to apprehend them, we had every reason to believe that they succeeded in taking these slaves to Madagascar.

On the 9th of September we left Tamatave, and proceeded to the north-west end of the island, where, after examining that part of the coast, we steered for Mayotte, and anchored on the 17th off the town, inside the extensive coral reefs that form the harbour.

Mayotte is one of the Commoro group, consisting of four islands, viz. Commoro, Johanna, Mayotte, and Mohilla, which we have before mentioned. Each of these islands was formerly governed, as all but Mayotte are still, by petty chiefs calling themselves kings and sultans. Mayotte now belongs to the French. How did the French obtain it? They hoisted their flag there, and said, "We want this island, we therefore take it;" and no one can say the island is worse off than it was before; and they are doing all in their power to obtain possession of the other islands, as we shall see presently; and although Johanna has been under British protection for about thirty years, which has prevented their monopolizing that also, it is within the bounds of probability, that the so-called Sultan of it may be induced to withdraw his dominion from our protection, and then there will be no difficulty in the way of the French obtaining it. If it remain in our possession it would make a good depôt for liberated Africans.

There is a very extensive slave-trade carried on to and from these islands, from the Portuguese Settlements on the West; indeed, it forms the staple trade with them here, as it does everywhere in the vicinity of the East Coast. A few years ago, in consequence of the reports made against the English Consul at Johanna; in reference to his possession of slaves, his authority as such was withdrawn from him: he still remains on the island, and if reports be true, so far as the slave-trade is concerned, with no great credit to our nation.

The very high-sounding titles of King, Queen,

and Sultan that these chiefs are invested with, put a serious aspect on the idea of usurping authority over them, much less of taking possession of their dominions, but we confess we cannot see the difference between them and the chief of a Chinese piratical gang; the one attacks and robs vessels with a few white men in them, and in some instances commits murder too; the others attack and rob towns and villages, not only of property, but of souls and bodies, of friends, relations, and all hope in the future, and commit murder to an infinitely greater extent, in causing the deaths of three fourths of the number of natives affected by it, and in many cases by the hands of the dealers themselves. What difference is there? Why in the former case, we hang the culprits or rather deliver them over to be executed, which they invariably are, and so limit the extent of the evil, while in the latter we allow the offenders to enter into a treaty with us, promising that they will not kidnap slaves again excepting in a limited degree. Is not that a difference? If the penalty were the same in the latter as in the former case, and two or three Arab slave-dealers were hanged, the trade would be stopped at once, and thousands of lives saved.

During the few days we were at Mayotte, we received great kindness from the governor, M. Hayes, and his amiable wife, with whom we made a tour of the island, and visited the Roman Catholic schools and convent, where there are upwards of a hundred native children under instruction; and I may here remark that there is no Protestant Mission on any of these islands, although the Jesuits are carrying on a very extensive work on them as well as in Mozambique and other places in the vicinity. Protestants are nowhere to be found on the coast, excepting at Zanzibar and Mombase, one solitary place north of it; these islands would be admirable places for mission work, and any earnest missionary would find there an extensive field for his labours, and might become as useful and as distinguished as that great and good missionary Mr. Ellis was in Madagascar.

From Mayotte we proceeded to Johanna. The miserable filthy hovels, forming the town there, ill becoming the beautiful country around, which except on its lofty peak, 6000 feet high, abounds in fertility. It is covered with palm and cocoa-nut trees, and abounds in pine-apples, bananas, and other fruits, sweet potatoes, arrow-root, &c. There is a large lake in the interior where quantities of wild duck are to be found, and an excellent stream close to the beach running through a cocoa-nut plantation, and of which the water is very good excepting in the autumn, when quantities of vegetable matter render it often unwholesome.

From this island we proceeded to Mohilla, where I found great changes had taken place since our first visit there in the "Pantaloon," two years previously.

Some account of what had occurred since that time may give an idea of the French method of acquiring possession of these islands and other places, and of advancing their own interests nationally and individually. A Frenchman who lived in the island of Madagascar, had managed to acquire certain grants from King Radama II., no one knew how or what for. On the death of that king, the Government refused to recognize those grants. Mons. L—— therefore left the island, and proceeded to Mohilla, where "by hook or by crook," he obtained similar grants from the Queen of that island; he then left to procure machinery, &c., for erecting a sugar factory there, but by this time the Queen and her chiefs, opened their eyes to the matter, and during M. L——'s absence, her Majesty was persuaded to abdicate in favour of her son (then thirteen years of age). On the Frenchman's return he was informed that his claims were no longer recognizable. The vessel that conveyed him back to the island was a French transport, the captain of which, on hearing of this, demanded an interview with the Queen, and on obtaining it threatened to fire on the island unless Mons. L——'s claims were acknowledged; he then left the place, but returned (from Mayotte) in company with a gun-boat, when an officer who was sent on shore for the reply from the Queen forced an entrance into her Majesty's chamber, where she at the time was in "dishabille," and for so doing was very properly kicked out of the house. This was an unwarrantable insult on the part of the Arabs, at least so thought the Frenchman; both vessels therefore opened fire on the defenceless island, without further warning, killing several people, and then landed a force and took possession of the fort (as it was called, but without any guns in it). The Queen escaped from the island to Zanzibar, and thence proceeded to France, to lay her complaint before the Emperor, who probably would have more sympathy with her now than at that time, as she gained little satisfaction.

It was soon after this occurrence that we arrived in the "Daphne." French troops had been landed from Mayotte, and Mons. L—— had established himself as guardian over the young king, and placed an Arab of his own selection over him as regent. This man's presence, and that of some of the other dupes of the Frenchman, accounted for the reserve of the boy and his attendants on my visiting him. On our arrival in the ship I proceeded to the shore in accordance with the usual custom, by invitation, and entered the old stone building, or what was left of it after the French bombardment. "All the forces" were the same excepting the men, that is to say, the veritable coats, hats, caps, firelocks, that I had seen two years before, but donned by other niggers. In addition to these, however, there was a train of about 100 Arabs, who formed two lines between which I walked from the entrance to a seat on the right of the throne, which looked like an old arm-chair, placed on a deal-table with half of each leg cut off. On this sat the handsome boy-king.

I endeavoured through the interpreter to ascertain the general feeling on the island amongst the Arab chiefs, but they would say nothing, purposely avoiding the subject, owing to so many of Mons. L——'s dupes being present; so after a few words I left the fort and returned to the ship.

On the 26th September, we arrived at Mozambique harbour, but I shall postpone till a later period in this narrative, any account of the Portuguese possessions on the coast, of what they claim as such, and of what they are really able to hold possession of, and also of the very extensive slave-trade carried on there.

From Mozambique harbour we proceeded to Zanzibar, examining on our way the Kiswara River.

On the morning after our arrival at this river, accompanied by Dr. Mortimer, I pulled some miles up to explore it, and to land for the purpose of getting some shooting. We landed at a point on the left bank, about three miles from the mouth, and walked into the interior; the country presented a picturesque scene of fertile undulating plains and wooded knolls, with gradually rising hills or slopes towards the interior; proceeding about two miles to the N.E. we found ourselves on the crest of a slope, at the foot of which lay a valley that only lacked cultivation to make it equal to any scenery in England. No wonder the land was uncultivated, for who would remain there to till it in the vicinity of that curse of the country, the slave-dealer, who while he can get a profit by seizing and selling those who alone would make the land what it might be, cares nothing for agriculture, to which, were the slave-trade put an end to, he would of necessity turn his attention. At the foot of this valley was a rivulet, then almost dry, and opposite was a wooded slope which would have adorned the finest park in our own country. On our right at the head of the valley in the distance were a few, perhaps a dozen, mud and straw huts, resembling somewhat in size, form, and colour haystacks in a farmyard. We had not yet seen anything to shoot, so we made our way to the village in order to ascertain, if possible, from the natives the best direction for us to take for our purpose; as we approached the huts, two women made their appearance and were walking towards what appeared to be a well, but on seeing us they ran back again and gave the alarm of our approach; when we had arrived at the village not a soul was to be seen at first, and the doors of the huts were all closed, but as soon as we could make them understand that we were friends and not foes, an old man came out, and after explaining to him in the best way we could what we wanted, he became as communicative as he could be under the adverse circumstances of neither party knowing a single word of the others' language; the inmates of the other huts sooned joined us, the women with the acute observation of their sex eyeing and scrutinizing us much in the same manner as children in a country village stare at an organ-grinder and at the dancing figures within that everlasting source of wonder and amusement to them, the organ. Having taken a thorough survey of us and of all our clothes, as well as our guns, which gave rise to a vast number of opinions and gestures amongst themselves, they became sufficiently assured to feel the materials of which our clothes were made, a process we did not encourage, as their hands did not promise to improve our garments, and from the force of imagination made one feel uncomfortable. We saw but few natives, and possibly a couple of dozen or so formed the entire population of the village; the men may have been at work somewhere else, for we only saw two or three in the place.

It is but little that these poor creatures can require. It was probably the only village for many miles round, the natives keeping as far as they can from any populous district, and retreating to places which the Arabs do not find it worth while to visit except upon very rare occasions, and where the Portuguese cannot intrude.

After assuring the natives in the best way we could that we were neither Arabs nor Portuguese, but English, who never stole negroes, their countenances lightened up, and they showed us that they understood what we meant and appreciated us; they then pointed towards the wood as the best shooting-ground, but we found no game and so returned to the ship.

Leaving the Kiswara, we steered for Revooma River, and on approaching it sighted and chased a dhow, which ran into the river and anchored close to some mangrove-trees near the entrance. On our ships anchoring off the river the chase was continued in the boats, and on boarding the dhow it was found she had been deserted by the negoda, who had left four slaves on board, and from the filthy state of the vessel inside, there could be no doubt that a cargo of slaves had just been landed; our boats were away all night, and the next morning a similar dhow was chased and captured by Lieutenant Acklom in the cutter, but not till it had been cleared of slaves and deserted. But the most exciting part of our cruise was yet to come.

ZANZIBAR HARBOUR, AND FLEET OF DHOWS.
(*From a Photograph by the Author.*)

[*Page* 153.

CHAPTER VIII.

Slave Dhows in Zanzibar Harbour—Important Information —Departure from Zanzibar — Domestic Slaves — Chase of a Dhow — Capture of a Dhow — Chase of another Dhow — Dhow stranded — Slaves in the Water — Rescue of Children in Life-boat—Another Slave Dhow stranded — Perilous Position of the Cutter—Capture of more Dhows—Another wrecked —Dreadful Condition of Slaves—Cruel Treatment on Board the Dhows—Arrival of "Star"—Departure from the Coast—Slaves on Board—Becalmed and drifting.

ARRIVING at Zanzibar, October the 12th, we found the harbour literally crowded with dhows of every kind, and among them several full of slaves, nominally bound for Lamoo, but from reliable information we received, we had no doubt that several of them were determined to run the gauntlet along the coast; there was some necessity for their doing this, because Lamoo, where slaves are not really required and which only serves as a safe starting-point for a vast number of them on their way to the more northern markets, was then overstocked with them, owing to war existing between two tribes on opposite sides of the Juba river north of it, which prevented the slaves being marched over-land to Brava, Magadoxa, and places farther north, as was generally done to avoid the risk of capture, and then reshipped at those places for the Persian Gulf. This route being closed by the war, they were compelled to convey them in dhows the whole way.

Our appearance in the harbour at this time was calculated to make them hesitate. I gave out publicly what my orders were on leaving Zanzibar, namely, to proceed to Bombay—without letting them know that I intended to examine the coast on my way north—and to confirm the slave-dealers in the belief of this, I undertook to receive a freight which some Banyans requested me to convey to Bombay, probably with the view of ascertaining whether I really was going there or not, never thinking we should hug the coast of Africa on our way, and on my accepting the freight, they came to the conclusion that there would be no vessel in their way on the North Coast. We received much information that threw suspicion on the legal traders in the harbour, besides definite information regarding the full slavers. From past experience I came to the conclusion that, excepting in these northern and the licensed slave dhows, there were no fittings in them to be relied on as evidence of their carrying on this trade, and even in these there was scarcely anything but the unmistakable bamboo deck; I had, therefore, made a rule never to detain any vessel but northern ones, from the fact alone of their having slave fittings, but only on the ground of their actually having slaves on board. The distinction at this time between what were domestic slaves, and what were *not*, there had never been any doubt about: it was a line easily drawn, and is now, in spite of the doubts that have been cast over it in India, by means of objections adopted to mystify it, reflecting on some officers who, on the first occasion of their serving on that coast had drawn the line correctly and distinctly, with a common-sense interpretation of their instructions. As an illustration of this difference between domestic slaves and others, I shall mention the case of two of the first dhows we boarded after leaving Zanzibar. On the 21st we steamed out of that port, through the north channel for Bombay, until clear of observation from the shore, and when about thirty miles off the coast, steered a course parallel to it, until we passed the latitude of Lamoo. We then closed the coast, and anchored on the night of the 24th off Brava. On the afternoon of the 25th we weighed and chased a dhow, and on boarding her we found it was a Zanzibar vessel. She had on board a crew of about a dozen negroes, *domestic* slaves, and a sister of the Sultan, who had three slaves with her—a man, and two women; these were *servants*, or *domestic* slaves in the literal sense of the term. On the 26th, we, however, boarded a vessel off the same part of the coast, a legal trader, which besides her crew of domestic slaves, had two boys in her that had been kidnapped at Pemba on the day of sailing; they were chased on the beach by the negoda and some of his crew, and being forced into the boat, were taken off to the dhow, and this story the negoda did not deny. Now, we maintain that even if such a vessel had been captured *within* the Sultan's waters, he himself would have been compelled by the treaty to recognize her condemnation, as he has in similar instances on many occasions, for she had no licence; but as she was captured beyond the limit of any treaty, by no stretch of interpretation of the instructions or orders, however much desired, could these two kidnapped children (two out of the many thousands who are thus forcibly carried to the northern markets) be brought under the nomenclature of " domestic slaves."

We therefore detained this vessel, and she, and several others (some of them full, and some with only a few slaves in them), were subsequently condemned at Zanzibar, and the condemnation approved by the Sultan. Another case of this system of kidnapping, was that of a woman and two boys who were stolen by the captain of a dhow from the shore, to be sold on arrival north.

In a former part of this narrative I described the custom of the captains and owners of legal traders of invariably taking a few slaves in by way of speculation. Now, if such a system were recognized as legal or excusable, there would be no occasion to convey large cargoes of slaves to the north, for the 2000 dhows that leave for the north at the beginning and close of the monsoon, would convey six slaves in each; 12,000 would thus be safely conveyed without loss or risk, and their capture would thus be entirely avoided. As well give up all endeavour to suppress the trade at once, as trifle in this way with the unfortunate slaves or the officers engaged in the suppression of it.

On the afternoon of the 28th of the same month a dhow appeared coming from the southward, so we immediately weighed and steamed towards her. It may here be remarked that owing to the strong current from the south, and light winds, the dhows, which are never calculated to sail on a wind, have no chance of escape from a vessel north of them. On nearing this dhow, which was running up towards us, close in shore, she put her helm up, and ran through the breakers on to the beach, becoming a complete wreck in a few minutes. We were close to her, though outside the breakers, and in time to see a crowd of unfortunate slaves struggling through the water from the ship to the shore. Many of them, no doubt, were drowned in the attempt, and others escaped up the hill before our boat could get near the shore. It was a question if the danger was not too great to risk the surf in the attempt to rescue any of them. We lowered the life-boat (one of White's five-oared), Mr. Breen, midshipman, and Richards, carpenter, slipping down the lifelines into the boat with me, and we shoved off. I intended, if the bar appeared too dangerous to cross, not to risk the lives of the crew; and I confess, after my experience, I never would allow a boat to attempt it again on this part of the coast; it did not look so bad outside. We gave way, and at this time we could see many of the slaves on the beach and in the water.

Suddenly we found ourselves amongst the breakers. A sea struck us abaft, and washed clean over the boat from stem to stern; and she must have broached-to if it had not been for the weight of two of us on the yoke line. Then another sea struck us, and then another, washing over the whole length of the boat and every one in it; but owing to her admirable construction, the seas went out over the bows, leaving only a few inches of water in her. In a few minutes we were over the bar, and inside it was comparatively smooth. But how was it possible ever to get out again? was the first thought that struck me, as I never saw worse-looking breakers, not even at Buffalo Mouth[1] or Algoa Bay. They extended the whole length of the coast for many miles, and from the inside we saw what they really were. When on shore we found we were too late to rescue many of the slaves; we, however, found seven little wretched children from five to eight years of

---

[1] Where we lost twenty-one men in four months, during the Kaffir war, of those attached to the Naval Brigade, including seven belonging to the "Castor."

age, who were unable from weakness to crawl away into the bush. One or two of them were doubled up with their knees against their faces, in the position, they told us afterwards, that they had been in for many days, and they were a week on board before they could stretch out their legs. There was a woman also there

FAC SIMILE OF THE CONDITION OF ONE OF THE SLAVES TAKEN OUT OF A DHOW CAPTURED BY THE "DAPHNE."

who was unable to get her child away with her. She came down to the boat, but while we were getting the children into it she disappeared. We at last got the seven little ones on board and were shoving off, when about twenty of the natives (Somallies) came down waving their spears and firelocks. When within about a couple of hundred yards I fired a rifle so as to strike the ground about twenty yards ahead of them. As I fired they threw themselves flat on their faces on the ground, and immediately got up, and taking the hint, remained where they were. We had still to cross the bar, and it was nearly dark. After attempting to cross it once or twice, and being carried back by the breakers, I thought, as we were armed, of hauling the boat on to the beach for the night, as there was no anchoring inside the bar, for excepting close to it there was only a white sheet of foam, which on receding left the boat nearly high and dry on the coral. At last, after waiting for about a quarter of an hour longer, there appeared to be a lull. It was now or never: the crew gave way with a will, and we succeeded in crossing, getting only one heavy breaker over us from stem to stern; the boat, however, going through it like a fish. We had the poor children stowed in the bottom of the boat. We looked anxiously round after we had passed to see if the sea had taken one of them out, indeed it was a miracle it did not. On inquiry we heard from them that the dhow was crammed with slaves, but that on seeing the ship the Arabs said, pointing to the smoke from our funnel, "White man is lighting a fire to cook nigger with," and by this they persuaded the poor creatures to risk jumping into the water when they grounded.

On the 29th we chased a full slaver on shore in the same way. The moment they saw us they steered through the breakers, and we could see one or two hundred negroes landing from her. Our boats were able to land clear of the surf, but only rescued one male slave, who was in such a wretched condition that he could not crawl from the beach. He told us that there were 119 in the dhow, that some of them, in the same state as himself, were carried up the hill by the other slaves.

On the 30th, another dhow full of slaves ran on shore and landed them. We had at this time but one left of the five boats belonging to the ship—two cutters, gig, whaler, and dingy—one cutter was detached on the coast, the whaler had just boarded a dhow some distance off, the gig was in chase of another, and the little dingy was made fast to a dhow in charge of a prize crew; the remaining cutter, under charge of Lieutenant Acklom, was sent in chase of this dhow, to endeavour to cut off and capture some of the escaping Arabs and negroes, as well as to overhaul the dhow on shore. Although no breakers were on this part of the coast, there was a heavy surf on the beach, and while the crew, after ineffectually chasing the runaways, were launching their boat in the surf, she was swamped, everything washed out of her, and in spite of every effort of those on shore, there seemed to be no prospect of their being able to get her head out and clear of the surf. We were about half a mile off the beach in the ship, without another boat to assist the cutter for some time; we had nothing but a signal-rocket staff supplied to the ship, and there was no possibility of sending a line the necessary distance by such means; and a canoe which we had, with one of the Sierra Leone Kroomen in her, started with the end of a line, but this too was found impracticable. At last, the gig answered her recall, and returned in time to render the assistance needed; the line was conveyed to the cutter, and towed by the gig, she succeeded in getting out of the surf, every one in her drenched and much exhausted. It was evident that it was impossible to prevent these vessels from running on shore, unless a boat could be so placed close in shore of them, and such a distance south of us, that the dhow would arrive abreast of her before she saw either the ship or boat; the latter could then board her or run up inside her until she had dropped down upon us; but the coast was so straight here, and the dhows sailed so close in, that they might be able to escape unless the boat were concealed; this plan could only be carried out, owing to the straight line of coast, about three miles south of Brava, where there was a coral rock, projecting about twenty or thirty yards from the shore, forming a point, or rather breakwater, stretching out beyond the breakers. We placed the cutters in charge of Sub-Lieutenants Farr and Henn, north of this point, and where they could not be seen from the dhows until abreast of them; we then steamed up to the north out of sight of this point, and that afternoon saw the cutters chasing a dhow which had to keep out from the shore to avoid them, and, consequently, to drop down upon the ship: she was a "*legal trader*," with twenty-one slaves on board, in a miserable and emaciated condition, lying on the top of her cargo; there were eight men, four women, and nine children. Before the boats could return to their former station, another crowded slaver hove in sight, and just as we got up to her, she ran through the breakers, and landed two or three hundred slaves. I may here remark that this was never done but by full slavers, the legal traders preferring to pass their few slaves off, if possible, as part of their crew, and of hiding some of them under their cargoes.[2]

On the morning of the 1st November, we observed the cutter, under charge of Mr. Henn, chasing a dhow outside her, which, on seeing us, lowered her sail, and a few minutes after she was brought alongside, with 156 slaves in

---

[2] It has been found impossible on some occasions to measure the dhows for tonnage, as they were wrecked in the surf and broken up in a few minutes; in such cases the boats cannot reach them and an estimate for tonnage has to be made by competent officers. Owing to the peculiar construction of these dhows, and to the fact that sometimes nearly one-fourth of their capacity is represented by the huge stern and peculiar raised poop of these vessels, the usual method of ascertaining tonnage is inapplicable. I have seen some of the smaller dhows, the whole outline of which much resemble in plan the section of a Minie rifle-ball, and with the exception of the northern *bateeles* and *badanes*, much superior vessels, and the largest of the dhows or *bugalas*, they are but floating tubs. The duty of measuring these vessels is very much disliked by officers.

The best plan I can suggest to prevent any misconception is, that the average tonnage of the dhows captured within the last few years be taken, and that in future, whatever the size of the slaver, the bounty be allowed for each dhow captured on the basis of that average. The average tonnage, according to the Blue Books of 1869 and 1870 was, in 1868, 113·487 tons, and in 1869, 109·598 tons. The average of those captured by the "Daphne" in 1868, was eighty tons.

her, forty-eight men, fifty-three women, and fifty-five children.[3] The deplorable condition of some of these poor wretches, crammed into a small dhow, surpasses all description; on the bottom of the dhow was a pile of stones as ballast, and on these stones, without even a mat, were twenty-three women huddled together —one or two with infants in their arms—these women were literally doubled up, there being no room to sit erect; on a bamboo deck, about three feet above the keel, were forty-eight men, crowded together in the same way, and on another deck above this were fifty-three children. Some of the slaves were in the last stages of starvation and dysentery. On getting the vessel alongside and clearing her out, a woman came up, having an infant about a month or six weeks old in her arms, with one side of its forehead crushed in. On asking how it was done, she told us that just

---

[3] The women and children are generally taken most care of, they having a greater marketable value, and in some instances we found them in good health and well cared for.

GROUP OF NEGRO MEN AND BOYS TAKEN OUT OF CAPTURED DHOW IN A STATE OF STARVATION. [*Page* 168.
(*From a Photograph by the Author.*)

before our boat came alongside the dhow, the child began to cry, and one of the Arabs, fearing the English would hear it, took up a stone, and struck it. A few hours after this the poor thing died, and the woman was too weak and ill to be able to point out the monster who had done it, from amongst the ten or dozen Arabs on board.

On the same day, the 1st November, we took a "legal trader," with fifteen slaves on the top of her cargo. These fifteen were in very good condition.

Again, on the same day we took another, with twenty-six slaves, unlike those in the former case, in the most wretched condition; some had been brought up from the country south of Quiloa, and fed with as much rice as they could hold in their hand and the half of a cocoa-nut shell of water per day. In some of these dhows, especially in the case of the fullest of them, unless the cargo happened to be rice or grain of any kind, there was never more than a bag or two on board, so that we were obliged to purchase rice out of other dhows, on our passage back to Zanzibar, to feed these negroes.

On the 4th November, the "Star," Commander De Kantzow, made her number, and I believe her appearance was hailed with pleasure by every one, as it was evident we had fallen upon a nest of slavers bound for Muscat, in accordance with the information received at Zanzibar. On the other hand, I was ordered not to delay longer on the coast; our coals were much reduced by this service, and our upper deck was now crowded[*] with slaves, for it was out of the question keeping them in the dhows, some of them unseaworthy, and in attempting to tow them they would have sunk. Mr. Churchill, C.B., Consul at Zanzibar, was on his way to Bombay in the "Star," but as I felt it necessary, under the circumstances, to leave the coast, I directed the "Star" to remain, to intercept the rest of this slave fleet, and invited Mr. Churchill on

---

[*] I have not mentioned each vessel taken, as the number eventually amounted to fifteen dhows on this part of the coast, having 322 slaves in all, and the story of the capture of each one would but be a repetition.

GROUP OF 322 LIBERATED AFRICANS ON THE DECK OF THE "DAPHNE."
(From a Photograph by the Author.) [*Page 171.*

to proceed with us to Bombay.... On the
.... and ourselves .....
two .... eighteen slaves
.... and cleared
.... of being
....
....
.... the sunset
.... precedes the mon..... of .... poorly
... as the sun....................
coast;..........................
of the gr..., we consequently found ourselves
with 822 negroes on board, and only ten tons
of coals left, nothing to be....... ordered
............................coast at
.................of two months and
.... eastward,
....
....
....
....
....
.... We

board, to proceed with us to Bombay. On the next morning, the "Star" and ourselves captured two slavers, ours having eighteen slaves, hers six. We then parted company and steered for the northward, with the intention of going to Aden to land the negroes, and condemn the prizes, but were unable to get farther than 4° 36′ north latitude, where we met the current that always precedes the monsoon about a month, and as the south-west monsoon had now nearly ceased, it did not reach so far north at this time of the year; we consequently found ourselves with 322 negroes on board, and only ten tons of coals left, drifting a knot an hour southward in the belt of calms that exists on the coast at this time of the year for about two months and extends for several degrees to the eastward; we therefore at first altered our course for Seychelles, with the intention of landing the negroes there, obtaining coal, and then going to Bombay, but we soon found this impracticable, as by the 18th November we had drifted so far down the coast, as to leave no alternative but to steer for Zanzibar. We were about three weeks returning from Brava to that port, expending our remnant of coals on the last day in steaming. We had on a former occasion gone over the same ground in four days. After completing with coals at this port, we sailed again with our living freight for Seychelles.

CHAPTER IX.

Negro Tribes — Gallas — Naming the Negroes — Marlborough—Negroes feeding—Several die—Small-pox breaks out—Examination of Negroes—Their Stories —Mary Careesey—First Lieutenant's Employment pus Patience—Peggy—Native Languages—Arrival at Seychelles—Put in Quarantine—Negroes Landed —Several marry—Arrival at Bombay.

I MUST now give some account of the slaves themselves, and their lives on board, &c. Of the three hundred and twenty-two, there were a hundred and eighteen men, a hundred and nine women, and ninety-five children, including thirty-two men and women from two wrecked dhows, surrendered on demand by the chief of Brava. Among these there were eleven different tribes, viz. :—

The Galla, an intelligent race which the Arabs do not class with the negroes.

Monheka, the tribe of the country adjoining the Gallas.

Legoha or *Messegora*, the tribe that bring ivory from the interior.

Minyemazer, next, or close to, the Legoha tribe.

Kamango, Machinga, Mazo, Makoo, Maheow, Nchassa, Monginda, more southern tribes.

Like birds of a feather, these negroes were always found in groups together according to their tribes, some of them being much superior to the rest in intellect, as well as in appearance.

The Galla tribe have none of the negro in their features; they are a handsome race; and those on board, both men and women, were so without exception; the men powerfully built, and the women positively graceful in form and movement, whilst their bright, intelligent faces and long curly hair gave them quite a civilized appearance, and could they but exchange the dark copper-coloured complexion for a white one, it would be almost impossible to make slaves of them. The Somallies, with whom they are always at war,

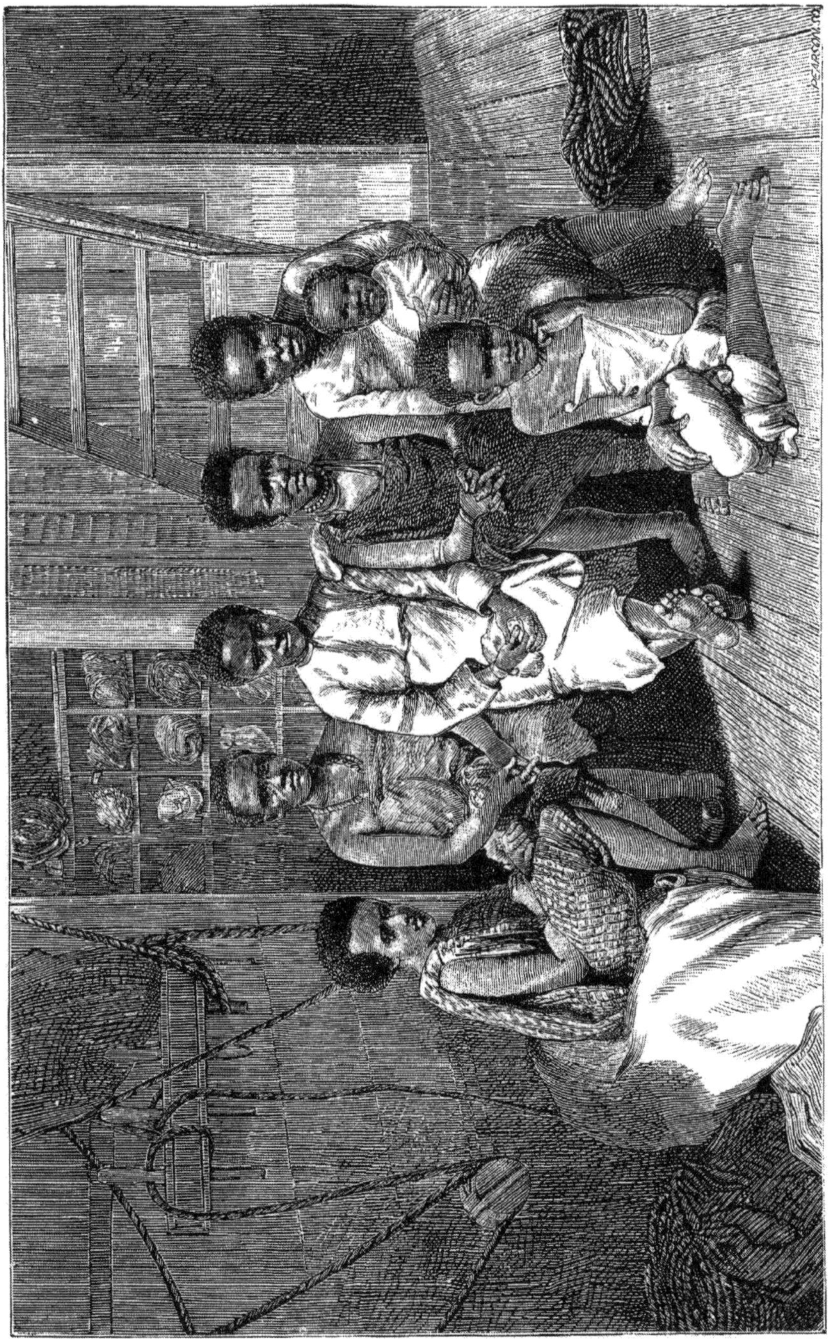

though considered the superior race, resemble them much in many ways, in intelligence, warlike propensities, habits, and manner of living, eating chiefly animal food, often obtained by hunting; they were the only tribe that almost *required* animal food on board. All the women were kept on the port side of the quarter-deck, and those of the Galla tribe, amounting to about ten or a dozen, located themselves amidships, between the engine-room and after-hatchways, where, being the best-looking ladies, I am bound to say they received more attention than any of the others, in the shape of an occasional basin of soup, or plate of meat and vegetables, brought up from the messes, the sight of which made the other ebony ladies eye them evidently with envy, hatred, and malice.

One of the first things, we are told, Adam did, was to name the animals, and one of the first things done by us was to name these slaves on their being received on board, at least the principal ones in each tribe; and among the Gallas we had Peggy, Susan, Sally, Sophy,

176 DHOW CHASING.

Mary, Tom, Jim, &c., &c. Peggy was a fine, good-looking woman, with a little boy of about twelve months old, who received the name of Billy, and who rejected every thing in the

SUSAN.   ANN.   THE TOAD.   SARAH.   THE ELEPHANT.
GROUP OF NEGRO WOMEN OF DIFFERENT TRIBES.
(*From a Photograph by the Author.*)

shape of clothing whenever it was attempted to cover him, toddling about in a state of nudity, and was often found in the arms of the boatswain's mate in the gangway, whose duty he appeared to think was to carry him. I believe he was never heard to cry during his six weeks on board.

Another intelligent tribe, though not to be compared to the Gallas, was the Maheows. Two of their women were called respectively "Betsy Jane" and "the Elephant," this last designation arising from the size of the person to whom it was given. There was not a man or woman in the ship to be compared to this huge monster.

Whilst there was not much distinction between the intermediate tribes, we must not forget to mention "the Monginda." Anything more repulsive than some of the females of this tribe it is impossible to conceive, for, unlike the men belonging to it, they are tattooed all over and have large holes in the upper lips, nose, and ears—holes made when they were born, and which the rings and ornaments suspended from them had enlarged to an enormous size; in the holes bored in the lobes of their ears they wear circular pieces of wood,

178 DHOW-CHASING.

like draughtsmen, inserted; and rings, &c., worn in the hole of the upper lip, had so stretched it that nearly all the lower lip was seen through it. In addition to this these

LUMPY KEBOKO.
(*From a Sketch by Mr. Churchill, C.B.*)

people are clumsy in figure, and have very small heads and large cheeks without one solitary look of intelligence to brighten them. I pointed one out to Mr. Churchill, asking him to name the tribe, and he replied that he considered it a new species altogether till then undiscovered; and for the benefit of natural historians he would call it "Lumpy Keboko," "Keboko" being the Arabic word for hippopotamus. Another of the same tribe acquired the name of "the Toad."

Amongst the men on board was one who belonged to the Monheka tribe, whose country adjoins the Gallas, and a finer specimen of a man could rarely be found. He had escaped from Brava on seeing the ship anchored about two miles off, by swimming against wind and current from the shore, and had actually swum two-thirds of the distance when he was seen from the mast-head and a boat sent to pick him up. On his arrival on board he told us he was the slave of a very cruel master and he wanted to escape. On being asked his name, he replied with something that sounded so like "Marlborough," that we gave him that name and made him captain of all the other niggers, to keep them in order and superintend the cooking, serving out their provisions, &c.—a duty he carried out well — proving a most useful fellow. For the purpose of cooking we rigged up a fireplace on raised blocks of wood, having a combing round it covered with sheets of copper, on which was erected a substitute for a stove consisting of raised iron bars for resting the copper vessels taken out of the dhows, and under them the fire was placed. Rice and grain formed the chief food; the grain was pounded up every morning by some of the men and women, boiled, and then as much as they wanted served out to them morning and evening, each tribe having theirs in one large vessel, round which they sat, despising spoons and forks and eating with their fingers. Each morning, whilst the decks were washing, the whole of the negroes would be assembled in the gangway and the steam-hose taken on to the bridge and water pumped over them; this was not only necessary, but very much delighted in by them, some of them remaining under it for several minutes. At times some new arrival would get close to the hose, not knowing its force, when he would soon be knocked down by the stream of water

GROUP OF SLAVE-CHILDREN ON BOARD THE "DAPHNE."
(*From a Photograph by the Author.*)

[*Page* 189.

GROUP OF SLAVE-CHILDREN ON BOARD THE "DAPHNE."

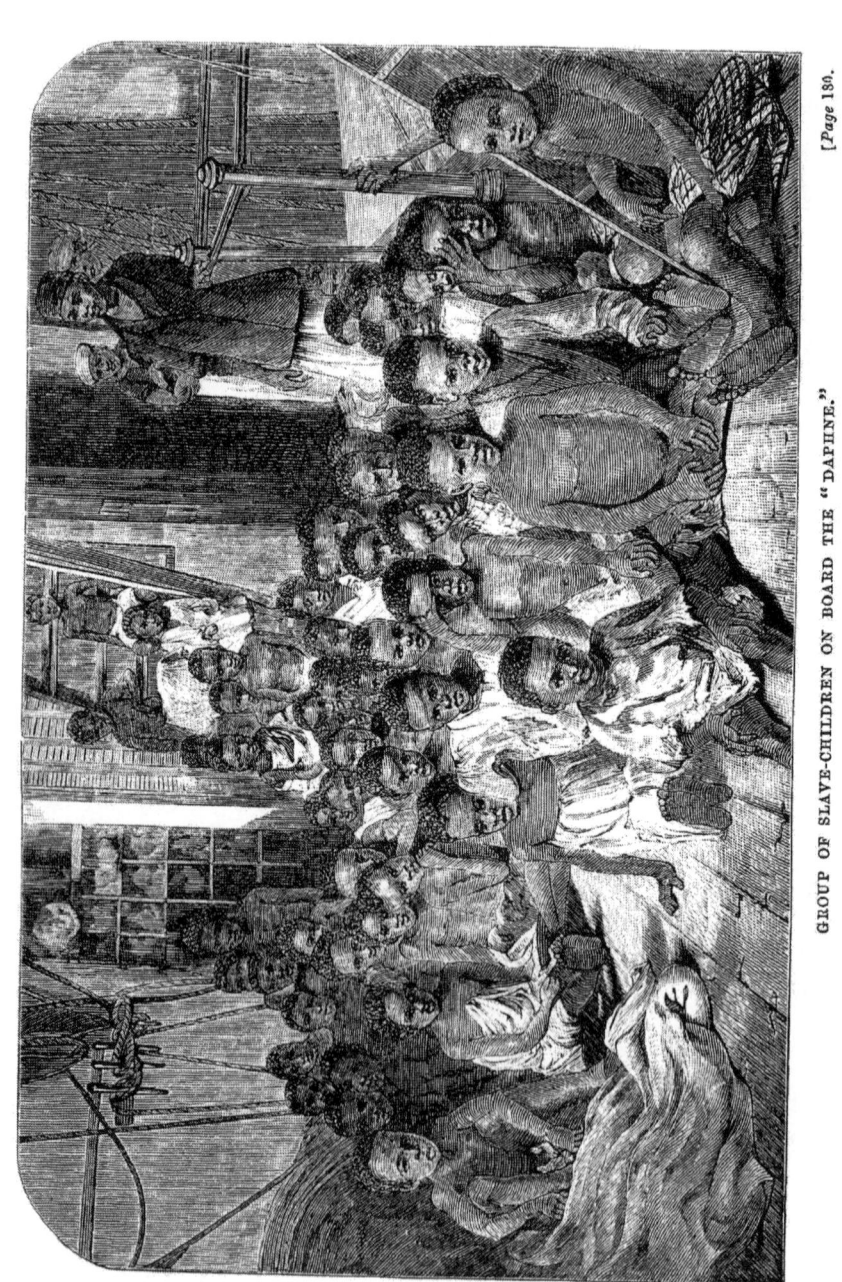

[*Page* 180.

and be seen sprawling along the deck, to the great amusement of the others. About a week after we left Brava, we had only three days' provisions for the slaves on board; fortunately, however, we fell in with a dhow that had a general cargo, and we were enabled to purchase enough to last us till we got to Zanzibar.

Among these poor creatures there were many seriously ill, and some of them died, though everything was done for them that could be done by Dr. Mortimer and others. They never rallied from the exhaustion produced by starvation on board the dhow. Dysentery was carrying them off, and amongst those ill, some were suffering from ulcers, and these had to be kept separate from the mass. But worse than all, the small-pox broke out just before we arrived at Zanzibar. After getting there we landed the only case at the time, hoping it would prevent the spread of the disease, and Mr. Churchill, while on board, being Judge of the Admiralty Court, heard the story of each slave separately, which facilitated our starting for Seychelles; but by the time we arrived there, we had buried in all, from various diseases, sixteen negroes, and there were fourteen more ill with small-pox, besides five of our own crew, and owing to the number of negroes [1] on board, and the sickness among them, it produced such an effect upon the health of the ship's company that we had as many as thirty-five besides on the sick-list, being the largest number we had had during our commission; the average number being about five or six.

I will now relate a few specimens of the answers to questions put by Mr. Churchill and myself to these Africans.

We sent for them one by one and questioned them through the interpreter.

---

[1] If the Arab passengers and crews of these slave dhows had been retained on board, it would have added upwards of 100 more to the number of souls on board. Some of these Arabs would have required guarding. How we should have fed them, and how far the additional crowding would have accelerated or increased the disease on board, is an experience yet to be purchased. At this time, however, it was not compulsory, but rested with the Arabs themselves, who invariably desired to be landed, knowing that it would be useless to return to Zanzibar before the next season. Indeed it would have been a punishment to take them back.

A woman of the Galla tribe was the first to come up. On the interpreter handing a chair to her, she took her seat in it as if she had been accustomed to one all her life, though perhaps it was the first she had ever seen.

"How did you get on board the dhow?"

"I was stolen with several others from a village."

"Where is your husband?"

"He was killed in the fight."

"What is the religion of your tribe?"

"When they wanted rain they went to a priest to get it."

"Did he pray for it?"

She didn't know.

"When their friends died what did they do?"

"They took the body to a priest, with a bullock, and he buried it."

"Who is your god?"

She didn't know.

"Who is the priest's god?"

She couldn't tell.

"When she died what would become of her?"

She didn't know.

"Was she glad to be free?"

She didn't know she should be free.

"Where are your other children?"

"All stolen from me."

The next examined was "Mary," another Galla, a remarkably pretty girl, about fifteen or sixteen years of age.

"What is your name in your own country?"

"Careesey."

"What part of the country were you taken from?"

"Teemeto, in Galla country."

"Are you married?"

"Yes; and my baby died."

"How were you taken?"

"Stolen with another girl."

"Who stole you?"

"I was walking with another girl from my hut to my mother's, and two Arabs came out of the bush and took us."

"How many days travelling were you from your house to the sea-coast?"

"One day from Chinacombo at top of river Toolo."

" Can you see Mount Killamanga from your home ?"

" Yes, not far off; but my country is flat."

" How long was it between your being stolen and captured by the 'Daphne' ?"

" Ten days."

"Did you cry or fret much after being stolen ?"

" Oh, yes! cry much for my father and mother."

" Were you glad when this ship captured your dhow ?"

She did not know she would be free.

" Are many people stolen from your country ?"

" Yes, often."

This girl was one of the first to die of the small-pox.

Examination of a boy about eight years old, one of those brought off in the life-boat from the wreck.

" What is your name ?"

" Zangora."

Recollected his mother. Men stole him.

" How many days were you travelling from your country to Quiloa ?"

"From when the corn was young to when it was cut; about three moons."

"How many slaves were in the dhow with you?"

"A great many; five died, and some were drowned in landing."

Arabs told them white man would eat them to make them go into the water and run away.

It would be impossible to give all the statements of these negroes here. There was a great similarity of detail amongst them, which might be summed up as follows:—"fights," "murders," "robberies," "separation from friends," "long journeys," "cruel treatment," and "sold at some market to be taken they know not where, with *the conviction that it was impossible ever to return to their own land or relations again.*"

Let some of those first Lieutenants who can appreciate the position of having expended the last pound of paint in completing the ship for an anticipated inspection, picture to themselves the position of Lieut. Acklom, who for six weeks had the mortification of seeing the ship turned into a depôt for negroes, who had no special regard for anything on board; and in addition to all this, finding himself thinking, acting, and settling every complaint and little grievance for them; for they soon discovered, somehow, that he was to be looked to for everything, and in their simple nigger view of it he possessed a supernatural power, so that they had only to speak to him to get all they wanted in life, and regarded him as a sort of "sultan," "prime minister," "foreign secretary," and "judge" combined.

On one occasion I came out and found him surrounded by niggers from every tribe talking away in their respective jargons to him, some wanting to have their disputes settled, rattling away as if they fully expected they were understood, others asking questions apparently about food, and some recounting with an air of the greatest mystery and importance something that had taken place between their tribe and another. "Huagu Yastakili, Kutiva, Katika, fumba," or some such words, were replied to with, "Oh! yes, of course, I perfectly agree with you." "Now suppose you, and Marlborough and Sally, and Jim and Peggy, go grindum cornum and boilum in the potum you have dinner, if not, you have none." Just then Peggy made her appearance. "What's the matter, Peggy?" Some Galla language unintelligible was the reply. "Oh! has she, poor old girl, lost her boy? Where's Billy?" This name was understood by her now, and she pointed to her boy in the arms of one of the men in the gangway. "Oh! that's not it. Well, what is it?" At last it was understood that Peggy wanted some fish for dinner as we had caught a shark that day. Such was the occupation of our senior Lieutenant, whose good-humour and equanimity never forsook him. He never wearied of doing his best for these poor creatures; and, ill or dying, as many of them were, they needed much compassion and patience to be exercised towards them.

Native Languages.

The language on the East Coast of Africa, from south of the Zambesi to Formosa Bay, the north extreme of Zanzibar, is chiefly

Swaheli; but this is not the only language, Arabic is also spoken. The Arabs who recaptured the territory of Zanzibar from the Portuguese about two hundred years ago, or rather reasserted claim to it, and drove the Portuguese out, adopted necessarily to a great extent the language of that part of the coast, Swaheli; and from the extensive monopoly of the trade far south of this, have transmitted that language into nearly every part of East Africa, excepting in the Somauli country and the interior, where it only exists to a limited degree. And it has more than probably become an improved language, owing to the intermingling of the Arabic with it. The negro slaves on arrival at Quiloa from the interior are often retained a few months there for the double purpose of recovering their health, and so making them more saleable, and of teaching them the Swaheli language, which is not only to some degree necessary, but increases their value in the Zanzibar market. It must not be supposed that of the eleven tribes on board the "Daphne," speaking as many different languages, that we could communicate with all; we could only be understood by those who had learned something, though very little generally, of the Swaheli language, by which our Arab interpreter, Jumah, could be understood; and those also of the tribes of which there happened to be amongst them one who had learnt a little Swaheli, and who could act as interpreter again between Jumah and his own tribe; but it was no very long or clear account even then that we could get, owing to their imperfect knowledge even in the case of those who understood Swaheli best, otherwise much might have been learned of these negroes, their country and their history, which was impossible to get at under the circumstances in which we were placed.

We were enabled to get a few words of the Galla language, the only one that appeared anything like complete and interesting; those of the inferior tribes seem but very limited in their words; broken ejaculations and oft repeated syllables produced monotony in the sounds, while they never seemed to carry on any long conversation between each other.

The Galla language struck some of us as resembling English in certain respects, others thought it more like the Italian, there was a little of the guttural, but more of the liquid sound, as they dwelt on and prolonged the vowels.

The following are words and phrases obtained from the natives, which may be interesting :—

Good morning,[2] *Nageeha fiah.*
What is your name ? *Myuntee stee una.*
What do you want ? *Nulla fidea ?*
You want something to eat, *Nulla fidea sagal.*
I love you, "Billy!" "*Billy*" *hanna adgee latee.*
You don't love me, *Soona hanna adgee latee.*

Good, *Dunsa.*
Bad, *Humta.*
You are good, *Atena dunsa.*
You are bad, *Atena humta.*
Head, *Mata.*
Eye, *Illa.*
Mouth, *Oofa.*
Nose, *Foona*
Neck, *Loub.*
Arm, *Arago or aretee.*
Chest, *Underaf.*
Stomach, *Kara.*
Leg, *Suga.*
Men, *Deerah.*

Woman, *Nadeane.*
Throat, *Loub.*
I, *Affood.*
You, *Nalam.*
Child, *Agolly.*
Baby, *Amnoo.*
Boy, *Gooreba.*
Girl, *Doobra.*
Foot, *Fan.*
Toe, *Koobein.*
Ankle, *Kooameto.*
Calf (of leg), *Serbia.*
Thigh, *Goodeate.*
Knee, *Gilbie.*

[2] The following words are spelt as nearly as possible according to the pronunciation of the natives.

Numbers.

1. Tate.
2. Lam.
3. Sadee.
4. Hafoo.
5. Shun.
6. Jah.
7. Toib.
8. Ladeate.
9. Sagal.
10. Kooden.
11. Kooden tate.
12. Kooden lam.
13. Kooden sadee.
14. Kooden hafoo.
15. Kooden shun.
16. Kooden jah.
17. Kooden toib.
18. Kooden ladeate.
19. Kooden sadal.
20. Illama.
21. Illama tate.
22. Illama lam, &c.
30. Sadamo.
31. Sadamo tate, &c.
40. Haffodo, &c.
50. Shun tom, &c.
60. Yah tom.
70. Toibatom.
80. Sadeatom.
90. Sagal tom.
100. Diss.
101. Diss tate.
102. Diss lam.
200. Lam diss.

Specimens of some of the questions put in the Swaheli language to slaves on board the dhows:—

Were you kidnapped? *Wewa muckamatwae.*
Were you bought? *Wewe uninunwa.*
Did they buy you? *We-me ku-nunuwa.*
Yes, *Udin-nam.*
No, *La (hetkuna).*
Where do you come from? *Utoka wassi.*
What tribe are you? *Kabila gani* (or *nitu gani*).
Where do you go? *Kuenda wassi.*
What trade are you? *Beashawa gani.*
Are you a slave? *Wewey M'turnwa.*

Examples of the Swaheli language, from a Book of Stories, published at the Zanzibar Mission House:—

HEKAIYA YA BRUCE NA BUIBUI.
Robert Bruce and the Spider.

ALIPOIHTAHIDI Sultani Brus katika ku
When strove   King Robert Bruce   to
khalisi 'nchi Skotland kwa nguvu za Ingreza
deliver   Scotland   from the forces of England
alikuwa akishindwa marra nyingi, na watu
he was conquered   many times,   and   his
wake wakatawanyika, na wangine wakawowa.
people   scattered,   and   others   killed.
Baadaye marra moja katika marra hizo, aliku-
After   one   of   these times,   he
wa malala katika nyumba mbofu, akazindu-
was asleep   in   a ruined house,   he woke
kana kwa nefsi yake, akakaa ku tafakari ka-
up   by himself,   he sat   thinking   a-
tika mambo aliwayakosa, akataghaiari moyo
bout the things he had lost, he was changed, in his
wake akamwona haifai ku ongeza juhudi.
heart he saw himself of no use   to prolong   efforts.
Bassi katika ku tafakari kwake, akaona bui-
Then amidst   his thinking,   he saw a spi-
bui hukwea katika kwenda mahali pake, aka-
der climbing   in   going to   his place,   it
anguka, akapanda tena, akaanguka marra
fell,   it went up again,   it fell   times
theletashar hali hiyo, hatta marra arobatashar
thirteen   thus,   till   the fourteenth time

akapanda, akafika mahali pake, akafanya ha-
it went up, reached its place, made its

riri. Akasema yule Sultani, alipoona haya,
web. Said that King, when he saw this

ya kwamba huyu buibui marra theletashar a-
that this spider thirteen times

lianguka, na mi nimefanya marra tatu ao
fell, and I have tried times three or

'nne. Akaazmia ku dumu nalo, akakusanya
four. He determined to persevere with it, gathered

watu wangine, akashinda Sultani Ingrez kwa
another army, conquered the English King in a

mapigano makuu, wala hakushindwa baa-
great battle, nor was he conquered aft-

daye hapo, hatta ya kuwa inchi yake milele
er this so as to be his land always

katika amani.
in safety.

On our arrival at Seychelles, it being known that small-pox was among us, we were put in quarantine, and the slaves were ordered to be landed on the Quarantine island, and the next day every slave was out of the ship. No one, however, but those belonging to the ship could land there, and we employed the Africans in building a large hut sufficient to hold all of them. We erected a hospital tent, for those of our own crew suffering from the disease on the opposite side of the little island, and there they remained till convalescent.

A few days after we had landed them, I went on shore to see them again, and found the interior of the large hut divided off into small huts or rooms, in some of which whole tribes were located, and in other smaller ones, married couples. Yes, indeed, they had taken upon themselves to make the best they could of a world that had treated them so badly, and thus to share their miseries together.

I took a list of these couples, with the names they had acquired or answered to, and sent it to Mr. Ward, Commissioner of the island, who promised duly to register the same.

This list was headed by

"Marlborough and Sally."

"Jim and Peggy."

Some four months later, when visiting these islands, we found that the epidemic had been fatal to about fifty more of the negroes, after we had left for Bombay. Our own men had quite recovered, and there was only one case on board after we left Seychelles.

On arriving at Bombay, we heard that the "Star" had captured many more slavers, and taken about three hundred liberated Africans to Aden, but some doubts were raised in the Indian Court there, as to whether they were domestic slaves, and whether it was not wronging the *poor Arabs*, to prevent their taking them to the northern markets, and, further, there appeared to be an inclination to give these *poor Arabs* the benefit of such doubts, and allow them to retain their slaves. I should prefer giving the benefit of any doubt to the slaves, and if either of them are to be abandoned to slavery, why not let the negroes take the Arab back to his country and sell him, as he might in some parts of it possibly, such as the interior of the Galla and Somauli country?

CHAPTER X.

Number of Captures in 1868 — Departure from Bombay — Cruise on Arabian Coast—Chase of Dhows—A Slave Dhow slips away — Maculla— Visit to the Sheik— Capture of two Dhows— Stories of Slaves on Board— Aden —Condemnation of Dhows — Departure for Seychelles—Capture of Slaver with fifty-two Slaves— Arrival at Seychelles—Visit to old Acquaintance.

IT may not be out of place here to make a few remarks on the future blockade of the coast, and on the necessity of a sufficient number of cruisers being stationed on it, if the subject is to be dealt with earnestly. In addition to other measures for the suppression of the slave-trade, it will be necessary to increase the squadron on the station considerably in order to make the blockade effective, and taking into consideration the fact that some of the vessels comprising the squadron will be required for stations in India, while some will be withdrawn at times for repairs, it does not appear, should the naval stations of East Africa and India remain combined as at present, that such service can be satisfactorily performed without a sufficient number of ships there to allow of seven being kept constantly employed upon it, which could not be the case with a squadron of less than ten ships (including the flag-ship); one half of these might be sixty-horse-power gun-boats, which could be easily beached for repairs at Zanzibar, and the rest of a larger class, and to each of them should be attached a steam launch or pinnace, for without one or the other, seven vessels would be quite insufficient for the service.

At certain seasons of the year, namely, when the monsoon sets in fully on the Arabian and Somauli coasts (and much earlier from the Red Sea,[1] on account of the heat), the ships would have to leave these parts of the coast, but on withdraw-

[1] There is an extensive trade in slaves carried on to the Egyptian ports in the Red Sea, through and from Abyssinia. See Dr. W. Schimpfer's letter in the Appendix.

ing they should remain as long as practicable in the track of the northern dhows from Zanzibar to Ras-el-Had.

As this is a question that will no doubt be more fully considered hereafter by the Admiralty and senior officers on the station, I shall content myself with briefly pointing out the manner in which the coast might be divided into several stations for the cruisers and steam launches.

1. On the Arabian coast, from Ras-el-Had to Haura, one vessel and two steam launches.

2. Red Sea, one vessel and two launches.

3. From Cape Guardafui to Formosa Bay, one vessel and one launch.

(The above would have to be withdrawn on the setting in of the monsoon.)

4. From Formosa Bay to Cape Delgado, one vessel and one launch.

5. From Cape Delgado to Macalonga river, one vessel and one launch.

6. From Macalonga river to Inhambane, one vessel and one launch.

7. From Commoro Islands to N.W. coast of Madagascar, one vessel and two launches; on

all these stations there are uninhabited islands, and other convenient places where these boats could be beached for repairs. In a very few years, no doubt, it would be possible to greatly reduce this squadron, as the slave-dealers would soon be convinced that England was in earnest, and that the slave-trade would become unprofitable and hazardous.

I would here remark that there were many circumstances tending to bring about in the year 1868 the capture of so many slave dhows. First, there was an increase in the number of slaves accumulated at the various markets, owing to the squadron being withdrawn for the Abyssinian expedition, and consequently absent from the coast at the commencement of the year, which the slave-dealers were anxious to take advantage of. Secondly, as we mentioned before, there was a war between two tribes on opposite sides of the Juba river, which cut off the land route along the coast from Lamoo to Brava and Magadoxa, by which the slaves are often conveyed, especially if there are any cruisers known to be off the coast, and also when the s.w. monsoon has ceased and they cannot get farther north in the dhows. And thirdly, the vessels of the squadron were so disposed of on the coast by Commodore (now Admiral) Sir Leopold Heath, that the slave-dealers never could find out where they were likely to turn up, but were surprised in every direction by them.

After refitting at Bombay, we sailed in company with the flag-ship and "Star," and for a few days were engaged in trying rate of sailing, in which the "Daphne," I am bound to confess, was always where the little boat was, as those of her class are likely to be, for though powerful steamers, they are perfect tubs in sailing.

We parted company with the flag-ship and "Star" on the 2nd April, and proceeded in accordance with our orders to Ras-el-Had and Kooria-Mooria along the Arabian coast.

On this coast we chased and boarded some fifty or sixty dhows, none of which had on board any, excepting a few domestic slaves.

On one occasion we sighted three dhows close together, and as soon as they discovered we were chasing them, they separated and steered in different directions, but soon finding it was of no use, as our boats were inside, they steered as before along the coast; we overtook and boarded these soon after dark; two of them we found to be legal traders, but on board one there were three or four slaves, including a father and son, who stated they had been domestic slaves in Zanzibar, but had now been sold, and were being taken to Muscat, to be sold again: the officer brought these slaves, and with them an Arab—who was said to be the negoda and owner of the dhow—on board the "Daphne" for further examination; but it was evident that he was not the negoda, for while they were on board, the night becoming very dark and blowing fresh, this dhow, leaving the other two alongside, slipped away, and we saw her no more, possibly the two other dhows by spreading out on first sighting us, were endeavouring to help this one in escaping.

We anchored off Maculla on the 26th April.

Maculla is an Arabian town with a large population of Arabs, and a larger one of slaves.

It is one of the principal markets on the Arabian coast to which dhows proceed when caught by the N.E. monsoon and unable to get farther towards Muscat. After leaving the African coast they cross over from Cape Guardafui to Maculla, which bears N.W. of that Cape, where they sell their slaves, some of whom may find their way to other places by land, but the greatest number remain there until the change of the monsoon again, when they are sent to the Persian Gulf.

Maculla is a genuine Arab town, the houses square built, with white-washed walls, giving the outside some appearance of cleanliness in the distance, but within the town, and within most of those houses, are filth and misery of every kind.

The country round is a barren, dried up mountainous district, with no vestige of vegetation to be seen anywhere near it from the sea. I went on shore to call on the Sheik, who appeared to be rather alarmed at our appearance, as he had unpleasant recollections of H.M.S. "Highflyer" having about two years previously enforced some demands on him with a few shot. I assured him our visit so far as he was concerned was a most amicable one, but we had reason to think there were large numbers of slaves often landed from the dhows, and that we were merely cruising off the coast with the object of stopping the slave-trade. He assured me that if it existed it was unknown to him, which statement coming from an Arab was not of great value, and he appeared much pleased that we were not about to repeat the "Highflyer's" bombardment.

On the 29th we captured two slavers, one a Zanzibar vessel having two slaves, purchased by the captain at one of the ports on the coast, to be sold again on arrival in the Persian Gulf. These poor fellows cried the whole time they were telling their story, and entreated almost in a tone of agony not to be sent back to the dhow. The other was an Arab dhow, the property of the captain. She was captured by the cutter under Lieut. Loch; on boarding her there was a faint attempt at resistance, a clattering of arms, and threatening attitudes, but they drew back on the cutter's crew boarding, and surrendered the dhow. She appeared to belong to some of the tribes on the Somallie coast, having no papers, and sixty negroes crowded on her deck. Of these there were about a dozen Somallies as merchant passengers—a tribe seldom made slaves of by the Arabs owing to their warlike character; the remainder of the negroes were probably owned by these, or the negado (i. e. captain), but from the fear they stood in of their owners, we could get information only from one woman and two children. Her story was that her husband had lately died, and that his brother was taking her across to Maculla to sell her to pay his debts.

The stories of the two children were that they were kidnapped by the captain about a month previously on the coast.

We towed these vessels to Aden for condemnation.

In the court the woman, apparently from fear of the negoda who was present, altered her story, and said that she was going to Maculla because her husband was dead, but immediately afterwards the man, whom she first had pointed out as her husband's brother who was about to sell her, came into court, not having heard her evidence, and swore she was his wife! Both dhows were condemned.

Leaving Aden on the 11th May, we captured a dhow with fifty-two slaves on board, between the island of Socotra and the Arabian coast. We now left this cruising-ground for Seychelles.

On our passage these liberated slaves appeared to enjoy themselves much; they were all in good health and condition: they chiefly consisted of women and children, who, as I have before said, are usually taken the most care of. It was interesting to see them every evening dancing to their monotonous nigger strains and tom-toms.

On arrival at Seychelles, some of us paid a visit to "Mr. and Mrs. (Sally) Marlborough," and "Mr. and Mrs. (Peggy) Jim." We found them in neatly built huts, and they told us they were very happy and contented.

CHAPTER XI.

Zanzibar—French Charlie's Shop, his Promptness—Trip to Dar-a Salaam—Our Party—The Town—Shooting Hippopotami—Mafamale Strangers—Fish Hawks—Mayotta—Marguerite.

FROM Seychelles we sailed for Zanzibar. After our arrival at that place the last-named dhow was condemned, and we made preparations at once for a three months' cruise towards the south.

Amongst the most important establishments at Zanzibar is the retail shop or store kept by a man known as French Charlie—why French I was unable to ascertain, seeing that he is really a half-caste Portuguese possibly he has adopted the appellation by way of entitling him to French protection, which it seems he has somehow acquired. To thoroughly describe the shop, and the premises of which it forms a part, would require the pen of a Dickens or a Thackeray, and indeed the former writer somewhat portrays it in his picture of Mr. Crump's establishment. In one of the narrowest and dirtiest streets of that pestilential town, and which of all in it most requires a strong constitution and a well-scented pocket-handkerchief to enter, is a rudely-built stone house, the main door of which opens directly into the shop and store of this worthy merchant of doubtful origin and inexplicable name.

The first things that attract the eye on looking around are great piles of mildewed bags and rusty preserved-meat tins stored against the wall up to the cobweb-covered ceiling, and presenting a good deal of the appearance of a barricade. It is dangerous, however, to pay too much attention at first to surrounding curiosities, as you stand a fair chance of a fall, for the ground of this shop—it has no flooring —might be taken for the model of a battle-field, or for a plan of Africa with its hills and valleys, woods and glens, rivers and lakes, but with a far larger population represented by millions of ants, while the wild beasts are replaced by innumerable spiders and cockroaches. Into this shop we were compelled to go, for it was the only one in Zanzibar that could supply what we wanted.

On entering, Bacchanal strains reached our ears from an inner room on the right hand, and as we passed through an archway or opening in the wall—these Arab houses have rarely any doors within—we saw, seated round a table saturated with the various liquors from overturned glasses, several Yankee merchant seamen, and half-caste negro women dressed in Arab costume, drunk, but still drinking. We had but a glance of this interior, and then gave our orders for a sufficient stock of everything we should require for the cruise, (for this Zanzibar merchant deals in everything—goats, fowls, preserved meats, ale and porter, tea, sugar, fruit, vegetables, &c.,) and having done so we speedily brought our first visit to the establishment to a termination, inwardly resolving that it should also be the last.

And, oh! Master Charlie, do we not remember well your downcast head and your eyes watching us so narrowly and furtively out of their corners for fear we should discover some *mistakes* in your long and numerous bills. Well, well! we would have said nothing about you, had it not been implied by a recent visitor to Zanzibar that he should have selected your society on the island, next to that of Mr. Webb's, if the latter had failed him; but though your "arrack" and tobacco may be preferred to the "British Consul's" mild "wine and cigars," yet, knowing the agreeable and enlightened people that are always to be met with there ready to welcome strangers of their own more refined tastes and manners, we do not think the expressed predilection in favour of Mr. Webb much of a compliment to the distinguished American Consul.

There was never any delay on the part of Master Charlie in the execution of orders; he had fully learned by experience the uncertainty of an English cruiser's movements—very often sudden and unexpected at Zanzibar—and the necessity of making hay while the sun shone. He was prompt in everything; he invariably brought the bill first with the announcement that—"Everyting is commeen (h)off in boat immedetely"—the advantage of this plan being probably, that instead of having to alter the bill, in case of the discovery that charges had been inserted by mistake for goods not ordered, or not supplied, he completed the stock to correspond with the charges in the bill, which was by far the more lucrative mode of making the correction.

The supplies being now on board, and Dr. Kirk being anxious for an interview with the Sultan, who was at this time residing at his palace on the mainland at Darra Salaam, asked me to convey him across in the "Daphne" previous to our final departure for the south; thither therefore we proceeded, having on board Dr. and Mrs. Kirk and their baby, for whom a patent cradle was constructed out of the lid of a box and two chairs.

Bishop Tozer also formed one of the party; he had had a severe attack of fever, and I had persuaded him to accompany us for change of air, that of Darra Salaam being cool and refreshing, as compared with the low, marshy, fever and dysentery producing isle of Zanzibar, and he returned with us at the end of a week quite another man; not, however, without the proverbial misfortune of "coming to grief," consequent upon having a Bishop on board, being realized, for as we were entering the harbour at the mouth of the river Kingani we touched upon an unknown patch of coral, but fortunately got off again almost immediately. And as on his coming on board I had, by way of a joke, mentioned my anticipation of some evil in consequence, it added to the circumstance a more ludicrous aspect.

The harbour of Darra Salaam is the entrance to the river Kingani, in which large ships [1] can make their way for more than a mile up.

It had just become the Sultan's new abode, he having built himself a palace here; another

---

[1] The "Daphne," 1081 tons, drawing seventeen feet of water, was the largest vessel that had ever entered the river at that time.

building had also been erected, a kind of official hotel for foreign consuls, or others, on their visits from Zanzibar, and there Mr. and Mrs. Kirk took up their abode, the Bishop remaining on board.

During the few days we were here Dr. Kirk accompanied me up the river occasionally for the purpose of shooting hippopotami, which abound in every part of the river; but there is one difficulty in getting possession of these animals, if you kill them in the water, they sink not to rise again perhaps for many hours or even days; if you only wound them, they dive and eventually escape to some other part of the banks and get away into the country, where the natives often find them. We had many shots at these huge animals, but our Snider rifles were of little use against their thick hides, and though we wounded many of them we never captured one.

At the end of the week we returned to Zanzibar, and on the following day sailed for the Mozambique harbour, where we arrived on the 17th July; thence we proceeded to Mafamale island, to which I had bid farewell just nineteen years before in the old pinnace of the "Castor," and which became the rendezvous of the "Daphne" boats for a few days. On landing in this little spot we found three strangers there, the only ones I had ever seen on the island; as we stepped upon the beach one of them left it and dashed into the water, and after taking one look at us—which gave us the opportunity of discovering that it was a seal—disappeared. The two other strangers who were evidently in a great state of alarm, chattering to each other loudly, were a pair of fish-eagles; with a Snider rifle I shot both of them, being much surprised that after the report of the first shot the second bird did not leave the island, but on the following day we found a nest in one of the trees, containing two young birds, which fully accounted for the fact of the parents not having left the island immediately they espied our approach. The largest of these birds measured five feet nine inches across the outstretched wings, and the other only a few inches less. I managed to skin them, but the only parts which we could preserve from the attacks of those destructive ants which swarm into ships on the Indian station were the talons, which were large enough to extend over the top of an ordinary sized breakfast-cup.

During the day or two that the ship remained at this island, the boats were sent up the river Antonio to obtain, if possible, information of any slavers; the Arabs informed the interpreter that a dhow was about to leave the river under French colours for Cape St. Andrew, with a cargo of slaves. At one part of this river on our boats entering it, although only fifty-six miles from the Portuguese island of Mozambique, and claimed by them as a part of their possessions, the Arabs and natives came down and prepared to attack the boats, which were obliged therefore to withdraw and proceed to another town farther up.

From Mafamale we proceeded to Mayotta. General Columb was at this time governor of the island. We arrived on a great fête day: a regatta was going on, and all the principal officials were being entertained by his excellency at a grand "De Jeuny," which fully accounted for the "Daphne" being put into quarantine for that day, as it was doubtless not thought convenient to invite British officers to meet half-caste and negro grandees; but this was all made up for the next day, when we were released from quarantine, by French hospitality and cordiality.

Amongst our kind friends there I must not omit to mention the Commissary-general[2], whose pretty daughter Marguerite, I fear, turned the head and captured the heart of more than one young officer of the "Daphne."

[2] A. Cahoüet de Marolles, Trésorier-Payeur des Finances.

PORTUGUESE POSSESSIONS.

PORTUGUESE POSSESSIONS.

CHAPTER XII.

Portuguese Possessions, their Claims—Population of Mozambique—Full of Slaves—Ibo—Cape Delgado—Quillimane—No other Portuguese Settlements—The Arabs in real Possession—Conducia—The Portuguese Slave-trade—Free Negroes—A Portuguese Schooner with Slaves in her—Defeat of Portuguese Forces—Their Power confined to one Island.

IN the year 1497, Vasco de Gama, a Portuguese commander, with three ships under his orders, rounded the Cape of Good Hope, and a few days afterwards anchored off the Zambesi river, thence he sailed to Mozambique, and northward along the coast, anchoring off several parts of it. At all of these places De Gama found what every one visiting that coast at the present day may find, that from Inhambane to Cape Guardafui the country is in the possession of Indian Banyans and Arabs, and is populated in the interior by both half-caste Arabs and negroes, with the exception of one or two solitary spots which the Portuguese have been enabled to hold, either because they were more or less separated from the mainland, or because the Arabs have not wanted them.

The Portuguese profess to be in possession of the whole of the coast, from Inhambane to Cape Delgado, but by what right or authority we cannot say, certainly it is not by right of conquest, seeing that they have not yet conquered it.

Mozambique is an island of one mile and a half in length, situated in a deep inlet of the sea, measuring six miles by five and a half: this inlet receives the waters of three small rivers within the island, and outside lie two small islets, on one of which, St. George's, stands a lighthouse with two men only upon it as lightkeepers.

The population of Mozambique was estimated

more than twenty years ago at about seven thousand, of which six thousand were negro slaves; the garrison did not number more than two hundred, the remainder consisting chiefly of Arabs and Banyans. The population is now much nearer twelve thousand, the increase being entirely in the negro population. To the self-interest of the Banyans, and also to a certain extent to that of the resident Arabs, may be attributed the continued possession of that island by the Portuguese, and were these two races to quit it, the latter could not hold it for a day.

Ibo Island is another Portuguese settlement: it is from four to five miles in length, and about three miles in diameter, and is the most important of all after Mozambique; moreover, with the exception of a small settlement recently made in Tongy Bay, Cape Delgado, for the purpose of collecting certain customs' dues, Ibo is the northernmost of the Portuguese ports; but they are not likely to retain their hold of Tongy Bay long, however, for it depends on the caprice of the natives, who are always very changeable. Ibo consists of fifteen or twenty stone houses of modern Arabic architecture, and many huts; the population consists of half-caste Portuguese, Arabs, Banyans, and slaves, and was estimated about twenty years ago at 2422, including the garrison, composed of creoles and negroes; but the trade, never very extensive excepting in slaves, has dwindled of late years so much that the population is now reduced to half the above number.

The Portuguese have one other settlement of importance to them, namely, a military station at Quilimane, consisting of a commandant, a few Europeans, and fifty or sixty native soldiers. Besides these three strongholds, if they may be so called, the Portuguese have no others; but there are one or two places where a half-caste Portuguese resident is to be found trading with the natives, who is allowed to remain there on sufferance by the Arabs, and is always ready to act as the representative of his country, if he can persuade any one that he has any authority in the place; sometimes indeed he will hoist the Portuguese flag, and there is always an Arab near who flies Arab colours, and allows the Portuguese ensign to sport in the wind on the principle that, "it pleases him and does not hurt me." But this is not always tolerated, and I could quote several instances to prove the utter powerlessness of the Portuguese to maintain their hold of this coast, if the natives were to make a determined effort to expel them.

In the Blue Book of 1870, a despatch from Mr. Pakenham, reporting the capture of a cargo of slaves in Madagascar, gives the defence of the captain of the vessel in the following terms:— "The King of Sangazy at Mozambique (that is a native), had sent them on board," &c., showing that the Portuguese had not then possession of this place. But we have had more serious proofs in circumstances unpleasantly affecting ourselves, that the Arabs are in actual possession of the country, for instance, our boats are frequently attacked on the coast; I have already mentioned one or two occurrences of this kind, but a more recent and positive instance occurred in the year 1864, at the distance of about fifty miles south of the Portuguese fort and town of Mozambique, an occurrence which is likely to happen again. A cutter belonging to H.M.S. "Lyra" in charge of Lieut. Reed and six or seven men, was swamped on the bar at the entrance of the river Mogincale, the boat being lost with all the arms, &c., and while the crew were sitting near the beach in the hope of seeing their ship appear, the natives in large numbers attacked them; some of the men escaped into the bush and remained there till the ship arrived, but two were murdered, and Lieut. Reed was seized, thrown to the ground, and secured with cords and taken with one of the crew into the interior. The Portuguese were appealed to, but could do nothing. But Mousa, a powerful Arab chief, to whom no less than a hundred and thirty minor chiefs are tributary, and who reigns over territory extending from within sight of Mozambique island to Angoxa river, and far into the interior, sent a messenger to the village where Lieut. Reed had been taken, ordering the minor chief to deliver Mr. Reed and the other captive to him, and they were marched through a large tract of country from the Mogincale river to Shangady on the Antonio river to the south of it, and on arriving there were received very kindly by Mousa,[1] who sent messengers to the mouth of that river, with letters to Captain Parr, assuring him of the safety of Lieut. Reed and the man who was with him, these messengers going through the country in which the Portuguese dare not show themselves: yet they call these Arabs rebels, an appellation which the latter treat with utter contempt.

"Why," say these Arabs, " do you (the English) refuse to acknowledge our power? if you did not, our subjects would not treat you as enemies,

---

[1] "It appears that the Arab chief Mousa has treated Mr. Reed and others that fell into his hands with great kindness, and in a manner which certainly accords with his profession of being a friend to the English; this is the same person whom the Governor of Mozambique refers to in his letter of the 30th of October, 1864, speaking of him as a rebel. Mousa has, evidently, from Mr. Reed's account, great power on this part of the coast, and owns the allegiance of 130 chiefs and 35,000 men; he is desirous of being recognized as an independent power." See Letter of Capt. Parr, Blue Book, 1865.

as they do the Portuguese; at any rate, supposing we are rebels, we have a right to be acknowledged as belligerents, and you see that we have actual possession of the country and always have had it. It is the Portuguese who carry on the slave-trade; we are ready, if recognized, to enter into treaties with the English for its abolition, but while other trades are cut off from us we are compelled to accept that which is forced upon us."

On the mainland, eight miles from the island of Mozambique, is the Arab port of Conducia, into which the Portuguese can only enter to trade. This is the principal Arab town on the coast south of Quiloa; it is separated from Mozambique harbour by the peninsula of Cabaceira. On the southern side of this peninsula, which forms the northern side of Mozambique harbour, are a few Portuguese villas, which the Arabs never molest while the Portuguese remain on peaceable terms with them in this neighbourhood, which they take care to do, as they have become far too weak to contend with the native population on the mainland.

Conducia has, however, a very large slave-market, and this extensive trade is carried on there, as at Mozambique, by the Portuguese.[2]

In the recent Report of the Select Committee, the following passage occurs:—"The slave-trade in negroes on the East Coast of Africa, is now almost entirely confined to the dominions of Zanzibar." And if there were any dependence to be placed on the fact that Portugal has nominally abolished slavery, the above might be true, but, unfortunately, we know that the trade is not only as extensive on this part of the coast as ever, but that it will be as difficult, if not more so, to stop it here, as in the Zanzibar territory.

[2] "I have reason to think that the slave-trade in dhows from the neighbourhood of Mozambique to the island of Madagascar has very much increased during the last year or so. . . . . It could not be maintained were it not for the false and mischievous claim set up by Portugal to the sovereignty of a line of coast from Quilimane to Cape Delgado, of six hundred miles, on which she does not possess any territory but the island of Mozambique, and by her commercial restrictions she has stopped the trade of the whole coast." Senior Officer, Capt. Gordon's Report, Blue Book, 1865.

The slave-trade is the principal traffic, even now, in the Mozambique Channel, and very strong measures will be required to stop it.

It is not difficult to arrive at the cause of such a conclusion, as that quoted above, being arrived at by the Committee. There was no one examined,—indeed, there was no one to be examined,[3]—who had ever had the opportunity

---

[3] Extract from Letter of Brigadier Coghlan's, relating to the slave-trade on the East Coast of Africa:—

"7. Difficult as it is, owing to the absence of any British agents on the coast, to secure accurate information of the full extent to which this nefarious traffic prevails within the Portuguese settlements, the foregoing facts are sufficient to prove that it has long been carried on without risk, and that, emboldened by impunity, its agents have within the last few years greatly increased their slave transactions in those parts.

"8. Further, it is equally certain, considering the penalties attached by the Portuguese Government to any participation in the foreign slave-trade, that such transactions could not be carried on in their African territories without the countenance of the local authorities. Their connivance is fully known to all the Arab and other traders on the coast, and I found the concurrent testimony in perfect accord with the statement of Colonel Rigby, that at the 'Portuguese settlements the slave-trade is carried on in the most shameless manner, all the Portuguese authorities aiding and abetting it, and dividing their nefarious gains.'

"9. Moreover, by all accounts, the cruelties of the traffic

of ascertaining day by day what was going on in the principal ports south of Quiloa and Zanzibar, as our consuls and others had had with respect to the Zanzibar trade, for we have

in the hands of the Portuguese equal in atrocity those so well known to accompany it on the Western Coast, and its late increase among them is fast destroying the last faint traces of civilization left in their once prosperous settlements on the East Coast of Africa. Large tracts of fertile country are becoming depopulated, and the remains of the semibarbarous tribes in the neighbourhood are being driven to a state of desperation, which threatens at no distant period to be the scourge and ruin of their degenerate and inhuman masters....

"14. But if the suppression of slavery in the Portuguese settlements is an object most desirable in itself, its importance is enhanced in view of any attempt on our part to abolish the traffic in the adjoining African territories dependent on Zanzibar. The fact of a neighbouring Christian people, known to be extensively engaged in the trade, is at once a precedent and a strong ground of apology to the slave-dealing Mahometans. No formal argument, indeed, is based on that plea; but hints as to our consistency in so strongly urging them to forego the practice, and doubts as to the disinterestedness of our motives in the solicitation, whilst our co-religionists are allowed to pursue the same course with comparative impunity, are frequently dropped by Mussulmans of those parts in all discussions regarding the abolition of the slave-trade. Submitting this remark as an additional argument in support of the energetic measures recommended for the suppression of the traffic in the Portuguese settlements."

never had an Englishman residing anywhere in the Portuguese possessions in the Mozambique Channel, nor, indeed, in its vicinity, with the single exception of one at the island of Johanna, and he possesses slaves himself, and has refused to give them up. In fact, there have been no other Europeans there, but the Portuguese themselves, on that part of the coast, for while we can venture with comparative safety on any part of the mainland belonging to the Sultan of Zanzibar, without much fear of being attacked, this cannot be said of any part of the coast south of it.

But there is another reason why the fact of the Portuguese sharing in this slave-trade does not come under observation; it is carried on by them in Arab dhows, under the Arab flag, and thus, when these vessels are captured, the stigma is cast on the sultan. Moreover, they have recently adopted the title of "free negroes" for the slaves, and have established a system of passports in vessels carrying their own flag, in consequence of which, detection, or, at any rate, capture and condemnation, are next to impossible. Ask any of the ten thousand negroes, that crowd the streets of Mozambique, where they come from, what they are, and how they got there, and the reply is the same as that of the slaves captured on board the dhows: —Stolen, dragged from their homes and families, sold and bought, sold and bought again, and brought from the markets on the mainland to this place, where they are worse off than they ever were before.

On the 6th September, we boarded such a Portuguese schooner as is referred to above, bound from Quilimane river, south, to Mozambique harbour, with several slaves on board; amongst them were four Monginda children, from five to ten years of age, whom a Banyan[4] of Mozambique, who was on board, claimed and showed passports for, under the name of "free negroes," signed by the Portuguese authority at Quilimane. These children could speak no language intelligible, either to our interpreter or to the Portuguese or Banyans on board the

---

[4] A British subject.

schooner, and although we put some questions to them, and tried by signs to make them understand us, it was all in vain, which proved they had only recently been brought from the interior. The case was most palpable, yet we could not take the risk of detaining the vessel, and sending her to the Cape, the only place to which we could legally send her, on account of the passports and her unseaworthiness. Never conceiving it possible, however, that the governor could have decided that these children and the other negroes on board were not slaves, I sent her into Mozambique, to obtain his opinion, with the intention of destroying her if they were declared to be slaves. This certainly was a severe test of the honesty of the professions of the Portuguese with respect to the abolition of the slave-trade, and it proved too severe for them; the governor assured me that they were "free negroes," and had passports!

In the beginning of the year 1869, the little power which still remained to the Portuguese was nearly annihilated on the coast, Sofala was again taken by the Landeen Kaffirs, and a strong force, under one "Bonga," had completely defeated the Portuguese troops on the Zambesi, the general and thirty-six officers being reported killed or missing, and the force, which had only recently been sent out there, nearly annihilated in the neighbourhood of Quilimane, which, it was feared, would be taken. Angoxa, which had been in the possession of the Portuguese for a few years, revolted, and was taken by some Arab forces; and to add to the difficulty of the situation, the Governor-General of Mozambique died of fever, when engaged in the above expedition at Quilimane. In short, the power of the Portuguese, and their only real stronghold, are now, as they have always been, practically confined to the island of Mozambique, their great slave-mart.

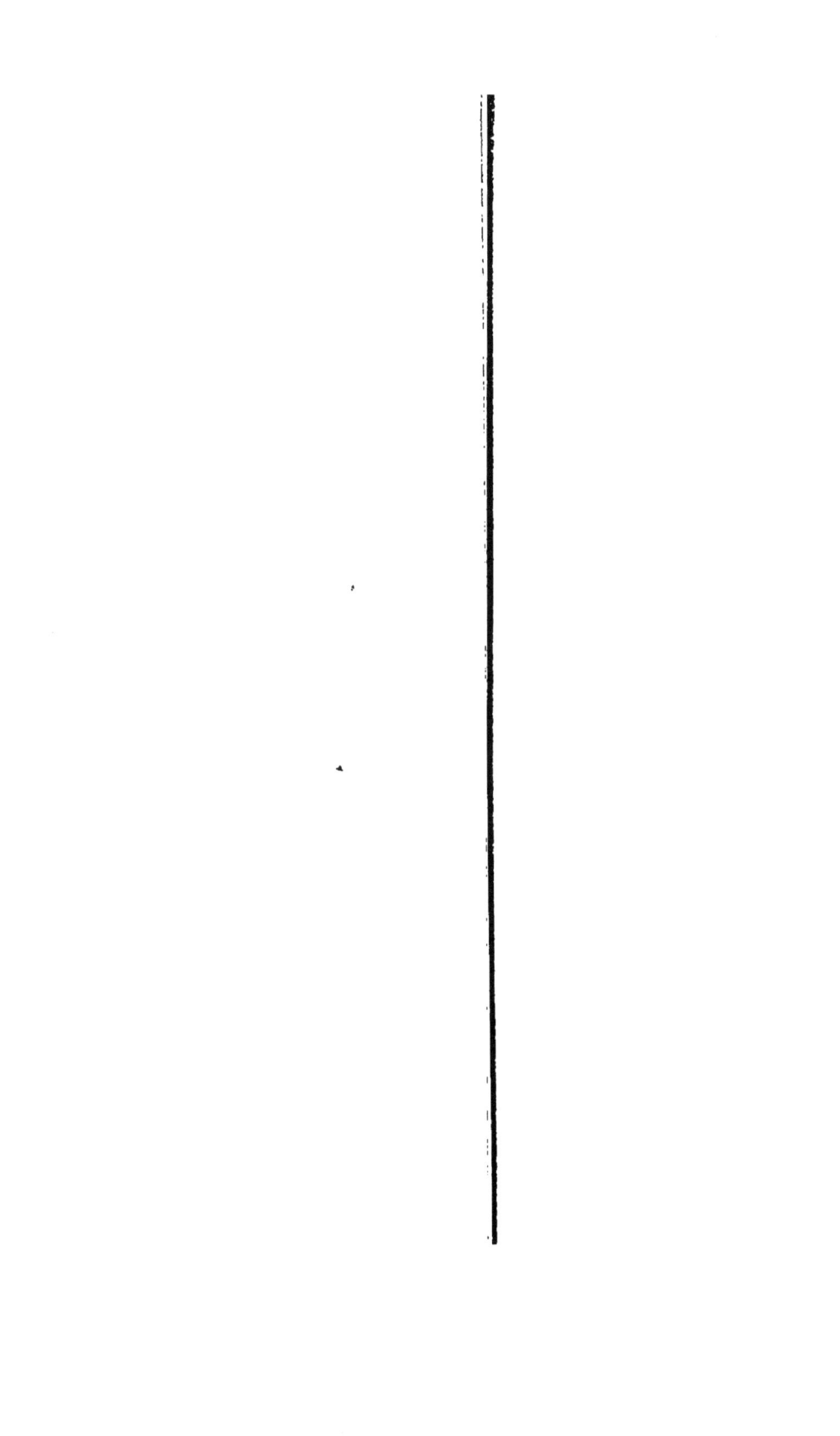

CHAPTER XIII.

Condition of Slaves in Portuguese Territory—Cruelty—A Slave flogged to Death—Slaves escape to "Daphne"—Slaves or "Free Negroes"—Refusal to give them up—Correspondence with the Governor—The "Star" in sight—My Promotion—Fernando Veloso Bay—An Interview with the Natives—Their Curiosity—A Mystery—The Rivers of Africa.

OF the condition of the slaves in the Portuguese possessions, one has only to visit Mozambique to learn the cruelties practised by their masters, who have the power of life and death in their hands.

Mr. Young, in writing on this subject, in the narrative of his research for Livingstone, alluding to the Portuguese, says, "Sent out here for a term of years, it best suits the powers that be if they are never heard of, least of all in their sole occupation, slavery and its attendant vices. . . . . The slaver in these dismal mangrove swamps leads a life of incessant terror, lest he should be overpowered by those under him. . . . . He is alone with his conscience, far from other white men, ardent spirits and debauchery cannot keep the spectre long from his mind, his plan is to rule by intimidation, nor will the death of a refractory slave here and there suffice to establish the fear he reckons on as his best defence against outbreaks. Mutilation, such as cutting off a right ear, or lips, is amongst the minor punishments; in the code of severe penalties, and in special modes of death, the horrors perpetrated on the wretched slaves, and on the women especially, leave it very hard to believe that the ingenuity of such men is a whit behind the cruelty of Satan. To detail things that have come to my knowledge, would make the reader sick at heart, wearied to think there could be such a chapter of human agony and torture upon this earth of ours."

It would be useless to add anything to the above statement, which is true in every respect;

but I have been led to refer to the condition of slaves, and to the slave-trade on this part of the coast, in consequence of the mistaken impression that seems to exist with regard to the abolition of slavery in the Portuguese possessions in the Mozambique Channel.

On the 14th July, we were anchored in Mozambique harbour, where I found a rumour in circulation which would have surprised me in any other place, not being Portuguese, on the coast, to the effect that a slave had been flogged to death in the town by his master, and that so many cruelties had been practised of late, that a complete panic existed amongst the slaves, and upon inquiry we found this was true. In the daytime, slaves would hide away in any nook they could find underneath the wooden pier, which extends sixty or seventy yards into the harbour, watching their opportunity to escape to the "Daphne," and as soon as the sun had gone down, and darkness had set in, the beach and pier were dotted with these unfortunate creatures, waiting anxiously for a boat or canoe to come off in.

At night, some of them not succeeding in finding any boat, would swim to the ship, one or two came on board every night while we were anchored there, begging to be allowed to remain. I questioned them as to their condition on shore, when they would point to old and recent lacerations on the back, which they said were produced by the lash; one of them had an iron bar or ring, about an inch in diameter, welded round his leg so tightly, that it was with great difficulty our blacksmith cut it off, and the pain it must have caused the poor fellow when it was soldered on can scarcely be imagined. Those who swam off, there can be no possible doubt, came from the Portuguese town, but to those who came off in canoes, I avoided putting many questions, as it would be required to be proved on the part of the Portuguese, that they had not come from the Arab towns on the mainland, forming the opposite side of the harbour, over which the Portuguese have no power or authority. Sixteen slaves in all came off to the ship to seek the protection of the English flag, and it rested with me as

Captain to decide on the application of a Portuguese in plain clothes, who, for aught I knew, was the man who owned them, whether I should deliver them up or not, but I had already come to the determination that I would not do so, as I considered, apart from the probability of their being flogged to death, that it would have been a disgrace to the flag, and dishonourable on my part, to surrender them.

On the evening when we were about to leave the port, and while we were weighing anchor, the person alluded to, who subsequently proved to be the chief of the police, arrived on board, with a newspaper under his arm, in which, he informed me through Mr. Breen, who acted as interpreter, it was stated we had several "free negroes" on board; I replied that we had no such on board, but that those which we had were slaves. He said they were not slaves, but "free," to which I replied that, if so, they had a right to come on board. "No!" said he; "they would require passports." I again repeated that they were slaves, that they came on board the ship for protection, and that I refused to surrender them.

On our return to the port a few weeks later, a correspondence took place between the Governor and myself on the subject, in which I maintained the position I had taken in the matter.

Two months from the time when these slaves had escaped from the shore to the ship, we returned for the second time to Mozambique; by this time, the negroes had become weary of the life on board, with the uncertainty of how long they might remain, and we had no opportunity of landing them at any place where they would be free, and, moreover, thinking probably that we intended giving them up to the Portuguese again, three or four of them swam to a dhow, with the hope of getting over to the mainland, or at least to escape somewhere out of the reach of the Portuguese. On hearing this, I sent for all the others, and told them that they were free to leave the ship if they liked to do so, when some, with hesitation, said that they would, being evidently tired of the ship. These were landed, but two others begged not to be given up, being in evident terror at the suggestion; I therefore retained them, and wrote a letter to the Governor, informing him that as there were some who wished to go on shore again, I had landed them. These, of course, were soon apprehended by the Portuguese, and had to make the best defence they could.

The most unmitigated falsehoods were published in the Portuguese papers (at Goa, I believe), and also at the Cape of Good Hope, which must have been conveyed there by the Portuguese corvette lying in the harbour of Mozambique at the time, on her way home; these falsehoods were only cleared up and proved to be such by a court of inquiry, on the "Daphne's" return to England in the following year.

At daybreak, on the 12th September, the "Star" hove in sight, and signalled my promotion. The greatest pleasure afforded by the announcement was that of the prospect of returning to England, an anticipation that will be appreciated by those who know what it is to be cruising off the East Coast of Africa for any length of time.

Our orders were to steer for Bombay again, where I expected to meet my successor, Commander Douglas.

On our way north, I was anxious to extend the survey that we had commenced during the preceding year, of Fernando Veloso Bay, thirty-five miles north of Mozambique harbour, and which we had found to be at least twice as large as it was represented on the chart; with this intention, we anchored in the snug harbour at the head of that bay, and, after having briefly examined the coast of the inlet, proceeded in the boats to the mouth of the river Fernando Veloso.

The entrance of this river at Sandy Point, is not more than a few yards across, with twenty fathoms of water in the centre, but shoaling rapidly on each side to eight fathoms, with such a rush of water, and a whirlpool at the narrow mouth, that except it were a small gun-boat, it would not be safe for any vessel much larger than a steam launch to attempt entering. I landed at Sandy Point, for the purpose of obtaining the longitude of it, with the artificial horizon, and, while so occupied, the natives made their appearance, at a distance of about fifty yards off in the bush. Hitherto, as we had pulled along the coast of the bay, and in among the mangroves they were to be seen paddling away from us, as if flying for their lives, in terror at our appearance; in vain we hailed them now and then, assuring them, as well as we could make ourselves understood, that we were not Portuguese, but English; they never stopped till they reached the shore, and then, jumping out of their canoes, ran off as fast as they could till out of sight; some of these natives, however, watched us for some time, and at last, on our beckoning them to come near, they approached us cautiously, a few of them having fowls and eggs; these we purchased from them, and they were delighted to receive a few presents into the bargain, in the shape of empty bottles and a little powder. Their curiosity to discover what I was about was unbounded; crowding around me, and peering into the artificial horizon, their wonder continued to increase, till at last I showed them the reflection of their faces in the quicksilver. They laughed and danced in ecstasies of astonishment, which were increased when I took some of the quicksilver out of the trough, and put it in their hands. The first man snatched his hand away, and dropping the quicksilver, saw it scatter into small globules, and then disappear amongst the sand of the beach, a look of serious surprise indicating a suspicion that there was some evil spirit concerned in the affair: but at last they took the quicksilver in their hands, and eventually expressed by their looks and exclamations that they had arrived at the conclusion that it was a mystery that "no fellow could understand!" After this they became more confident of our peaceable intentions towards them, and came on board the ship, with a few articles of food for sale. I tried on several occasions to direct their attention to the white ensign, and to explain to them that those who sailed under that flag never hurt or stole the niggers, and I believe that many of them understood me.

The river Fernando Veloso, just above the mouth, opens out immediately to a greater and apparently increasing breadth, presenting a vast sheet of water as far as the eye can reach, the depth increasing on both sides for about half a mile, which we sounded and found no bottom at twenty fathoms. Surely, if the source of the Nile is still somewhat of an interesting mystery, so are the sources of these extensive and unexplored rivers of the east coast, Fernando Veloso, Rovuma, Lufigi, Kingani, &c., and it is to be hoped that we shall yet see the day when the dhows, and that strange vessel, the Metapa barge of Africa, shall be engaged in conveying cargoes of grain, ivory, and even cotton, and perhaps precious metals, down these noble rivers, instead of the tortured living freight they now carry.

CHAPTER XIV.

Jumah's Death—Visit to his Widow—Arab Mourners—Time of Mourning—Prospect of being married again—The Slave-market—Wretched Scene—Disgusting Conduct of Dealers—A Farewell to Zanzibar and its various Inhabitants, &c.

WE arrived at Zanzibar a few days after. Since we had left that port Jumah, our interpreter, had died of dysentery. He was a great favourite, and an amusing old rogue. I was anxious to see his poor wife, —that is to say, his principal and favourite wife, the others could hardly be considered as wives,— to tell her that arrangements would be made for her receiving the balance of pay and prize-money due to her late husband, whose death she had been informed of before. With Abdala, Jumah's servant, who had acted as our interpreter since his master's death, I went to the house, but was at first refused admittance by the male relations, or authorities, until I assured them that unless I saw Mrs. Jumah before I left it would be very difficult to make arrangements about her receiving the pay, &c.; and at last, after much ado about so unheard of a proceeding as a Christian obtaining an interview with a mourning Mahometan widow, the objections were overcome, and I was ushered up the stone steps, or stairs, to her room. On entering it, I saw sitting on a couch on the right hand, six or seven women, one of whom, from her age, appeared probably to be the mother of Jumah, the others were some of his wives. As I entered, the whole of them lifted up their hands, and with upturned eyes began a most plaintive wail, which they continued for some time, poor Jumah's name being often repeated. This sorrowful wail was taken up by an invisible person within curtains drawn round a bed on the left-hand side of the room. This was Mrs. Jumah superior, and I was offered a chair close to these curtains at the head of the bed. Through the interpreter I promised that everything should be arranged so that she should receive what was due to her late husband through the Consul, and answered many of her questions about poor Jumah's death, &c. She seemed glad to see me, and though unable to speak English appeared to understand it a little. During this conversation she drew the curtains on one side, and then I saw that she was dressed and sitting in the middle of the bed. I asked her, through Abdala, how long she was going to remain there.

"Five months," she replied.

"Five months on that bed?"

"Yes," she said; "that is the proper time for those of my religion to remain on their bed mourning."

"Well, what then?"

"Oh! then I get married again."

This, I suppose, was a calculation she had made on the prospect of the pay and prize-money to be paid to her, and, after such a calmly expressed intention, I thought she was likely to mourn with very natural tears the anticipation of such a long imprisonment. As I quitted the room the wailing was commenced again by the other wives, whose prospects of marrying again in five months I did not inquire into, but probably their chance was not so great, seeing that they had no pay or prize-money coming to them.

Before we take our leave of Zanzibar let us walk through the town and look at the slave-market. Wombwell's menagerie makes a great sensation in our country towns and villages, but the cockney looks upon it in a very different manner, he has seen it a dozen times before, and if he steps in, it is merely by accident; if you watch him for a moment you will see that his attention is attracted more by the strangers around him than by the wild beasts. The indifference with which he regards the noble animals encaged there as compared with the wondering gaze of the rustic, presents a fair parallel to the different sensations which a European experiences on his first view of the slave-market on his first visit, and at subsequent periods when familiarity has blunted the keen feelings of overflowing pity and compassion for the slaves, though not his hatred and contempt of the slave-dealer. Those more vivid feelings are not so engrafted even in the Christian's nature as to bear too severe a test, and while we find them benumbed by familiarity with such sickening scenes, those of anger and hatred, being more innate in us, last longer; and, for myself, I could never see a slave-dealer without a strong desire to hang, or at least to horsewhip him.

Will my readers now accompany me through the town, in a walk of eight or ten minutes from the British Consulate? It will be well, however, while doing so, in consequence of the many offensive odours, to turn our heads on one side often, as Mr. Henn is said to have done on one occasion here, an act for which we do not blame him. But it certainly was injudicious of that energetic—not "effervescent" officer, as Mr. Stanley has thought fit to call him—to talk of shooting African lions in the presence of one who was impressed with the idea that there were no lions in Africa but himself and Livingstone.

Passing the Sultan's palace, the good-looking exteriors of the houses of the "well to do" Arab population, and through filthy streets, we emerge by a narrow lane into a small square—large for Zanzibar. Here the first thing that meets the eye is a number of slaves arranged in a semicircle, with their faces towards us and the centre of the square. Most of them are standing up, but some are sitting on the ground; some of them, in fact, utterly incapable of standing upon their feet, miserable, emaciated skeletons, on whom disease, and perhaps starvation, has placed its fatal mark. If those who are sitting down had evinced half the stubbornness on the mainland that they do here, they would have been knocked on the head and left a prey to the wild beasts; but there is a limit to such treatment in Zanzibar, on account of the presence of the Europeans. Inside this semicircle are half-a-dozen or more Arabs talking together, examining the slaves, discussing their points, and estimating their value, just as farmers examine and value cattle at an English fair or market. Near the middle of the square are groups of children, also arranged close together in semicircles, and sitting down when not under inspection by would-be purchasers. Children, young as they are, some not more than five years old, looking old already. Native children, whom I have seen in their homes, and who have not passed through the bitter experiences which these miserable little creatures have endured, are like all children, black and white, fond of toys, even though it be but an "old shoe" or a "dead kitten," and the ever-present doll, though made of a mere bit of stick or scrap of straw-matting. But these unhappy slave-children had passed all that; they had no inclination to play, they sit in silence, or rise up when required; they utter few words amongst themselves, for they have long lost parents and friends, and those in the same position sitting around them are utter strangers, often foreigners, to them.

In another portion of the square are a number of women, forming several semicircles; their bodies are painted, and their figures exposed in proportion to their symmetry, with barely a yard of cloth around their hips, with rows of girls from the age of twelve and upwards exposed to the examination of throngs of Arabs, and subject to inexpressible indignities by the brutal dealers. On entering the market on one occasion we saw several Arab slave-dealers around these poor creatures; they were in treaty for the purchase of three or four women, who had been made to take off the only rag of a garment which they wore. On catching sight of English faces there was a commotion amongst the Arabs, and the women were hurried off round a corner out of sight. And this is the only expression of shame that occurs on the part of these slave-dealers, who, knowing the opinions of the English respecting the trade, are unwilling that they should detect them in the perpetration of all their enormities.

Bidding farewell to Zanzibar, to the east coast of Africa, and to all kind friends we had found there; bidding farewell also to Arabs and half-caste Arabs, to Portuguese and half-caste Portuguese, to Banyans and half-caste Banyans;

to tortured negroes and torturing half-caste negroes; to markets where human flesh is sold; to fleets of filthy dhows, comparable only to the Black Hole of Calcutta; and to scenes of misery and suffering not surpassed in any age, or in any country,—we left for Bombay, where I handed over the command of the "Daphne" to Douglas, and returned in the mail steamer to England.

CHAPTER XV.

Immense number of Slaves released—Misconception of the term "Domestic Slaves"—Many Slaves conveyed under that Name—Distinction quite clear—What are Domestic Slaves and what are not—What has become of liberated Africans—Tariff of Wages—Efforts to improve their Condition—Missions—The Jesuits.

ON the East Coast of Africa, there were released 1071 slaves in the year 1868, and in the following year 1108, this latter number was perhaps the largest that had been set free for many years, and so alarmed the Indian authorities for fear, I presume, that it should rouse the anger of the Imaum of Muscat, and the petty chiefs of Arabia and the Persian Gulf, that a Commission was organized to inquire into the circumstances attending the captures. I have not seen the Report or the evidence given before that Commission, and I gather from the letter of Admiral Sir Leopold Heath, which accompanied his observations on that Report (See Blue-Book, C.B. 1870), that he had not seen the evidence either, and I further gather from that letter that that Commission reported that many mistakes and improper seizures were made by officers; as I am not one of those to whom these charges can refer, seeing that the vessels we captured had slaves on board and were condemned, I may perhaps be allowed to show that the mistakes, if any, were on the part of those who had given evidence before the Commission.

I am aware that there are many facts relating to this subject which may reflect, perhaps, on the Indian authorities, relative to the view taken by those acting under them, and which it might be unbecoming an officer serving in those seas, though under the orders only of the British Government, to refer to; but I have a copy of a document before me now, which throws much light on the cause of the mistakes, and proves those mistakes or misapprehensions not to have been on the side of the officers engaged in the suppression of the slave-trade, but on the part of those who did not fully understand what orders and instructions the naval officers had been directed by in this service, and who were led into error by a mistaken conception of what the term "domestic slaves" implied.

The Secretary of the Government of Bombay, writing on the 13th April, 1869, to the Political Resident at Zanzibar, after referring to a capture made by H.M.S. "Star" which had what he is pleased to call "six domestic slaves on board," but which was proved at the time of the capture to be engaged also in legitimate trade, says,—

"I am desired by the Government in Council to inform you that a Zanzibar vessel proved at the time of capture to be engaged in legitimate trade, and laden with a considerable cargo, but having on board six domestic slaves employed as sailors, and not slaves for traffic, is not, under the treaty with the Sultan of Muscat (Zanzibar), liable to capture and condemnation."

On the first impression after reading this one might be inclined to say, "Well! we knew that before!" but officers in the position of commanders of ships do not require to have their instructions reiterated or interpreted for them, therefore there must be something else implied, and on looking at the case again we find that there is something not quite clear; there is no reference to the place of capture, or whether it was within the limit of any treaty, and judging from the circumstances alluded to and from the facts that we have since learned about this capture by the "Star," we are led to infer that the Government in Council implied that when there are not more than six slaves in *addition* to the crew, they are to be considered as "domestic slaves." If such be the case I not only differ from such an opinion, but I assert that any officer who should take that view of the case and act upon it, would be neglecting his duty.

There seems to be an impression that the crews of these dhows are "domestic slaves," and in one sense such may be the case, but there are no men practically more free, many of them are actually so, than those composing the legitimate crews of such vessels who are trained from their boyhood as sailors, and who if they were tired of such a life have ample opportunities of escaping from it when visiting India, the ports of Aden, Suez, &c., which they are sure of doing occasionally; and, further, it is impossible for officers with the least experience of the coast to make any mistake with regard to these men. The stamp of the negro sailor himself, who is so differently treated on board the dhows, and whose intelligence is evidently so superior to any other negroes found there, and the absence of the look of submissive despair in the expression of his countenance, are sufficient to distinguish him, and I know of no mistake of the kind ever having been made.

As evidence of the fact that these pretended "domestic slaves" are not such, and that they never return from the northern markets, it may be stated that while hundreds of dhows have so-called "domestic slaves" on board besides their crews, when going *north* in the south-western monsoon; those vessels which we boarded as they returned south in the north-eastern monsoon never had any, and their crews were invariably much smaller than they were in those going north. It might be well if commanding officers were in future to make a return of dhows boarded, classed according to their tonnage, especially mentioning the number of negroes on board those steering north, and those going southward.

It should be remembered also that not only northern dhows, but northern Arabs in any dhows, have no legal right to convey negroes or domestic slaves from any part of the African coast northwards. I must add that there appears to have been culpable oversight of this and similar points, in the conduct of certain persons whose conclusions have been erroneous, but whose opinions have had too much weight. And with the facts staring us in the face, that while seventeen hundred slaves are all that are required for domestic service in Zanzibar territory, according to the lowest estimate twenty thousand, but in reality at least fifty thousand negroes are imported annually into that country, and consequently re-exported to other places, is it not preposterous to talk of respect for dhows having, so-called, "domestic slaves" on board and on their way to the northern markets? I am sure that every officer who has been on the African coast, and has had any experience of the trade there, will agree with me that, not one in a thousand of those on board are "domestic slaves," or ever return to Zanzibar territory again.

Slaves, as we have already said, are marketable articles, kidnapped, stolen, or purchased to be sold at markets, without or beyond the dominions of the flag the vessel is flying, and nothing can make "domestic slaves" of them, but if six, or any, such are allowed to each dhow, you may as well withdraw the squadron engaged in the suppression of the traffic altogether, as all would be conveyed to the northern markets in that way.

"Domestic slaves" are servants, labourers, or artificers, such as are to be found in every country where slavery is allowed, and when they are on the high seas under the flag of that country they are not to be interfered with;

but those referred to are not "domestic slaves," but poor creatures dragged from their homes in the interior, and up from the Mozambique to Quiloa and the Zanzibar markets, to find their way to the northern markets, in legal as well as illegal traders, by twos, by tens, and by thousands.

It is seen by the numbers given that the sum total of slaves set free in two years, 1868-69, amounted to 2179. I am not acquainted with the exact number landed at each place, more than half of them I believe were landed at Seychelles, the remainder—with the exception of a few taken to Bombay, and a few children, selected for his school by Bishop Tozer, in 1868, to Zanzibar—were carried to Aden. What has become of them? and, Have we in any way improved their condition? are fair questions; there is no institution on this coast similar to that at Sierra Leone on the Western.

At Seychelles, however, I ascertained that the rescued slaves were farmed out to the Creoles for five years, after which they were supposed to be able to shift for themselves.

Their wages at the time we made the inquiry were 1lb. of rice per day, 6lbs. of fish per month, and one dollar per month, and they had to find themselves in clothes. This state of things was not very satisfactory certainly, but it was rectified subsequently, and the following is the tariff of the weekly wages as supplied by the Commissioner of the island in the following year, the blacks, I presume, having to find their own provisions and clothing:—

	1st year.	2nd year.	3rd year.	4th year.	5th year.
	s.	s.	s.	s.	s.
Seven years of age	2	3	4	5	6
Eight „	3	4	5	6	7
Nine „	4	5	6	7	8
Ten to twelve	5	6	7	8	10
Thirteen to fifteen	6	7	8	9	10
Sixteen to eighteen	6	7	8	10	12
Nineteen and upwards	7	8	10	11	12

In a religious point of view the liberated Africans, even at Seychelles, are not a whit better off that we are aware of than before. Mr. Vaudry, the clergyman there, does all that he can for a few of the children, but it is almost as much as he can do to attend to the old population or residents, to whom, besides his weekday services, and his work in the excellent schools there, he has to preach three times every Sunday, one sermon in English, and two in French. I have heard from his own lips how anxious he is to extend his labours so as to include the slaves, but, with the exception of the few children who have been received in the schools, he is unable to do anything for them for want of assistance, and while we have a Bishop and clergymen, besides several Nonconformists' establishments[1] at Sierra Leone on the West Coast, for the benefit of the emancipated slaves, there is nothing of the kind on the East Coast. The consequence is that at Seychelles they unlearn nothing that was evil in their former lives, while they increase it tenfold by drunkenness and debauchery of every kind.

The Jesuits, however, are strong at Seychelles,

---

[1] The Nonconformists are not represented on the East Coast, except at one place, Mombase, by the Free Methodists; there is an immense field for their labours out there.

as at many other places on the east coast, and they appear to have around them the great majority of those in the island who profess any religion at all; they have schools too, but they have not much occasion to work amongst the blacks, for the Creole masters, if of *any* religion, are Romanists, who are not likely to care much for their negroes, except that they do not go to a Protestant church, for, judging from the morality of Seychelles, that is the only thing they look upon as sin.

CHAPTER XVI.

Aden—Negroes worse off—Somallie Boys at Aden—A good Field for Missionaries—Bombay a worse Place for them—Duty of England to instruct them—Depôt necessary on Mainland—Placing them on Islands an Injustice — Zanzibar the worst Place for them — Johanna preferable, but Mainland only suitable — Possibility of returning to their own Country.

AT Aden there is no accommodation for the negroes, they are kept on a small rock or island until they can be sent to Bombay, Mauritius, or Seychelles, and there is little or no employment for those who remain at Aden. Some few have been farmed out to the Parsees, a doubtful advantage to them temporally, certainly none religiously, and many we fear have found their way back to slavery again.

Slaves are sometimes taken from Aden to

Mauritius,[1] but I do not know of any efforts being made towards benefiting the negroes there,[2] beyond freeing them, and obtaining employment for them. They find their way, much in the same manner as at Seychelles, amongst the French planters,[3] where they

[1] "You are aware that two or three cargoes of rescued slaves were discharged at Mauritius seven or eight years ago, and the children sent to the Powder Mills Asylum: a very large proportion of them soon died, and many were afterwards carried off by the epidemic." (Extract from Letter of the Rev. S Hobbs.)

[2] A lady long resident in the Mauritius informs me that the captured slaves brought there were treated with the greatest kindness and sent to the Orphan Asylum at the Pamplemousses, under the care of Mr. and Mrs. Ansorgé, where, as soon as they could be made to understand anything, their religious education was most carefully attended to; some of them were taught trades at the asylum, others were hired out as domestic servants, and every care taken to place them where they would be kindly treated. It must, however, be remembered that a very small proportion of liberated negroes have been taken to that island for many years.

[3] "In the case of those who are sent to the Mauritius, I believe, they cost us nothing; the planters give a premium which covers the whole expense of maintaining them.

"73 *Mr Kinnaird*] You have heard no complaint of their treatment in the Mauritius?—No; on the contrary, I believe the negroes are happy there.

"74. The Mauritius is a very excellent outlet for these

are often to be seen in the same state of nudity as in their own country, and are frequently lost sight of, with the exception of a percentage of the children who get into the schools.

But Aden teems not only with liberated Africans, but also with Somallies, natives of the opposite side of the Gulf (north coast of Africa), an intelligent but bigoted Mohammedan negro race, who find their way there to trade, and often too for safety, their lives not being safe in their own country, where duels and murders are the only ways of settling disputes. Numbers of Somallie boys are to be found in Aden, who get their living by running on errands, by diving for coppers beneath the sterns of the mail steamers for the amusement of the passengers, and of fighting together " Englis fash," as they call it, at the doors of the hotels for sixpences, bestowed by the same persons who have gone

liberated slaves ?—I have no doubt they are happy there, but I still think that our taking them to our own Colonies lays us open to the charge that we are putting down the slave-trade for our own purposes." (From the evidence of the Hon. C. Vivian.)

on shore for a little recreation. Right well have these desperate little urchins learned to use their fists "Englis fash;" they mostly speak broken English, and if you ask them what they come to Aden for, and why they do not return to their own country, they reply, drawing their fingers across their throats, "Englis no cut throat." "Me like Englis best."

Surely with such a field as this, there is no need to send all the missionaries to the West Indies or the Figi Islands, &c. Better save these from Mohammedanism and Hindooism, than when become such, trying to convert them again to Christianity. Mission schools here, and in many other depôts for the liberated Africans, would be of incalculable benefit, especially if the stream of these Africans could be directed back into the interior. At present the garrison church is the only one at Aden.

Have we nothing more to offer the liberated negro but his freedom? enhancing as we do in releasing him the misery of ten others of his own race.

There is only one greater evil for the negro

than that of being kept at Aden, and that is to send him to Bombay (see Sir Bartle Frere's evidence,[4] 436, A. B., book 4) where he obtains freedom, and perhaps, for a time work, to eventually fall amongst those with whom from his colour he is obliged to mingle namely, the Hindoos, when, if he adopts any religion, it is idolatry.

I maintain, therefore, that it is England's bounden duty to give at least two years' instruction to every adult slave she liberates, and a fair education to the children.

If we liberate a thousand negroes a year, which is improbable, we should never have more than two thousand under instruction at a time —which would not be a very costly undertaking when we consider how much money is spent at home in education.

To locate liberated negroes on any distant island such as Seychelles,[5] Mauritius, or Zan-

[4] See note, page 287.

[5] The Seychelles group of islands contain in all but 30,000 acres, many of which are rocky and unproductive, so that the number of liberated Africans sent there must of necessity be limited.

zibar, is little better than condemning them to penal servitude, and is a positive injustice. You may rescue the London street Arab from the profligacy of a locality, or the barbarous treatment of parents or neighbours, and captive mountebank children from the cruel bondage of their torturers, but to lock them up for life in a reformatory, which you only do for a limited time even when they have committed some crime, would surely not be freeing them. On such ground, therefore, I say that we are bound to establish a depôt or depôts on the *mainland* for all liberated Africans.

Mr. Vivian in answer to a question as to the possibility of taking them back to their own country, said, "I think, however, it is very doubtful whether we are justified in taking those slaves into our Colonies ourselves; I think it justly lays us open to the charge of making use of our crusade against the slave-trade for our own purpose." But why not create a colony for them in their own country? It has been suggested that the liberated slaves should be placed at Zanzibar, but even supposing Zanzibar to become English property, I believe it would be worse than any other place for them, as it must of necessity remain populated by its present inhabitants, who would prevent the moral improvement of the negroes who would in a great measure remain in their employ; moreover, they would always be liable to be stolen or enticed away in the dhows, and thus find their way into slavery; besides which, the extreme unhealthiness of this low island, and overpopulated, pestilential town, renders it uninhabitable for any large number of Europeans, and many other objections⁶ might be cited.

⁶ Extract from Bishop Ryan's Letter :—

"The beneficial results obtained by the labours of the Church Missionary Society on the western coasts supply the strongest encouragement for the application of the same benevolent principles and methods of action on the east.

"The proposal to make Zanzibar the depôt is one which I would respectfully but earnestly deprecate for the following reasons. In the first place, because of the impracticability of upholding an institution containing liberated negroes in the midst of a population of slaves of the same race, brought in most instances from the same localities. Secondly, from the difficulty which would be raised in the way of all efforts to evangelize those whose rescue by a Christian nation involves the obligation to endeavour to impart to them the knowledge of Christianity. Thirdly, because the establishment of a

The late Lord Clarendon in a letter to the British Consul at Zanzibar, dated June 16th, 1870, says, "It is also my desire to promote the supply of free labour in Zanzibar by landing most of the liberated slaves there, and placing them under the *jurisdiction of the Sultan*, after they have been registered at the British Consulate; under the understanding, however, that his Highness will undertake to afford them sufficient protection against the slave-dealers, and will prevent their again becoming slaves." Now, in the first place, his Highness is unable to prevent

depôt for free labour at Zanzibar, providing a regular supply of natives to work in Réunion and elsewhere, would directly lead to the very same operations in the interior of Africa, against which the late Earl of Clarendon, as Foreign Secretary, remonstrated so strongly some years ago. The system of the 'libres engagés' led to most of the bad consequences of the slave-trade in the interior of Africa itself. An Arab chief on being told that it was not slavery but free labour, replied to this effect :—

"'All same ting to me. Old time you call it slavery, now you call it free labour; I go catch men, sell; you give the money; all right.' And it sure would be a strange result of British interference for supplying the slave-trade that the plantations should be worked by labourers procured by us from the hold of slave-ships, and then placed beyond the reach of our protection."

his own slaves being stolen, kidnapped by hundreds annually, by the northern Arabs; and, however willing he might be, he is unable to give such guarantee, and further he is a cunning Arab and is not to be trusted; he might sell dozens of them, and declare that they had been stolen by the northern Arabs, and no doubt when the number of such freed negroes became great, and the price of a slave in the Persian Gulf raised, as it would be, to three or four times the present rate by the suppression of the slave-trade, the temptation would be too great for many of the Zanzibar Arabs to withstand; but above all this, I assert that such freedom in Zanzibar under the Arabs, if the term could be applied, would be far worse for the negro than his being carried to the markets at the northern limits of slavery, where I believe, though in bondage, they find permanent and, for them as compared with anything at Zanzibar, comfortable homes and better masters, and being, as already stated, at the extreme limit of the slavery mart, they would not be likely to find their way into any slave-market again.

Without considering the question of our own convenience, the feelings of those who wish only to get rid of the slaves, no matter how, or the trustworthiness of the Sultan or merchants of Zanzibar, but looking at the subject solely with regard to the slave himself, I have no hesitation in saying that it would be better for the poor negroes to let them be taken without hindrance wherever the dealer wished than to leave them at Zanzibar, and it would not be more ridiculous for the police authorities at home to enter into an agreement with the thieves and burglars of various dark localities of London, and say, "Now! you have in your possession a quantity of stolen property, we take it from you, and we who know to whom it belongs, will not punish you, but will give you back the plunder, provided that you promise us that you will not sell it, and will not steal any more." This we think would suit the Zanzibar Arab very well.

The island of Johanna, which would be much more easily acquired, would be immensely preferable to Zanzibar, or to any other island; it is about the size of Madeira, and not unlike it in appearance; it is healthy and fertile;[7] and seems to me preferable to any other island in those seas for the purpose; it is, as we have already stated, under British protection, very little would be required to purchase it, and with a good English town created, it would serve also as the Madeira of the Indian Seas for invalids.[8]

Still, I maintain, that the mainland is the only suitable place for liberated Africans; without such a place, whatever we may do for the negro,

---

[7] "The mountains are covered with trees, chiefly forest and palm trees, the valleys are rather narrow, but they contain in some places much level ground which is partly cultivated and partly planted with trees; the continually changing variety of the landscape offers many highly picturesque views, and Sir William Jones does not hesitate to give them the preference over the forest views in Switzerland and Wales; the climate is said to be mild, the heat at least not being oppressive in July." ('Knight's Geographical Cyclopædia.)

[8] "The fertile and salubrious island of Johanna, three degrees south of Delgado, with its secure anchorage, and its reigning Sultan decidedly favourable to our interests, would form an eligible haven for the cruisers on the north; whilst the hitherto neglected British possession of the southern portion of Delagoa Bay might constitute a convenient station for those destined to watch the line of Portuguese coast from that point to the mouths of the Zambesi"

we cannot prevent the waste and depopulation of the country going on, and that must still go on for some time whatever efforts we may make to suppress them. Nor will it offer him the opportunity of finding his way back to his own country, which he would be enabled to do if the interior were opened up, and gradually became known, as even now it is to some extent as regards the relative and approximate position of the various tribes.

CHAPTER XVII.

A Bulwark on the Coast necessary — British Stations—Abolition of existing Treaties—Basis of future Treaty—Future Treatment of liberated Africans—Darra Salaam — Indian Garrison — Road to Interior — Intrenched Stations—Instruction, &c., of Negroes—Cost of undertaking a Company—Practicability of Scheme.

IN reply to the question put by the Select Committee as to the practicability of sending these negroes back to their own country, one witness declared that it was impossible, but I differ entirely with him on that head—it is by no means impossible; and every slave so liberated and returned to his own country by us would strike a "heavier blow" to the slave-trade than ever yet has been dealt against it. I propose, presently, to show how this may be done.

The embankments of the great African reservoir of humanity have been broken down by the slave-dealers; it is of no use trying to catch a fraction of the escaping stream and leave the breach in the walls of the reservoir, we must repair the breaches, not only by abolishing existing treaties and blockading the places of exit, the ports and rivers of embarkation, but we must also build up the walls and, to some extent, turn back the stream; and this can only be done by establishing a bulwark on the sea-coast, to which all liberated Africans should be taken, and to which the wealth of the country would inevitably flow, under the protection and encouragement of the English, whom the natives, far in the interior, even at Lake Nyassa (see Young's Narrative) have learnt, to some extent, already to trust from repute, though they know little about us; and who hearing that there were British towns and stations in Africa would have no fear of approaching them with the produce of the country, whereas they now live in such continual dread of seeing a foreigner, especially if that foreigner be Portuguese (who, though in the country for centuries, has been a greater curse to it than all the wild beasts it contains);

that they are satisfied to be left alone, contented if they can only supply their bodily wants, and run and hide themselves at the sound of every rustling leaf, lest it should be caused by a man-stealer.

I now propose to consider how such a bulwark is to be established.

I take it for granted that the issue of Sir Bartle Frere's mission to Zanzibar will be the total abolition of the slave-trade; so far as treaties are concerned they have been violated in every respect; and in order that any future negotiation may be effective, the absolute prohibition of the slave-trade and the declaring it Piracy is the only basis possible; and in this all nations worthy of consideration will join us. The petty Eastern chiefs will then see that their game is played out, and will be glad to come to any arrangement we may propose. As their subjects, conducting this trade and conveying the negroes over the seas, on finding that nothing can save their vessel and its cargo from capture, instead of continuing their course run her into the boiling surf with the bare chance of saving a few of the slaves, though they risk their own lives in the attempt, so will these piratical potentates come to any terms that may be dictated to them with the chance of losing all before their eyes. The Arabs are crafty, and if the Sultan can get compensation for any sacrifice he may make he will; but we consider that it would be shameful of England to purchase from him the freedom of the negroes which is their right, especially when the purchase-money would consist in a permanent annual payment. If we were purchasing cattle or the right to preserve game in his territory this would be all very well, but if we are expected to compensate him, why should we not equally demand compensation for the injuries done to the negroes and the payment of the expenses of their maintenance?

Recollecting what it has cost us in the past— I do not confine the meaning to a pecuniary sense—and regarding the difficulties and perplexities which any half-measures will certainly produce in the future, I am of opinion that the only conditions for another treaty with the Sultans of Zanzibar and Muscat must be:—

1st. The total abolition of slavery and the slave-trade.

2nd. The acknowledgment of the obligation not to supply the vacancies occurring among the domestic slaves of the country from any people beyond that country.

3rd. That domestic slavery, of any kind, should only continue to be recognized for a limited period, say ten years; and

4th. That the trade be declared *piracy* and the penalty on conviction, whether in the interior of the country or in Africa, *death*.

Such measures, I have no hesitation in declaring, would put an end to slavery in five years, and save thousands of lives.

Supposing these views to be carried into effect, the next thing to be considered is how best to deal with the liberated Africans; some place on the mainland of the coast must be occupied by us, either a portion of that territory which is now infested by the marauding tribes of half-caste Arabs and negroes, or, which would be far preferable, a station purchased, if necessary—no matter at what cost—of the

Sultan of Zanzibar. The best spot for this purpose would be the line of coast from Darra Salaam, inclusive, to the south entrance of the Lufigy river; this would embrace a line of coast about eighty-five miles in length.[1]

Darra Salaam, which I propose to make the main station, and which is represented in an engraving taken from a photograph, is on the left bank at the mouth of the Kingani River: it is as healthy a place as could be selected on the coast, certainly more so than the island of Zanzibar, and could be improved by forming reservoirs for fresh water, into which vegetable matter could not find its way. At this place should be stationed one native Indian regiment of foot and a large detachment of horse, with a detachment of fifty or a hundred volunteers from acclimatized European troops in India. Darra Salaam should be the basis of operations in Eastern Africa, and the only depôt for

[1] Although this would include the island of Monfia, that island would be of no use; it being perfectly uninhabitable, owing to an extensive lagoon and quantities of fever-producing mangrove-trees and marshes. No natives can live on this island.

(From a Photograph by the Author.)

and

Sultan's Palace. PANORAMIC VIEW OF DARRA SALAAM. Official Hotel.

[*Page* 286.

liberated Africans, having for its further object the development of the trade of the country, communication with the interior, and the surveying and exploration of it. To this station might be conveyed at once, the last two thousand of liberated Africans, including as many as can be found of those landed at Aden and Bombay;[2] and with the aid of these, the formation of a main road might at once be made to Lake Tanganyka, over the best known tracts. At intervals of ten or twelve miles, as the road progressed, should be established intrenched

---

[2] Sir Bartle Frere, in his evidence before the Select Committee (457), says, in answer to the question—"How are liberated slaves disposed of at Bombay or Aden?"—"When there were very few of them, about twenty years ago, they were made over to the police of Bombay, and the chief magistrate of police was charged with the duty of finding employment for them; ... after a while a very large number of children were brought, they quite exceeded the power of natural absorption [Does this term mean absorption by the Hindoo races, &c., to learn idolatry?] or any means at the command of the police. There were some very painful cases, some of the men were kidnapped, and some of the women were found in a state of prostitution in the bazaars, and the Government at the time took the advice of the Missionary Societies, and the Missionary Societies took *some* of the children...."

villages, peopled by some of the liberated slaves, who should, however, have been detained at the main station for at least a year or two, for the purpose of teaching them to speak and read English and the first principles of religion, for if we neglect to teach them these, it would be better for the honour of England, to avoid the terrible responsibility, and to withdraw from the undertaking altogether, for, depend upon it, "from whom much is given, much will be required."

From the most intelligent and the most advanced of the educated negroes should be selected chief and petty magistrates, with limited power over the intermediate villages between Darra Salaam and the main stations, which I propose should be formed at intervals of fifty to eighty miles along the road.

I do not, however, propose to throw the burden of this undertaking entirely on the Government, though I believe it would be as economical a plan as any, the land being purchased and a sufficient force being established for its defence by the Government, would be all that would be required of it. A company might then be formed to carry out the rest of the plan, with a guarantee from the State for a certain number of years; such a company, I am convinced, would find the plan not only feasible, but highly remunerative, from the commerce and wealth that would ultimately flow to it from the interior of the country. London should be the head-quarters of this company, which should have power to frame laws and bye-laws for the settlement, and which should be represented by a governor at the main station, Darra Salaam, and eventually, probably, at some more salubrious colonial city in the fertile mountainous districts of the interior.

It may be objected that such a plan is impracticable, that none such has ever been carried out on the western coast. To this I reply that the interior of that coast, from all we can learn about it, is by no means so rich in cultivation, climate, or trade, at any rate, that nothing of the sort has ever been tried there; if it had been, we might have now been reaping some return for all our efforts on that coast.

It may be supposed that we should be invading or interfering with the territory of the natives. To this I reply that we should only be reinstating the rightful owners, for the native element on the eastern half of Africa is all but annihilated, and the country is occupied by marauding parties of Arabs and half-castes who are living by war with, and sale of, what is left of the genuine native population.

The land adjacent to the main road in the fertile parts of the country, should be apportioned to a certain number of the negroes not otherwise employed, or who have served their allotted time to entitle them to their freedom, and should possess all the privileges of British subjects under the laws of the company; and, further, these villages should be made "cities of refuge" for all natives who might seek their protection.

Such is an outline of the scheme which I venture to propose. Now as to the practicability of it.

Let us look at what took place in Abyssinia —not that I propose that as much should be done in as many years as was accomplished in weeks there—namely, that of making a road into the very interior of the country, but circumstances may be quoted in connexion with that campaign in support of the feasibleness and of its probable advantageous result. No sooner was the road made and stations established there, than there flowed to the latter the produce of the adjacent country; everything brought in was immediately weighed and measured, and paid for in coin accordingly; and though the natives, on the first appearance of our troops, did not know the difference between the value of a penny-piece and half-a-crown, they could, before the expedition quitted, give you change for gold or silver with accuracy in silver or copper; and they not only appreciated the justness and straightforward dealing and uniform kindness they met with, but, even in that short time, had learnt to entirely trust our countrymen; and I am convinced that nothing is impossible with the natives of Africa in any part of it that we have penetrated, and that no means are so effectual in penetrating and even civilizing the country as those which gain their confidence and unhesitating trust. This having been effected, there would be no limit to our success in any part of Africa. With the Abyssinian Expedition and the success of the Suez Canal in our minds, we must either have become apathetic amidst our luxury or have lost the spirit of enterprise, hitherto so characteristic of our countrymen, to regard such an undertaking as that proposed as unfeasible.

With the vastly increasing population of all other parts of the world, and with young Englishmen seeking a maintenance in every foreign clime already well populated, would it not be possible to create an English Colony in the healthy, mountainous country in the interior of Africa, where there would soon be a far better opening, and a greater certainty of obtaining a living for those thousands of emigrants leaving our country only to be disappointed in Canada, the United States, and still more so in the yellow-fever and pestilential countries of South America?

Such a scheme, however extravagant it may

appear at first sight, would, I am convinced, prove eminently successful, first, by bringing the slave-trade to a speedy termination; and, secondly, by the immense profits which would be derived from trade with the interior of the country, which would develope its grand resources. On the other hand, it is evident that the present "jog-a-long" system, which entails continual expense and occasionally an almost utter forgetfulness of the existence of any slave-trade, except by those who are engaged in its suppression, may go on for ever without producing any really substantial results.[3]

[3] The intelligence received since Sir Bartle Frere's arrival at Zanzibar is that the Sultan asserts that the abolition of the slave-trade will be the ruin of Zanzibar; but to this we reply that Zanzibar is a small portion of Africa, and that the slave-trade there has been the ruin of half the country. The Sultan adds that if the slave-trade were abolished, the Somalli Arabs would "desert the place and go elsewhere:" we would rejoice if they did, and say "Joy go with you." Their own statement shows that while they remain there no other trade is likely to be developed in East Africa: we fear as yet we are not sufficiently advanced in our manner of dealing with this question of slave-trading, and that the tendency is to consider the interest of the Zanzibar Arabs as superior to the far greater number of the human race in Africa.

Africa has to be civilized and Christianized, and eventually must be. When is the work to be commenced? Are we to postpone it for future generations to accomplish? to sit on the cushions, stuffed by our forefathers, and wear them out, leaving no feathers for our descendants? If nations and individuals are judged, so also will generations be, for omission of good as well as commission of evil, and the evil begins where the omission of duties ceases. The tides are either ebbing or flowing; they do not cease to flow in all places at the same time, there are always eddies running out before the flow has ceased entirely, but in the end the whole turns. Unless the tide of civilization continues to advance, unless we as a nation continue to be of some use, as instruments in the hands of the Almighty, as we have been hitherto, in moulding and planing the world into a civilized form, as the Anglo-Saxon race has been forward in doing,—we shall surely be put aside like a blunt instrument, and one of a keener edge taken up instead.

APPENDIX.

APPENDIX.

EXTRACTS FROM EVIDENCE TAKEN BEFORE THE SELECT COMMITTEE OF THE HOUSE OF COMMONS.

MR. CHURCHILL, C.B., called in; and examined.

287. "I will ask you whether you are acquainted with the statements of Dr. Livingstone with regard to the slave-trade?"—"Yes; I have read his book, and I do not think them exaggerated at all from what I have heard from Dr. Kirk, who accompanied Dr. Livingstone. In conversations with the former, I have gleaned that the road between Nyassa and the coast is strewn with the bones of slaves that have been killed or abandoned on the road, and the villages which, on their first visit were flourishing, were on their second visit quite abandoned and destroyed; in fact, the whole place had been reduced to a state of desolation."

288. "You would not think the statement ex-

aggerated, perhaps, that for every slave brought to Zanzibar there is a loss of four or five additional lives?"—"No, I think it is not exaggerated; they are better taken care of, of course, after they reach Zanzibar; there, they become comparatively happy. I do not even think they would return to their own country if they had the offer to do so; but the land journey is very trying, and in the course of it they are subjected to great cruelty, as is also the case when they are carried by sea, particularly when they fall into the hands of the northern Arabs."

298. "What are the last accounts you have had from Zanzibar as to the slave-trade?"—"They are very bad; from a private letter I have received, I learn that the slave-trade had increased in activity; the policy of Seyd Burgash towards the British agency had also altered; he was at first rather frightened at the attitude of the agency towards him; he did not know exactly what the British Government might do, and he was particularly anxious to please; but afterwards, seeing that nothing came of the insolent language he had held immediately after his accession, he changed about again, and became as insolent as ever; as far as the slave-trade is concerned, I believe he has not changed his views."

299. "What course would you recommend to be adopted to put a stop to the increase in the slave-trade?"—"I think the Arabs do not understand forbearance at all; they put it down to impotency; they think you are not in a position to insist upon anything, and they misunderstand the motive; in my opinion, the best plan would have been to have adopted strong measures towards the Sultan, and to have forced him to a certain extent."

415. "Has the late or present Sultan, to your knowledge, ever offered to sell or cede the island of Zanzibar?"—"No, never; he on one occasion said, 'If you go so far as to demand the total abolition of slavery, and the carrying of slaves on my coast, you had better take the island away from me altogether.' But that did not mean that he would either give or sell it."

416. "Would a free settlement on the coast tend to prevent the slave-trade, do you think?"—"I think so."

417. "Where would you suggest it should be established?"—"I should think Monfia, to the south of Zanzibar, between Kilwa and Zanzibar, a very good place."

418. "What would be the cost of protecting such a settlement?"—"It would not be very considerable. I think it would pay itself in the

course of a few years; you would have to have a governor there, I should say; and 200 or 300 men would protect the whole place; it is a small island."

419. *Lord F. Cavendish.*] " Whom does it belong to ?"—" It belongs to the Sultan of Zanzibar. I do not think he would offer much difficulty to our securing it."

420. *Chairman.*] " Would it be possible to prevent the slave-hunting in the interior; and, if so, how ?"—" Only by a decree from the Sultan; that is to say, that he should prevent his own subjects from engaging in that trade; and it is generally his own subjects who go up country with merchandise and set the negroes fighting against each other for the purpose of obtaining slaves."

SIR BARTLE FRERE, G.C.S.I., K.C.B., called in; and examined.

453. " What is the nature and extent of the Indo-African trade, exclusive of slaves ?"—" It is very considerable. Some of the reports before the Committee give the figures. But the point that should be noted especially is, that it is a very old and reviving trade. Before any authentic Greek history, it is quite clear that there was a very considerable trade on this coast, and India had a very considerable share

in it. It is more than probable that a good deal of the African trade, such as it was, which found its way to Tyre and Syria, was carried on then, as now, by Indian merchants, who had their houses of agency at African ports. The earliest travellers, both those who came from the north and those who came with the Portuguese round the Cape, found Indian traders at every port along the coast, and a very considerable Indian trade carried on between Africa and India. And that trade was only crushed for a time, or very much lessened, at all events, by the action of European and Arab piracy. All the novels of Defoe's time speak of piracy in those seas very much as we refer to expeditions into the Far-West of America; and it is quite clear, if you read the Memoirs of Captain Singleton, or any books of that kind, that active young men went into those seas and plundered everybody, but especially the Indian merchants, almost without any sense that they were doing wrong. It was only when the trade had got to be almost entirely confined to large ships that piracy came to be less profitable. Of late years this trade has revived, and judging from all analogy, there can be no doubt that if it were properly dealt with, and not impeded, as it is impeded, by the slave-trade, it would increase very rapidly. I may mention that almost all of what we may call the banking business at those ports is done by natives of India, who have their homes in Scinde, Kurrachee, Kutch, Kattewar, and Bombay, and some as far south as Cananore and Cochin. They never take their families to Africa; the head of the house of business always remains in India, and their books are balanced periodically in India. The house in Africa is merely a branch house, though many of those people will assure you, and they give very good evidence of the fact, that they have had branches in Africa for 300 years, and possibly for much more. When you have that kind of network of indigenous activity existing as a mercantile agency, it is impossible to believe but that the traders will be as ready to push legitimate trade as they have proved themselves to be in India."

454. "What is your view of the comparative importance of those African traders to England and India?"—"I should say the trade is equally important to both."

455. "But I mean with regard to the amount?"—"With regard to the amount of it, the trade used to be almost all carried on through Bombay. The first change was that a portion of it was taken to the *entrepôt* at Aden; but latterly a great deal of it has come direct from Europe to Africa. There is a considerable and

increasing American trade, or rather there was before the American war, and the German and French trade is very rapidly increasing. The German trade has become a matter of very great interest to all German mercantile men and political economists, and German attention has been very much directed to that coast. But notwithstanding the large direct trade that has grown up, the Indian trade continues to increase almost as much as the English trade, and there seems to be an almost inexhaustible field for trade on that coast. I had the advantage of having Dr. Livingstone living with me for some time, between two of his expeditions to Africa, and he is, as the Committee are aware, one of the most keen and careful observers that one could possibly meet with. He was extremely struck when he had travelled a little in Western India; he made two or three journeys to a short distance from Bombay, and he was extremely struck with the immense apparent facility for a very large mutual trade being carried on between the two continents. Dr. Livingstone pointed out that there was an almost unlimited power of producing food in Africa. We had been in the habit of supposing that in India we should never have to import food from anywhere else; but it so happened, during the time he was with me, that in one province of India famine was threatened, and the prices were at once lowered by importation from the Persian Gulf. He remarked the fact immediately, and pointed out that the grain that was imported was grain that could be produced to any extent in some of the high lands at a little distance from the coast of Africa, and that grain of different kinds, suited to the Indian taste, could be laid down on the coast at a rate which would render its transit to India a matter of commercial certainty."

456. *Sir John Hay.*] "The grain being cultivated by free labour, I suppose?"—"There was very little free labour known then, but he spoke rather of the capabilities of the coast; he spoke particularly of the coast round Mombaza, where there are a few Englishmen settled, I think, who belong to the Church Missionary Society."

448. "I think you heard a portion of Mr. Churchill's evidence, and probably you have read his evidence given on a former day; have you any remarks to make on that evidence?" —"I have no doubt with regard to the facts of the case that Mr. Churchill's evidence is very full and accurate; but I entirely disagree with the remedies he proposes for putting a stop to the slave-trade. It appears to me that the

cardinal evil which you have to deal with is the oscillation of our own opinions in the matter. Up to about the time when Lord Palmerston died, for many years the general opinion of all parties in England had been in favour of a determination to put a stop to the slave-trade wherever we could possibly do so without infringing the rights of other nations, and the whole weight of the Government influence had been put on the side of suppressing the slave-trade. But of late years it has been manifest that there has been very considerable wavering of our own opinions upon the subject. Many of those who were most active in promoting measures for the suppression of the slave-trade in former times have thought, perhaps, that the work was done, and because the work was effectually carried out on the west coast of Africa they have rather relaxed their efforts, and one sees in public writings a good deal of a kind of excuse for slavery, which certainly would not have been put forward some years ago, and would not have met with any kind of public favour and acceptance. That seems to me to be the cardinal evil with which we have to contend, and our Government, representing public opinion, appears to me of late years to have been very half-hearted in the matter. The first thing to be done seems to me to be to make up our own minds with regard to what is to be done, and whether we really are in earnest as we were twenty-five or thirty years ago."

523. "Is the east coast of Africa an unhealthy coast?"—"The lower parts, at the mouths of the rivers, are, I believe, very unhealthy, but directly you get through Deltas, and the low country on the coast, you get to a country which has been described to me as remarkably healthy; you rise up a kind of steppe into a table-land, and you find that is healthy."

ADMIRAL SIR L. HEATH called in; and examined.

684. "Was much trade carried on which you were not able to prevent?"—"The official custom-house returns at Zanzibar state, that on the average about 20,000 slaves a year are imported into Zanzibar; besides that, there must be a large number of slaves exported from the mainland which do not pass through the custom-house at Zanzibar; Zanzibar cannot want anything like that number, and therefore you must presume that the surplus is carried away for export to foreign countries."

685. "What number in the year did you succeed in capturing?"—"For the year ending

December, 1867, eighteen dhows were captured, and 431 slaves were emancipated; those being the cargoes of the eighteen dhows. During that year, the squadron were all employed in Annesley Bay in the Expedition against Abyssinia, and the efforts against the slave-trade were comparatively small. In the year ending December, 1868, the total number of vessels captured was 66; the total tonnage of these dhows was 7233; and the total number of slaves liberated was 1097. In the year 1869 the total number of dhows captured was 32; the total tonnage of those dhows was 3431; and the total number of slaves liberated was 1117. During the second year's cruise my ships were distributed principally along the coast of Arabia, from Ras-el-Hadd as far as Maculla, one being stationed near Socotra, and two down in the Zanzibar neighbourhood. The vessels boarded during the spring season were upwards of 400 dhows; out of those 400 dhows there were but eleven slavers, and in those eleven slavers there were 958 slaves. I am exceedingly puzzled to know how it is that the enormous number of slaves exported get along the coast without being found out. I believe that very few dhows could have passed the squadron during those months; and though, comparing the wants of Zanzibar with the known importations at Zanzibar, there must have been not many short of 20,000 slaves exported, yet it appears that there were not above 1000 slaves on board these 400 dhows. This rather shows that naval efforts alone will not put down the trade."

686. "As to those 400, were you satisfied that all except the eleven were perfectly free from any complicity in the slave-trade?"—"I think it is morally certain that scarcely any guilty dhows escaped amongst that 400."

687. *Sir John Hay.*] "Do I rightly understand you to say that scarcely any dhows escaped going north with slaves?"—"I cannot understand how they could have passed us, distributed as we were."

689. *Chairman*] "According to that it seems to be utterly hopeless by any efforts of the cruisers to put a stop to the trade?"—"By any efforts of cruisers in numbers such as we have now, I think it is hopeless."

690. "But the number would appear to be sufficient in this case, because you say that you think hardly any guilty dhows escaped?"—"I think the cruisers should be near the rivers and places of export, at the same time as they are near the places of import. I had not ships enough to do both."

691. "Then with an increased squadron you

think something more might be done?"—"I can only say I hope something more might be done."

692. "One may collect that you do not anticipate any complete stoppage of the trade by any efforts of the cruisers?"—"I think we have gone on for twenty-five years and have done no good whatever."

695. *Sir J. Hay.*] "Supposing you were appointed again to the East Indian command, and you were told that you might have for three years, or two years, or till the trade was suppressed, an unlimited number of ships, both for the blockade of the Arabian Coast and the Persian Gulf, and the portions of Africa from which the slaves were exported; will you state for the Committee, what number of ships you would conceive to be necessary to enable you to carry out with certainty the total annihilation of the slave-trade?"—"I do not think any number would suffice with certainty, but I should ask for ten ships to begin with."

696. *Chairman.*] "Ten instead of seven?"— "Yes."

697. "Do you think that would very materially increase the number of captures?"—"I think the number would be increased."

698. *Sir J. Hay.*] "I think you have had con-

siderable experience on the west coast of Africa?" —" Yes."

699. " Are you aware of the number of ships that were employed on that length of coast, as compared with the number employed along this length of coast; was not the number of ships employed on the west coast of Africa very much more considerable than that for which you now ask ?"—" Very much more considerable, and the nature of the sea is far more favourable for blockading operations."

700. "Not looking to the economical question, or to the probability of the number of ships that you might ask for being given you, assuming that the country was determined to put down the slave-trade on the east coast of Africa in the same way as on the west coast; would you say that ten ships, or anything like ten ships, would be sufficient to cover the 4000 miles to be blockaded on the east coast ?"— " No matter how many ships you have, there will of course always be some vessels which escape being boarded; it is quite possible, that, though we boarded 400 dhows during the season I have spoken of, there may have been 400 others that passed outside us; but when I said that I thought we must have boarded nearly all dhows that came up, I referred to those that passed along the coast; the Arabs

have very good information; I do not think that they knew what I intended to do, but it is quite possible that they did."

701. *Chairman.*] " Do you think that by having more Consular Agents along the coast, you would have the means of deriving better information upon the subject of the slave-trade?" —" I think the appointment of Vice-Consuls along the coast, would be a most valuable thing, not only as regards giving us information, but as regards pushing our political influence."

704. " Was there anything in your instructions that in any way impeded your success; any limitation of your power ? "—" There was nothing whatever in my instructions to limit my action till the issue, by the Admiralty, of a circular dated 6th November, 1869, which appears at page 94 of Class B, East Coast of Africa Correspondence from 1st January to 31st December, 1869. That circular made an unpleasant impression upon all the officers commanding the ships under my orders. Its manner was accusatory as to the past and threatening as to the future; its matter was, principally the forbidding the capture of dhows for having domestic slaves aboard."

705. " Do you think there were many slaves carried in that way in those dhows which were

not classed as guilty dhows?"—"There is no doubt that a very large number of slaves must have been carried in that way. At page 75 of the same Blue Book are extracts from letters found in some of the dhows, being inclosures in my letter to Sir Seymour Fitzgerald replying to a complaint of Sir Edward Russell, the Judge of the Vice Admiralty Court at Aden, as to dhows being captured for having domestic slaves on board. These show that domestic slaves are frequently carried to sea for sale."

707. "In 1868, 66 dhows were captured, while in 1869 only 32 were captured; but if this order did not come till November 1869, it would not have any bearing upon that decrease?"—"No; the larger number of captures in the earlier year was, because in the previous year the slave-dealers had been left alone, owing to the Abyssinian War."

708. "There is a large difference between those captured and those who appear from the Custom House returns to have been exported, and which are unaccounted for in any way?"—"Yes."

709. *Sir R. Anstruther.*] "What means have you of distinguishing domestic slaves on board a dhow from any other slaves?"—"The Admiralty in that circular have laid down as a definition of what are to be considered domestic slaves,

'where the slaves found on board are very few in number, are unconfined, and appear to be on board for the purpose of loading or working the ship, or attending upon the master or the passengers, and there is no other evidence that the vessel is engaged in or equipped for the slave-trade.'"

710. "I may take it as your view that the action of this circular to which you have referred has been more or less to impede the squadron in the capture of slaves?"—"If you put it in the future tense it will have that effect very largely, I think. I should like to quote, as illustrating my views on that point, a portion of my annual Report of 22nd January, 1870 (it is in the Correspondence for the year 1870): 'On the 6th November, their Lordships issued "Instructions for the Guidance of Naval Officers employed in the Suppression of the Slave-trade." Those instructions forbid the detaining of vessels having slaves on board, if there are attendant circumstances showing that the slaves are not being transported for the purpose of being sold as slaves; and there is added, as an example of the nature of those circumstances, "Where the slaves found on board are very few in number, are unconfined, and appear to be on board for the purpose of loading or working the ship, or attending upon the master or the passengers,

and there is no other evidence that the vessel is engaged in, or equipped for, the slave-trade." I believe that, just as it is said a drunkard can only be cured by total abstinence, so the slave-trade by sea can only be put down, if at all, by a rigid forbidding of the carrying to sea of any slaves of any description. As I have before remarked, even what is called a domestic slave is not only a salable article, but an article which is very often sold; and the return of those embarked to the port they originally left, depends solely upon whether or no a good offer has been made for them at the ports they have visited in the interval.'"

711. *Chairman.*] "Seeing that the fleet you have had under your command is not sufficient to prevent the escape of a very large proportion of the slaves exported, has your attention been directed to any measures which might be adopted to prevent the continuance of the slave-trade?"
—" In answer to your question, I will quote part of my letter dated 1st March, 1869, addressed to the Secretary of the Admiralty, in the Blue Book, containing the correspondence of 1869: 'I observe that it is not unusual to close these reports with an expression of hope that the heavy blows which have been dealt at the trade during the past year, will go far to check it for the future. I can express no such hope. The

trade is far too profitable, and will not be affected by a risk so small as that incurred by the proceedings of her Majesty's ships. It supplies a want which has not been left unsatisfied for many centuries past; a want which, sanctioned by the religion of the country, has grown almost into an instinct. To put down this trade, requires far more effort, and far more energy than England has yet shown in the matter. Twenty-five years have elapsed since the first treaty with Muscat, and all that time we have been contented with the capture of a very small percentage of the total exports; a percentage large enough to irritate the legal traders, who are harassed and annoyed by the visits of our cruisers, but too small to affect materially the illegitimate trade. We must do far more than this to insure success. We must double or treble our squadron. We must establish vice-consulates at the ports of export, but above all, we must force the Government of Zanzibar into active acquiescence in our views, and, if necessary, purchase or take possession of that island.' In subsequent letters urging the same view, I have altered this last sentence, and said, 'purchase the sovereignty of the island.'"

712. "Is that the only thing that occurs to you as a means of putting a stop to the trade?"—"I think that if a treaty is made in the sense

of Lord Clarendon's proposals to Mr. Churchill (page 30, Correspondence of 1870), if that part of the existing treaty which is supposed to allow domestic slavery afloat is abrogated, and if the squadron is increased so as to make it difficult to evade that treaty when made, we shall have a chance of success; but I still hold that the only radical cure will be the making Zanzibar a centre from which British civilization can radiate into that part of Africa."

713. " You mean becoming actually possessed of it as being a colony of Great Britain ? "— " Yes."

714. " Or a protected state ? "—" That is a matter for the Foreign Office to determine."

715. " Zanzibar is not a very healthy place, is it?"—" Zanzibar is undoubtedly an unhealthy place, but I do not know that it is more so than many other tropical colonies or English settlements."

717. " Are you able to give us any information as to the healthiness of those parts of the coast where it is proposed that vice-consuls should be stationed ? "—" The only fact I know as to that is, that a Mr. Heale, an Englishman, engaged in the purchase of hides at Brava, lived there for some months, and I never heard that he was seriously affected by the climate."

Mr. Edward Hutchinson called in; and examined.

1336. *Chairman*] "You are one of the Secretaries of the Church Missionary Society?"—"I am."

1337. "Has your Society been instituting inquiries with respect to the suitability of Seychelles as a place to which to send liberated slaves?"—"I may say shortly that the whole of this matter has been before our committee for the last four years; we have been investigating it thoroughly for that time, and we arrived at this conclusion, that the Seychelles was the most suitable place at which a depôt for liberated slaves could be established; and, in anticipation of the Government agreeing with our view, we sent a missionary there with instructions to purchase a property there, and commence a training institution; we did not do that till we had ascertained from the fullest evidence we could collect upon the subject, that Seychelles was the best place for the purpose. We sent a gentleman from the Mauritius to the Seychelles, who sent us a report, an epitome of which I have here, and he also procured for us a report by Mr. Swinburne Ward, the Government Commissioner at the Seychelles, speaking in the most favourable terms of the Seychelles as being suitable for a depôt for liberated slaves."

1338. " Would your Society be prepared to send agents to the Seychelles for the instruction and civilization of liberated slaves who might be sent there ?"—" We have an agent there now, and he was quite ready to set to work, but a stop was put to the whole matter by the Government refusing to send any more slaves to the Seychelles. If any number of liberated slaves had been sent to the Seychelles we were prepared to have applied for a sufficient number of lads and children to train and teach, with the hope, at some future time, of their returning to Africa. And I say this because the Committee may perhaps not be aware, that Dr. Livingstone, when he last went to Africa, took with him nine lads from our institution in Bombay; that is the institution to which the Government of Bombay sent slave children captured in the Indian Ocean; and from that institution Dr. Livingstone selected nine lads to accompany him in his travels into the interior of Africa, and who are now with him; and in a report in 1866, by Dr. Livingstone, which is to be found in the papers before the Committee, he mentions that one of those lads met his own uncle at the very village from which he had been torn as a child, and the uncle, finding the value that this lad would be to him, having been taught agriculture and carpentry at Nassick, proposed that he should stay with him, but the lad's answer was, 'No,' he preferred staying with his master, Dr. Livingstone."

1339. " Is there anything else which you wish to state to the Committee ?"—" I should like to say that we have given this subject very careful consideration, and we believe that the recommendations contained in the Report of the Committee which sat at the Foreign Office are very valuable, but there is one particular in which we dissent from them, and that is, the recommendation contained in paragraph 64. We dissent entirely from the proposal that those children should be liberated at the island of Zanzibar, and there handed over to any master from whom they might take wages; it is a proposal which we think is entirely opposed to the whole policy that our Government have hitherto adopted in dealing with the slave-trade."

1340. " It was your Society principally which drew the attention of the Government to this matter, was it not ?"—" We have pressed this matter upon the Government at various times. Two years ago we went on a deputation to the India Office, which resulted in the appointment of the Foreign Office Committee."

1341. "The Bishop of Mauritius brought the matter before you?"—"He brought the matter before us in 1867, and since that time we have been perpetually working to bring public opinion to bear upon it."

1342. *Mr. Kinnaird.*] "Is there any other place besides the Seychelles which would be suitable for the establishment of schools for the liberated slave children?"—"I might say at the Mauritius itself there is a large establishment, which has been superintended by our missionaries, and there the Mauritius Government have done what the Government did at Sierra Leone, namely, they have given 6d. a-head per diem for every child we would take and train. That has been carried on for a long time very successfully indeed; and Governor Barclay, in one of his letters, says, if we could establish a similar institution at the Seychelles, he has no doubt that the Mauritius Government would make a grant for the purpose.

1343. *Mr. Kennaway.*] "You would prefer that any settlement of slaves should be under the British flag?"—"We take that position, because a liberated slave is a British subject; the present Act of Parliament requires that slaves shall be liberated in British dominions; that is the point from which we start."

1344. "Do you think, supposing the liberated

slaves were congregated at the Seychelles, you would be able to isolate them from the immorality of the place; it has a bad character at present, has it not?"—"It has a bad character; the Seychelles consist of a group of seven islands, and the evidence we have rather leads to the conclusion that Mahe would be the best for our operations; but we have no doubt that we should be able so to train the emancipated slaves as to prevent them from being affected by any immorality there may be in the place; and, moreover, they are only children; and it is a point which it is important to bear in mind that a large majority of the slaves captured are children."

1345. *Mr. Kinnaird.*] "The Church Missionary Society are willing to undertake that work?" —"Yes."

1346. "You only ask the Government to contribute a small payment?"—"Sixpence per head per diem would completely cover the expense; that is what the Government have given us at Sierra Leone."

1347. *Mr. J. Talbot.*] "Why would not such a settlement at Zanzibar be satisfactory?"— "There seems to be very little evidence as to the power the Sultan could bring to bear to protect liberated slaves there. Besides, from what I have read I should say that Zanzibar is a very unhealthy place; the only place where a depôt could be established would be in the interior of the island, which General Rigby has told us is extremely unhealthy."

1348. *Mr. Kinnaird.*] "If the depôt were established in Zanzibar, would not you be afraid that they might be taken as slaves again?"— "That would depend on the measures that might be taken with a view to their protection; if ample measures were taken, and the place became civilized, then the children might be secure, but at present the children would be as likely to be kidnapped as not."

1349. *Mr. Fowler.*] "Have you any mission at Zanzibar?"—"No."

1350. *Mr. J. Talbot.*] "If they were put under the protection of the British flag at Zanzibar, what objection would there be to their being kept there?"—"It is an open question; if the Government decide on Zanzibar for a depôt, no doubt our committee would consider the propriety of going to Zanzibar."

1351. *Mr. Kinnaird.*] "The experiment at Nassick has answered thoroughly, has it not?" —"It has been most satisfactory."

REAR-ADMIRAL C. F. HILLYAR, C.B., called in; and examined.

1152. "Looking to that, do you think that the

occupation of Zanzibar, or some other arrangement that would give us the control there, would be the proper mode to stop the slave-trade on the east coast?"—"I have no doubt that the occupation of Zanzibar, or the cession of Zanzibar to the British Government, would very materially tend to suppress the slave-trade on the east coast. I think it is the focus of the slave-trade on the east coast much the same as Lagos was on the west coast."

1153. "You do not anticipate at present that any operations on our part will stop the slave-trade so long as it is the interest of the Sultan of Zanzibar to continue it?"—"As long as the Sultan of Zanzibar derives his main revenue from the slave-trade, I think he will encourage it, either openly or under the rose."

1154. "With reference to the number of ships you would think it necessary to employ, if you were sent there for the special purpose of stopping the slave-trade on the coast of Arabia and on the East Coast of Africa, will you indicate to the Committee what number of ships you would think necessary for that purpose and the class of ship?"—"I should say a dozen ships of the class that are at present on the south-east coast, which have been highly reported on as efficient vessels; the same description of vessels that are at present employed."

1155. " You think twelve would be enough ?"—" Yes."

1156. " Both for the coast of Africa and the coast of Arabia ?"—" Yes, those vessels should be supplied with good boats, and should be specially fitted out for the suppression of the slave-trade."

1157. *Chairman*] " With steam launches ?"—" Steam launches are a most valuable auxiliary."

1190. " Do not you think that a much smaller class of vessels than corvettes of 1000 tons would answer the same purpose as the larger ones, and cost much less ? "—" A smaller vessel would not have the advantage of being able to send away boats cruising; small gun-boats would only be able to do the duty themselves, without the assistance of their boats."

1191. *Sir J. Hay.*] " Had your squadron smokeless fuel when you were there ?"—" Whenever we could get it."

1192. " Did it make much difference whether you had it or had it not, in betraying the position of the ships? "—" I should say it would make a very material difference. It was always the object of the cruisers to have coal that would not show smoke. I recollect, in one instance, in the 'Centaur,' on the west coast, chasing our own smoke, which had banked with the land breeze before daylight."

MAJOR-GENERAL C. P. RIGBY; called in and examined.

560. "Is the profit of the trader who buys slaves at Zanzibar and on the coast adjoining Zanzibar, and exports them to the Red Sea, very large?"—"Apparently it is very large, that is to say, a slave sold in the market at Zanzibar for, say 20 dollars, would be resold in Muscat for 60 to 100 dollars, but the mortality during the sea passage is so very great that it very much reduces the profit."

561. "What occasions that very great mortality?"—"The way they pack the slaves in those small dhows; the want of proper food; the state of filth they are in; the want of water; and if they happen to sight an English steamer at sea the slavers frequently cut the throats of the whole number of the slaves on board and throw them overboard."

562. "Then the sufferings of the slaves on board are rather increased by our cruisers being stationed on the coast?"—"Very much indeed; there is no doubt of it. I remember the case of a dhow that was captured in the harbour of Zanzibar by the ship 'Lyra.' I had had information that that dhow had got slaves on board, and just before she sailed I went with Captain Oldfield of the 'Lyra,' and boarded the dhow. There were 112 girls on board her, evidently

selected to be sold at a high price for the harems of Arabia and Persia. The dhow was taken alongside the 'Lyra,' and these slaves were taken out. A fatigue party from the 'Lyra' was sent into the dhow to take out the provisions, but each man as he went into the hold of the dhow fainted away; the doctor then gave orders that the vessel was to be towed out and scuttled, and he said from the frightful stench, and the state the dhow was in, if she had gone to sea, there could be no doubt that in a week the whole of those slaves would have died; that I think is a very common case. They go to sea so ill provided, that the sufferings of the slaves are very great, and particularly if they have put off their departure to the last, or if the northern winds set in earlier than usual, and they cannot beat up against them; then the sufferings are frightful."

563. *Mr. Shaw Lefevre.*] "What is the average length of the voyage to Muscat?"—"Thirty to thirty-five days; if they have any slaves on board, they have to put in at two or three ports for water; and that circumstance gives great facility to our cruisers to check the trade, because they have only to watch a few ports on the coast to the north, and they are sure to catch a great many of those dhows."

564. *Chairman.*] "Do you think by active

exertions on the part of our cruisers, the trade could be prevented, looking at the large profit there is on the slaves?"—"I have not the slightest doubt that within five years it could be entirely stopped; but to stop it, we want what we have never yet had, viz. system; one year you get an active officer on the coast, who enters into the spirit of the thing, and checks the trade a good deal; then he goes away, and another man comes with quite different opinions; or you get a captain of a cruiser who takes the advice of the Consul and pulls with him, and he does a great deal of good; and then, perhaps just as he has become acquainted with the secrets of the trade, and begins to know where the slaves are shipped, and where the dhows put in for water, and can distinguish between a legitimate trader and a slave dhow, which it takes a long time to do, he is ordered away and never goes back again."

590. "Is Zanzibar itself unhealthy?"—"The town is not, but it is almost certain death for any white man to sleep in the plantation. Some years ago the commodore went with several officers and a boat's crew to one of the Sultan's country houses in the interior of the island, a distance of about fifteen miles; they only slept one night in the interior, and a few days afterwards the only one of the whole party alive was

one who had slept in the boat, the vegetation is so dense and rank."

591. " Do the natives suffer from the climate?"—" Not in the same degree, the Arabs do, very much; I think very few Arabs of pure race reach manhood."

619. "Whose subjects are the northern Arabs, who chiefly carry on this trade?"—" They are chiefly the piratical tribes; the tribes who in former years gave us a great deal of trouble."

620. " Are they subject to any power?"— " That is the difficulty in dealing with the slave-trade; a great many of them are nominally under the jurisdiction of the Imaum of Muscat, but in reality the Imaum of Muscat has no power at all over them; he can do nothing effective."

621. " To what ports do those northern Arabs chiefly take the slaves?"—" A great many now go to Macullah and Ras-al-Had, and other ports in Arabia, and a great many go to ports in Persia."

622. "You think that the chiefs having control over those ports, would not have sufficient power to stop the import of slaves, if they wished it?"—" In dealing with them I should send an English man-of-war round with proclamations in Arabic, which I would have read out by the sheikhs and elders of the tribes, giving them distinct notice that after a certain date the

provisions of our treaties with all those chiefs, declaring the slave-trade piracy, would be rigidly enforced, and that the commander of every dhow found with slaves on board would be hanged."

575. "Nothing having been done to carry that out for a good many years, do you think it would still have the same effect?"—"We might well say to the Sultan we have left it to you to act up to the treaties, and to abolish this horrible man-stealing; you have not done it, we do not say you are wilfully and knowingly keeping up this slave-trade, but it has been, chiefly through the instrumentality of the English Government, suppressed in every other country in the world, and we will no longer allow you Arabs to be an exception."

576. "We have no treaties with them which prohibit man-stealing altogether?"—"No, but we should simply say we will not allow this; I think the Arabs quite understand that way of putting it. I often said to the Sultan, You Arabs come down here because you find a very pleasant and fertile country preferable to your own barren deserts, but that does not give you any right to depopulate half Africa, and to go and steal the population and sell them."

577. "You consider we should be justified in interfering with a strong arm in the interior of

Africa to prevent the stealing of the natives?"—
" By means of an efficient squadron you would be able so to check the trade that in a few years it would be given up; we could not interfere in the interior."

596. . . " Zanzibar is also becoming the emporium for the sea-borne trade of Madagascar, the Mozambique, the Comoro Islands, and the whole of the east coast of Africa. It is now the chief market in the world for the supply of ivory, gum, copal, cloves, and cowrees, and has a rapidly increasing export trade in hides, oil, seeds, dyes, &c., whilst sugar and cotton promise to figure largely amongst its future exports. The foreign trade of Madagascar has increased with extraordinary rapidity since the ports of this island have been opened to commerce. It is impossible to foresee what may be its extent in a few years. As one example of this increase, I was informed by the United States Consul at Zanzibar, that during the north-west monsoon of 1865, upwards of sixty large bungalows and dhows proceeded from Zanzibar to the western ports of Madagascar, to load rice for Kutch and Kattiwar, in consequence of the deficient harvest in those provinces. All this valuable trade is at present lost to British merchants, because until there is a postal communication with Zanzibar it is impossible for them to compete with the

foreigners, who at present have it all in their hands, and whose vessels, arriving with the latest state of the markets, they are thus enabled to regulate their purchases and sales. Nearly the whole of the local trade of Zanzibar is in the hands of British-Indian subjects, viz. Banyans, Khojahs, and Borahs, some of whom are very wealthy. The American, French, and German merchants conduct nearly all their business through these natives of India, who would however much prefer trading with English merchants, as they know that all disputes arising would then be settled by the British Consul, and according to the same law for both parties. The way in which the want of postal communication operates to prevent any of the trade being carried on by merchants at Bombay, may be illustrated by the following example of what several times occurred during my residence at Zanzibar:—A wealthy native firm at Bombay chartered a large British ship to proceed from Bombay to Zanzibar to load a cargo for London; the letter of advice to their agent at Zanzibar to purchase a cargo being duly sent by the mail steamer to Aden. There being no postal communication between Aden and Zanzibar, the letter does not reach the latter port for several months. In the meantime, the ship arrives at Zanzibar; the agent, having no advice, has no cargo ready; the foreign merchants, acting on an agreement existing between them for the purpose of excluding British merchants from any participation in the trade, run up the price of all produce in the market 40 per cent., sharing whatever loss there may be amongst each other. The ship, after waiting in vain for a cargo, comes on demurrage, and is finally despatched to London in ballast, entailing a heavy loss on the charterers in Bombay, who give up in consequence any intention of establishing a trade with Zanzibar. The expense of establishing a monthly communication between Zanzibar and the Seychelle Islands in correspondence with the French mail steamers running between Aden and La Réunion, and which call at Port Victoria, Island of Mahe, would be inconsiderable. The distance between Zanzibar and the Seychelle Islands is about 800 miles, almost due east from Zanzibar. Both monsoons are a fair wind, but there are frequent long calms, and the navigation on the Seychelles, bank is tedious and dangerous for sailing-vessels, owing to the very strong currents. A small steamer would consequently be preferable to a sailing-vessel. I think that if a regular communication were established with the Seychelles, a considerable trade would soon arise; natives of India residing at Zanzibar would be attracted to those lovely and salubrious islands, and the expense of keeping up a small vessel would be in part or entirely covered by freight and passage."

597. "You would look to the increase of commercial intercourse as having considerable effect in diminishing the interest which the natives have in the slave-trade?"—"I would; it is impossible to calculate what the trade of that coast might become in a few years if the slave-trade were once abolished."

598. "In what way does the existence of the slave-trade prevent the growth of a legitimate commercial trade?"—"The great export of able-bodied labourers from the country deters free labourers from coming to settle at Zanzibar or along the coast, because they know that as long as the slave-trade is going on they are not safe for a day."

608. *Lord F. Cavendish.*] "You have read the Report of the Slave Trade Committee of 1869, which sat at the Foreign Office?"—"Yes."

609. "What do you think of the terms of the treaty which it recommends should be negotiated with the Sultan of Zanzibar?"—"*I do not think any treaty would have the slightest effect; treaties with Arabs are mere waste paper.*"

610. "You think we should get rid of our present treaty?"—"We can easily do it, by say-

ing, 'This treaty has never been observed by the subjects of the Sultan of Zanzibar or of the Imaum of Muscat, and it is of no use having a treaty in force that is never observed.'"

611. "Would you at once forbid all export of slaves to the island of Zanzibar?"—"The worst part of the slave-trade is that from Lake Nyassa to the south, Kilwa being the port of shipment. The whole of that vast and rich country is becoming depopulated. Banyans who have been for years at Zanzibar have told me that they remember, when they first came to the coast, the whole country was densely populated down to the sea-coast, and now you have to go eighteen days' journey inland before you come upon a village almost. That is fully confirmed by Baron Van der Decken and Dr. Rosher, who travelled that route. Baron Van der Decken talks of miles and miles of ruined towns and villages the whole way up towards Lake Nyassa, where there is now no population at all. Every year this slave-trade is extending farther and farther inland. A great number of the slaves are now brought from the western side of Lake Nyassa; the Arabs have got dhows on the lake on purpose to convey their slaves across. I had a proof at Zanzibar of how the slave-trade extends from nation to nation in Africa. I found, in registering all the slaves I emanci-

pated, that amongst the recent arrivals most of them gave the names of their tribe as Manganga. I could not at that time exactly fix the position of their country; however, shortly afterwards I saw a letter of Dr. Livingstone in the paper, saying that he had recently travelled through the Manganga country, where the whole population was engaged in the cultivation and working up of cotton; and he said that he had never seen such a wonderful cotton country in his life, or such a fertile country. I think, a year or two afterwards, he went through the same country, and found it entirely depopulated, all the huts being full of dead bodies. The children had been carried away, and most of the adults slain. That is one of the worst features of the slave-trade in that country. When the slave-traders go into a district, they kill all the men and women, and burn the villages, and carry off the children. The reason they give for taking the children only is, that the children are driven more easily, like flocks of sheep, or they are tied with ropes and chains; the men they lose more by desertion on the way."

612. "My question was whether you would prohibit the present trade which we allow between the mainland and Zanzibar for the purposes of Zanzibar itself?"—"Unless the Government choose to do what I think is the proper

course, viz. to stop it with a high hand at once, and say we will not have this trade go on, it might for the sake of the Arabs in Zanzibar be permitted for a short time between Mirama and the island or coast opposite Zanzibar; there is not the same atrocity in that traffic, because it is not carried on on the organized system that the other trade is; probably from what is called Mirama, 4000 slaves are annually brought to the island of Zanzibar; that would be sufficient to keep up the supply in Zanzibar and Pemba; they are men and children who have been kidnapped. The slavers do not burn towns and villages, and murder the grown-up people to get those slaves."

613. *Sir J. Hay.*] " Are they exported from Darra Salaam ? "—" Mirama is the coast district opposite the island of Zanzibar; Darra Salaam is quite a recent creation of the late Sultan of Zanzibar, and it is now going to ruin again."

614. *Lord F. Cavendish.*] " When you speak of stopping the slave-trade with a high hand, do you mean by a squadron, or by any interference on land ?"—"By a squadron; I do not think the squadron need be very strong; but it would be ineffective without an experienced naval officer, an officer whose heart would be in the work."

615. " If the trade were allowed from one port only to the island of Zanzibar, would not there

be a danger of slaves being taken overland, even from Lake Nyassa to that port?"—"That could be checked, because there is such a marked difference in the tribes; I would severely punish any man who should export natives of those southern tribes; you could easily stop that."

626. *Mr. Crum-Ewing.*] "You mentioned that at one time a considerable trade in slaves was carried on with the French Islands; is that entirely given up now?"—"We have no recent information, I believe, about that. Two or three years ago Lord Campbell carried a motion in the House of Lords for an Address to Her Majesty, to appoint a Consul at Mozambique. I think it is a most unfortunate circumstance that that has never been acted on. Not only have we no Consul at Mozambique, but the consulate at the Comoro Islands has been abolished, so that from Zanzibar to our own territories in Port Natal, there is nobody to watch British interests, or to interfere with the slave-trade. In consequence of the ports in Madagascar having been thrown open to foreign trade since the death of the old queen, there is such an immensely increasing trade in the products of Madagascar, that they have begun to import slaves into Madagascar very largely, in order to cultivate their rich land; and,

although the Portuguese Government have abolished the slave-trade in Mozambique, I must say I do not believe it is abolished, or will be abolished without a British squadron to watch it. Up to recently there was no trade whatever in the Mozambique dominions except the slave-trade; the whole business of the Portuguese population was men-stealing and men-selling. At the five chief ports, Ibo, Mozambique, Inhambane, and the mouths of the Zambesi, the only trade was in men. Large parties of half-caste Portuguese, led very often by Portuguese, scoured all the interior, and brought those slaves down to be sold."

627. "Do you think that slaves are still taken to Réunion?"—"I have no recent information about it. We have now a Consul at Réunion, and I should think he would be able to state whether they are still importing slaves under the name of free engagées."

628. "What are the products of the interior of the country about Lake Nyassa?"—"All sorts of grains and vegetables. In the valleys of those large rivers opposite Zanzibar, within the Sultan's dominions, they are now cultivating sim-sim, from which most of our fine olive oil is made, which goes very largely to Marseilles. In the last few years a great trade has sprung up in orchilla, which is a purple dye, and sugar

is grown to a great extent. I believe very few people know what a fertile country that is. Baron Van der Decken, whose very interesting work has lately been published, speaks in the very highest terms of the fertility of the country, and of the opening there is for trade there. He describes a good deal of the country, a little to the north, as being a mountainous country, very much resembling Switzerland, and he says the chiefs are very anxious to have Europeans come and settle amongst them."

629. *Chairman*.] "You mentioned that Dr. Livingstone had found one district near Lake Nyassa where cotton was being cultivated?"—"Yes, the Manganga country towards Lake Nyassa. He describes the whole country as being a field of cotton, all the people of both sexes being busily engaged in spinning and weaving."

630. *Mr. O'Conor*.] "You think it useless to make treaties with the Sultan?"—"From my knowledge of the Arabs treaties are utterly useless. I understand that some of the witnesses who have been examined have suggested that the Sultan might be induced to give up the slave-trade if the 40,000 dollars which he annually pays as subsidy to the Imaum of Muscat were remitted. I am convinced that he

would never fall into that arrangement. When the Mission was over here that was a point the Secretary urged upon me more than any other. He said the Sultan of Zanzibar would rather give up the country and go to live at Mecca for the rest of his days. I think any negotiations upon that basis would be sure to fail. The Sultan would look upon it as a great humiliation, and it would be so considered by all the Arabs. They would say then, 'Is the Sultan of Zanzibar become a paid servant to the Feringhee?' and the chances are that he would lose his life."

669. "Did I rightly gather from the early part of your evidence that you approve of the suggestions of the Committee which sat at the Foreign Office?"—"Yes, generally; I think they recommend that all slaves should be exported from Darra Salaam only."

MR. H. C. ROTHERY called in; and examined.

815. "Have you learnt whether there is any difficulty in distinguishing a legal trader from a dhow?"—"I have always understood that there is very little difficulty in distinguishing between them, except in the case of legal traders, who do sometimes take a few slaves on board. There is no distinction in appearance, I am

told, between legal and illegal traders, but when a slaver has a cargo of slaves on board, there is no difficulty in distinguishing whether they are domestic slaves, or whether they are slaves carried for sale."

816. "Have you been able to learn from any papers that have come before you, whether domestic slaves are often taken to sea for sale?" —"I should have thought not; I should have thought it exceptional; the captain of the dhow perhaps might, if he had a good offer for a slave, sell him, but I should have thought, generally, that the slaves he had on board would be so valuable to him, as hardly to make it worth his while to sell them."

817. "If they are trained for mariners at all, they would be much more valuable on the ship than on the mainland?"—"Many of these dhows have perhaps half their crews composed of slaves, and, if they sold them, I should have thought a master would have great difficulty in navigating his dhow home again."

818. "How do you know a domestic slave from a slave intended for exportation?"—"I have always understood that the slaves when they got to Zanzibar were well-treated, that they became more civilized, and got into better condition; whereas the slaves exported from Kilwa, which is the chief port of exportation,

are generally in a state of the greatest emaciation."

819. "Are the two descriptions of slaves differently guarded?"—"I should have thought so."

820. "Are the slaves for exportation in the hold?"—"Not always, I believe; when they have only small cargoes of slaves that would not be necessary."

821. "Can you give us any assistance in suggesting means for the suppression of the slave-trade?"—"No other suggestions occur to me than those which we made in the Foreign Office Committee Report."

822. "From any information you have obtained subsequently, have you had reason to change your opinion at all?"—"Not on any point."

Rev. E. STEERE, LL.D., called in; and examined.

1044. "Can you speak to the healthiness of the country?"—"I have no reason to think that the climate of the country is worse; we all thought that the mainland opposite, particularly at Darra Salaam, was likely to be more healthy than Zanzibar itself. I have been at Darra Salaam, which is very finely situated; it has an excellent harbour, and there are some very fine buildings; but I am told that it is now to be abandoned.

It was always thought that Seyyid Majid intended it as a place of security against his brother, the Imaum of Muscat, the town not being so accessible from the sea as Zanzibar is."

1056. "Are there a large number of dhows engaged in that particular trade?"—"There have been generally a large number of them every season."

1057. "Have you any idea of the number of dhows engaged in that trade in the course of a year?"—"There is so much secrecy about it that I do not think anybody can tell accurately; there is a certain build of dhow one knows, and one used to see eight or ten of them in the harbour at a time. I do not know how many of them there would be in the course of a year."

1058. "You saw many dhows in the harbour at a time, which in the night would load their slaves and go away?"—"Dhows which everybody knew were there for piratical purposes if the opportunity offered."

1059. "Would they carry off a great number of slaves?"—"They would carry as many as they could on board; there was one taken by the 'Wasp' that had, I think, 380 on board."

1060. "Do you look forward to any considerable increase of commercial intercourse at Zanzibar, supposing the slave-trade were put down?"

—" Yes, I think commerce will go on increasing, and I think commerce tends to suppress the slave-trade; the legitimate commerce of Zanzibar is so large that the slave-trade is being rather squeezed out by it."

1061. " Do you think that the export of slaves is now decreasing rather than increasing?"—" Yes."

1062. " For how long has that been the case?"—" It has been chiefly, I suppose, since cloves began to be planted in Zanzibar."

1063. " That has given rise to a great trade?"—" To a very great trade."

The Hon. C. Vivian called in; and examined.

33. "I suppose, as far as female slaves are concerned, they are, to a great extent, taken to the harems of the Imaum of Muscat and the Arabian chiefs?"—" I believe that most of the slaves are taken to Muscat itself and Soor, and from thence they are exported to various ports on the Persian Gulf, and to Persia itself, wherever the market is the highest; they go even up to Bussorah and Mohamrah, and from thence I have no doubt some find their way into Turkish harems."

34. " In point of fact, I suppose, at Muscat there is a recognized slave-market?"—" Yes."

35. "I need hardly ask you whether the system of obtaining slaves and exporting them involves great hardships and misery?"—"In answer to that question, I cannot do better than read the beginning of our Report. 'The slaves required, as well for the legal as for the illegal traffic, are obtained from the interior of Africa. Formerly they could be procured from the countries bordering on the coast, but constant slave-raids have so depopulated those districts, that the slave-dealers are now forced to go far inland for their supplies. Year by year further tracts of country are depopulated and laid waste, and at the present time it is chiefly from the neighbourhood of Lake Nyassa and beyond it that slaves are obtained. The persons by whom this traffic is carried on are, for the most part, Arabs, subjects of the Sultan of Zanzibar. These slave-dealers start for the interior well-armed, and provided with articles for the barter of slaves, such as beads and cotton cloth. On arriving at the scene of their operations, they incite and sometimes help the natives of one tribe to make war upon another. Their assistance almost invariably secures victory to the side which they support, and the captives become their property, either by right or by purchase, the price in the latter case being only a few yards of cotton cloth. In the course of

these operations thousands are killed, or die subsequently of their wounds or of starvation; villages are burnt, and the women and children carried away as slaves. The complete depopulation of the country between the coast and the present field of the slave-dealers' operations attests the fearful character of these raids. Having, by these and other means, obtained a sufficient number of slaves to allow for the heavy losses on the road, the slave-dealers start with them for the coast. The horrors attending this long journey have been fully described by Dr. Livingstone and others. The slaves are marched in gangs, the males with their necks yoked in heavy forked-sticks, which at night are fastened to the ground, or lashed together so as to make escape impossible. The women and children are bound with thongs. Any attempt at escape, or to untie their bonds, or any wavering or lagging on the journey, has but one punishment, immediate death. The sick are left behind, and the route of a slave-caravan can be tracked by the dying and the dead. The Arabs only value these poor creatures at the price which they will fetch in the market, and if they are not likely to pay the cost of their conveyance, they are got rid of. The result is that a large number of the slaves die or are murdered on the journey, and the survivors arrive at their destination in a state of the greatest misery and emaciation.'"

185. "... I wish to read to the Committee two or three extracts from important despatches received since I last gave my evidence, which may be of use to the Committee. The first is dated from Zanzibar, the 20th of March this year. Dr. Kirk says, 'The whole subject (this is about the disposition of liberated slaves), of the disposal of slaves on shore here, is one requiring much consideration and careful organization before being practised to any extent. In the absence of some official thoroughly conversant with both the Zanzibar people and the tribes of the mainland, I consider that it would be most dangerous to allow beings so helpless as a cargo of freed slaves to go into the hands of any proprietor here. Properly directed, I believe, that a greater influence can be obtained for the abolition of slavery through those freed slaves than in any other way; and nothing can be more disgraceful than the present mode of dealing with them at Aden and Bombay. I am certain, however, that it will be found expedient, if not necessary, so long as Zanzibar remains a free Arab government, for us to have a free settlement somewhere on the coast, possibly not an English possession, but certainly under our administration. On such a station only

could a mass of freed slaves be properly and advantageously dealt with for the first five years of their freedom, and a settlement of this nature on the coast, would be a break in the land route, that will at once be opened when the sea transport is prohibited and blockaded.'"

23. "What is the approximate annual export of slaves from the dominions of the Sultan of Zanzibar?"—"We estimated it in our Report at about 20,000 a year, but it may be more. I was looking at Dr. Kirk's returns, in which he says, as I understand him, that between 1867 and 1868 the Sultan got 270,000 dollars for his tax upon slaves; if that is the case, that amounts to about 56,000*l.*; we only calculated it at 20,000*l.* a year on 20,000 slaves."

24. "You suspect that the number would be double?"—"Yes, upon that calculation; but I am not quite sure whether Dr. Kirk included in that the sale of slaves as well as the tax; you can safely take it at 20,000, it certainly is not less."

25. "Have you any reason to doubt the statement made by Dr. Kirk, and confirmed by Dr. Livingstone and the Rev. Mr. Waller, that four or five lives are lost for every slave delivered safe at Zanzibar?"—"I have no reason to doubt it, and the hardships the slaves encounter

become greater every year. As the country near the coast becomes depopulated, and the slave-hunters have to go farther into the interior for slaves, so does the march become more horrible and deadly to the slaves."

26. *Mr. Kinnaird.*] "From the last accounts, how far does it appear that the slaves are now brought?"—"According to the last accounts they are brought from Lake Nyassa."

27. "Have you any idea what the distance would be?"—"No; several days' journey."

75. "What did the Committee of which you were a member recommend should be done with the liberated slaves?"—"That they should be landed at Zanzibar itself, under due precautions, where a depôt of liberated slaves should be established, so as to substitute gradually free labour for slave labour: that we should form a colony there of free labour to compete with slave labour."

76. *Mr. Kennaway.*] "Would they not be liable to be carried off if they were taken to Zanzibar?"—"Of course they would, unless under very strong precautions."

77. *Mr. Kinnaird.*] "The great objection to it would be, that unless the Sultan of Zanzibar behaved better than we could expect him to behave, in all probability they would be recaptured?"—"Yes, the Sultan could not do

it himself; we should be obliged to help him."

78. *Mr. Crum-Ewing.*] "The northern Arabs would be too strong for him?"—"Yes; it was only the other day that the northern Arabs were found engaged in a plot to kidnap his own slaves, and take them away to the north."

186. "I wish to read a report from Admiral Cockburn, which is dated from Zanzibar, the 31st of May, 1871: 'I take an early opportunity after my arrival here, to write about the slave-trade; I am sorry to be obliged to give a bad report. It is without doubt a fact, that the trade is as busy and profitable as ever it was; in spite of all our exertions, every new plan adopted by us is quickly met by a cunning device of the Arabs encouraged by the Sultan, if not actively, certainly negatively. It is painful to any naval officer to be obliged to acknowledge this. Under existing treaties, and the recent instructions respecting domestic slaves, the Sultan having the power to give passports to any number of vessels laden with poor living creatures to be transported to different parts of his dominions, it is rendered almost impossible for a cruiser to take a dhow anywhere south of Lamoo, and during the south-west monsoon it is very difficult to keep cruisers sufficiently near the coast to intercept

them running with a fresh breeze. I assure their lordships it is a matter of sneer and jeer by the Arabs, our impotent efforts to stop that horrible abomination; yes, my lords, even the Sultan says the English will talk and bully, but can't or won't stop the trade. It is positively evident that a new system must be adopted. I propose that the money we annually expend in this course be employed in a more profitable and useful manner; I suggest that a stationary ship to act as a depôt and guard-ship, with a steam launch, be sent here under a captain who has had some experience in this duty; that a certain sum per annum be paid to the Sultan, on condition that he gives up the slave-trade, importing only a few to fill up vacancies in his dominions. Your Lordships are aware that the Sultan receives about 10,000*l*. per annum, by a tax upon the entry as well as the exit of slaves. The sum given to the Sultan would be recovered by the saving in bounties for captured negroes; and the stationary guard-ship would be cheaper than a cruiser; a large frigate without steam would be the best vessel, jury-rigged, and kept like a man-of-war, with a commander's complement of officers and men. This ship would be a military support to the Sultan, if he agreed to our own terms. I would add the advantage of a stationary officer at this port is greatly increased by the known fact that the East India Government do not encourage their agent in his efforts for the destruction of the inhuman traffic, which of course hampers him, if it does not damp his zeal. I visited the slave-market here yesterday, and a more painful and disgusting sight I never saw. Hundreds of poor negroes of both sexes, ranged about in all sorts of conditions, some living skeletons, others fat and well-dressed, pulled about with a crook stick and examined just like sheep or other animals in a market. I will take another opportunity to give further information, but I would not delay the request for the stationary depôt and guardship.'"

REV. HORACE WALLER, called in; and examined.

921. *Chairman.*] "I believe you are now a clergyman in England?"—"I am."

922. "Have you been on the East Coast of Africa?"—"I joined the Universities' Mission to Central Africa at the end of the year 1860, and I was there till the year 1864, when I returned to this country and took Holy Orders."

923. "In what part of Africa were you?"—"On the river Zambezi and in the neighbourhood of Lake Shirwa."

924. " You remained there for four years ?"—" In that part very nearly three years."

925. " What distance were you from Zanzibar?"—" A very considerable distance to the southward of it."

926. " Towards Nyassa ?"—" To the south of Lake Nyassa, within 100 miles of Lake Nyassa, in the part of the country from which slaves were principally collected to be sent down to the coast, and also down the river Zambezi into the Portuguese dominions."

927. " Were there very large exports of slaves from that part of the country ?"—" At that time the exports were very large, perhaps they had never been so large before in that part of Africa. The whole of the country to the north of the Zambezi was for the first time invaded by slave-traders, who took advantage of Dr. Livingstone's previous explorations, using his good name and fair fame amongst the natives, and saying that they were the same sort of white people that they had previously seen; and in that way the natives allowed them to come into their country. Before that time no Portuguese had ever been into that part of the country. I may state that the slave-trade that was opened out there was of two descriptions. In the first place, the Kaffir tribes to the south of the river Zambezi had been fighting for a great number

of years amongst themselves. No slaves are taken from the Kaffir tribes for the slave-trade which we have under consideration, but owing to the hardships of warfare, nearly all the women and children had disappeared from those tribes, and the Kaffirs were most anxious to replenish and strengthen the tribes, and therefore they told the Portuguese that they no longer wanted muskets which burst, and with which they were very much cheated, but they would prefer to have women and children sent to them. The Portuguese thereupon collected all the women and children they could in the highlands bordering on the river Shiré, and sent them down to Tette, which is the principal Portuguese port on the river Zambezi, whence they were sent to the Kaffir tribes in the interior of the country, and traded away for ivory and gold dust. Then again there was at that time another very large export of slaves to the mouth of the river Zambezi, to Quilimane, another of the Portuguese settlements. The French engagées system was then in full force, and a large export of slaves was going on from Quilimane. Besides those there was also a trade carried on to the north by Arabs, the slaves for which trade were taken from this part of the country to Kilwa, to be exported to Zanzibar, and they were also taken in very large numbers to Mozambique, whence they were exported to the Comoro Islands and to Madagascar, and some of them to Réunion."

928. *Sir J. Hay.*] "Slaves of all sexes?"—"Of all sexes."

929. *Sir R. Anstruther.*] "And of all ages?"—"In a gang of eighty-four slaves that Dr. Livingstone and two or three of us liberated, there may have been seven women of twenty-one years of age; there may have been ten men of nineteen years of age, and the rest were boys and girls of from seventeen down to six or seven. I must explain that for those Kaffirs the Portuguese collected women and children only; it was useless sending them young men of eighteen or twenty; the Kaffirs wished for women and children only. The slaves collected for the French engagées system would be principally of the age of eighteen to twenty-five, because they could be put on the plantations at once, but in all slave-gangs by far the largest proportion consists of children. The slave dealers prefer children because they are not so troublesome to drive, they are much easier caught if they attempt to escape, and they very soon settle down in their occupations, and they do not pine as slaves of greater age would."

930. *Chairman.*] "When you say children, what age do you mean?"—"From seven years of

age upwards; you will find in every slave-gang a great many children of seven to ten years of age; they are, perhaps, the most valuable slaves that can be captured."

931. *Sir R. Anstruther.*] " Can you form any idea of the proportion of children that have been exported lately?"—" I know from letters which I have received from Dr. Livingstone, and which I would have brought had I known I was going to be examined to-day, that the same devastation is going on up to the latest dates; he has been through an immense tract of country which is now entirely depopulated; on all sides there are signs of this slave-trade having swept away the whole of the population."

932. *Chairman.*] " Where is that?"—" The country between the east of Lake Nyassa and the coast."

933. " How far is Nyassa from the coast?"—" I should say 300 or 350 miles."

934. " Do you mean that all the country, from the coast to Lake Nyassa, is depopulated?"—" It is depopulated to within a short distance of Lake Nyassa."

935. " You referred just now to slaves collected for the purpose of being employed on the French engagées system; that has entirely ceased now, has not it?"—" The French engagées system has entirely ceased, but it was so profitable a trade

that the Portuguese on the river Zambezi sold off nearly all the slaves they had on their farms to supply it, and therefore during the latter part of the time that I was in the country they were getting fresh slaves down for the cultivation of their farms; and the whole of the country in which we were was depopulated for their trade."

936. "That was not for export?"—"Not for export at that time, but if the opportunity offered they would have exported those slaves."

937. "If they could have got for them such a price as would have compensated them for the loss of their labour on their estates?"—"Yes."

938. "Our attention is rather directed to that portion of the trade which you have described as being carried on by the Northern Arabs?"—"If you will allow me I should very much like to avail myself of the opportunity of describing the cruelties I have seen connected with the collecting of the slaves. I think I am not asking too much to be allowed to state this, because I know that many of the slaves taken from the part of the country we were in find their way to Mozambique, and that many of them find their way to Zanzibar. Dr. Livingstone recognized slaves at Zanzibar that had been brought from that part of the country, and I have recognized at Mozambique some who had

recently been taken from the highlands, and indeed the slaves themselves told us where they had seen us, so that we could at once identify them as having been drawn from the country we had been in. I think that attention should be prominently called to the condition of those unfortunate people in their transit from the interior, because, though I can quite see that one's mouth is rather closed as to the status of a slave when he gets to an Arab master, that has nothing to do with the sufferings connected with his capture. It is true that a slave is well treated by his Arab master; as has been well observed, a man will not ill-treat his slave so as to hurt him, any more than he will his horse, but life is so cheap in the interior of the country that this rule does not hold good at all, as far as regards what takes place before the slave is finally sold. When I first went there in 1861 (and the state of things was even worse when I left in 1864), the ordinary price of a slave was two yards of calico—that is to say, for a boy ten years of age. A woman would fetch something more if she was likely to be sold to the Kaffirs, or if she was likely to go on to one of the Portuguese farms, or to go to any of the Portuguese in Mozambique: she might have fetched eight yards of calico; but the price varied very much. The process of catching the slaves is this: the slave-dealer goes into the country with so many muskets, and so many pieces of calico, and he finds out the most powerful chief, and he gives him spirits, and keeps him in a state of semi-drunkenness the whole time, and tells him he must have more slaves; he gives him muskets and powder on account, and the man immediately finds out an opportunity to settle some old outstanding quarrel with some other chief, and therefore a war breaks out. As soon as war breaks out, favourable conditions are created for the carrying on of the slave-trade, because famine is sure to follow in a country where the people are dependent on one wet season for tilling the ground, for it is only during the wet season that corn can be sown. Then a chief without food, and without the means of buying food, will sell off his people very cheaply indeed. Captures are made in war. Kidnapping is prevalent all over the country, which leads again to all sorts of petty disputes and retaliation, and the more disturbed the country is, the cheaper slaves become; so cheap do they at last become, that I have known children of the age of from eight to ten years bought for less corn than would go into one of our hats, and you may easily imagine where they are bought so cheaply, and where they fetch so large a price on the coast, it pays the slave-dealer very well to collect as many as he can, knowing that he must lose a certain proportion on the way, but also knowing that the remnant he saves will pay him a very large profit. It is like sending up for a large block of ice to London in the hot weather; you know that a certain amount will melt away before it reaches you in the country as it travels down; but that which remains will be quite sufficient for your wants."

939. *Chairman.*] " Can you give us any idea of the comparative price of a slave on the coast, and in the interior where they are bought ?"— " I ascertained the price of slaves at Mozambique, and I found they were worth there about eight dollars, the same slaves having been bought in the interior for a few yards of calico."

940. *Sir R. Anstruther.*] " What is the proportion of waste of life in the transit ?"—" It is very difficult to say what is the waste of life in the transit without having travelled with a slave caravan the whole way. Sickness may break out; they may cross a part of the country where there is very little food, and then many die of famine. Then, again, if there is anything like insubordination in the slave-gang, the axe and knife are used very freely indeed, and an indiscriminate slaughter takes place amongst

all those who are strong enough to be at all obstreperous. We liberated a gang of eighty-four slaves one morning, and within a few miles of the place where we liberated them we were shown places in the bush where slaves had been killed only that morning; one poor woman had a child on her back, which she had recently given birth to, and which she was too weak to carry farther, and the slave-dealer took it by the heels and dashed its brains against a tree; another woman was ill herself, and could not keep in the line, and the slave-dealer dashed her brains out with the axe, and she was cut out of the slave thong. They are all united in a long string, the men being yoked in heavy forked sticks, which are kept on their necks from the time they are captured till the time they are delivered to the slave shipper, sometimes for six weeks, and sometimes even three months at a time."

941. *Chairman.*] " What is the time generally occupied in the transit to the coast?"—" It varies; the slave gang is made up as the dealers travel about; they do not collect all the slaves at one place and go straight to the coast, the slaves are marched to and fro in the country, to a chief here and to another there, wherever the dealers hear that slaves are to be sold, and then they are all eventually taken to the coast. The

travelling is very slow; I should say it is no uncommon thing for a slave-gang to be some three months from the time it is first formed to the time it reaches the coast. The loss of life is very terrible indeed, owing to the hardships of the transit, and owing to the brutality of the drivers."

942. "Dr. Livingstone, in one of his letters, estimates that about one-fifth reach the coast; do you think that that would be a fair average?" —" I should say that one-fifth do reach the coast, perhaps more; but I would also state this, that the Doctor believes that for every slave that comes to the coast perhaps ten lives are lost in the interior."

945. " Dr. Livingstone mentions one part of the country which at one time he found well cultivated, and where a great quantity of cotton was grown, and which on a subsequent visit he found entirely depopulated?"—" Yes, that is the country I am speaking of in which so great a change took place. Many of the Doctor's statements have been discredited, but he is not a man to exaggerate in any respect; I know that contrary opinions about the country have been stated, and it has been hinted that he has coloured things rather too highly, but when I was there I had opportunities of seeing the remains of villages in all directions, the popula-

tion of which had been entirely swept away; I have seen as many as three villages burning in one morning within two hours, and I have seen hundreds of captives carried away from those villages."

946. "The villages are set on fire, and, in the confusion, the men, women, and children are captured?"—"Yes."

947. "Within what time did that change take place from its being a flourishing cotton-growing country to its being depopulated?"—"In about two years."

948. "Do you remember in what year Dr. Livingstone saw it in its flourishing condition?"—I think the Doctor came home to England and represented the flourishing state of affairs in 1859, and we found the altered state of things in 1861; the inhabitants of that district were a very industrious and intelligent race; they had an immense quantity of iron all through the country; coal also was found there, and gold; and copper was taken away to the coast in the form of malachite."

949. "They have been swept away?"—"Entirely swept away. I may say that the country was formerly so thickly populated that you might have travelled for seventy or eighty miles, and have come to a village at every two miles; in many places you would have found a village at

every half-mile. It is thoroughly well watered, and it is hardly necessary in any case to take any precaution about water. Another proof of the great population in the hill country is this: that there was no game to be found at all, with the exception of a few guinea-fowl."

950. *Sir R. Anstruther.*] "The consequence of this depopulation is that all this land is lying waste?"—"The Doctor, in one of his last letters to me, speaks of having to cross a tract of 120 miles where they found not a human being of any kind. All this land that I am speaking of is perfectly swept of its inhabitants, and I have no hesitation in saying that every bit of this damage and misery has been caused by the slave-trade."

951. *Chairman.*] "Where are the slaves obtained from now?"—"The slaves are now brought from great distances in the interior. The belt of country between the Lakes and the east coast is denuded of its inhabitants, and, therefore, they have to be brought from the west side of Lake Nyassa; they are transferred across the lake in Arab dhows; there are settlements of Arabs on both sides of the lake, and the Doctor in his travels has given very accurate accounts of the slave-trade crossing the lake."

952. "To what power are those Arabs subject?" —"They are not subject to any one; they are

perfectly lawless; they have no master at all; the greater part of the slaves that go to Zanzibar now are brought from the vicinity of that lake, the great proportion of them from the west side of the lake, simply because the rest of the country is depopulated."

953. "Of course the farther the slave-dealers have to go inland for the slaves, the greater the waste of life?"—"The cheaper they are to buy, and the greater the loss of life there is in bringing them down to the coast."

954. "You do not know anything as to what is going on now, I presume, except from the letters of Dr. Livingstone?"—"I am in constant correspondence with Dr. Kirk; and I may state that Mr. Young, who went up to search for Dr. Livingstone in 1867, went through the greater part of the country I am speaking of, as far as the middle of Lake Nyassa, and according to his account the same state of things was going on at that time. I have since heard from more recent accounts that it is still going on, and, in fact, it must go on as long as slaves are exported from the east coast."

955. *Sir J. Hay.*] "Are those slave-dealers of whom you are speaking Portuguese subjects, or Arabs?"—"Most of them are Portuguese subjects; some of them are Arabs."

956. "Have the Portuguese Government no

means of restraining them?"—"I speak of things as they were; I can only say that the Portuguese who were sent out there, were sent out to shift for themselves; the Home Government did not wish to hear anything more of them, and the slave-trade was never interfered with in any way except on paper."

957. *Mr. J. Talbot.*] " Did you accompany Dr. Livingstone on any part of his travels?"—" Not as one of his expedition; I went out with Bishop Mackenzie, but I was with Dr. Livingstone, off and on, for nearly four years; I joined him because we wished to save the lives of a great many of those poor men and children who had been liberated by us, and the Doctor and myself were working together for that purpose for some time; eventually he sent me down to the Cape with them, and a great many of them are there at the present time."

958. *Chairman.*] " Have you any suggestion to offer to the Committee with the view of suppressing the slave-trade on the East Coast of Africa?" —" Having listened with much interest to the evidence which has been given here, I should like to suggest that which seems to me to be one very good plan, and which I think might be adopted. The suggestion has been made that vice-consuls should be placed at different parts of the coast to watch the slave-trade, and

to aid the fleet, as they certainly would be able to do in a most valuable way. General Rigby thinks that it would be difficult to get men to undertake that office, on account of the unhealthiness of the coast, but I think that difficulty might be removed in a measure, by having what I have heard called a "Floating-consul;" that is, a consul who should have a yacht at his command, and who should ply between, say Zanzibar and Madagascar; he might spend some part of his time at Kilwa, and some part of his time in Mozambique harbour; he might cross to Johanna, where a large slave-trade is going on, and he might cruise along the coast of Madagascar if need be, though perhaps that would be too large a field. At all events, I think the danger to a man's life would be obviated by his being able to move about. To put a man in a very unhealthy place is not only likely to kill him in a short time, but it makes him non-efficient very quickly indeed. The result of two or three attacks of fever is very serious; if the man is not moved away, he, in some cases, becomes morbid in his ideas, and, in other cases, he becomes exceedingly nervous. In some cases I have known men become really demented as long as they have been within the reach of the malaria that has made them ill. It is necessary, in that country, to be moving about. You may undergo any hardships as long as you move about, and are in active employment; but once be stationary in an unhealthy place (and there is no place so unhealthy as a small Arab town), and your life is very much hazarded. I would add that I think there are also other advantages in such a plan. I think the slave-dealers would then never know where to expect this officer; he would be master of his own actions and movements much better than he would if he had to be dependent on calling upon a man-of-war to take him from one place to another. I do not think the expense of such a service would be very great; it would be a popular service, and many men would be found who would enter heart and soul into it."

959. " Do not you think the same service could be performed by one of the fleet cruising about in the same way from port to port ?"—" I think not so well, because I attach importance to the vice-consul being enabled to reside on shore for a short time, by which means he would be able to obtain information which he otherwise could not obtain. The floating-consul might go to any of those ports, and remain a short time at them; and then, without the necessity of asking any one's leave, he might weigh anchor the next morning, and communicate with any of the fleet."

960. "Have you any other suggestion to make with a view to putting a stop to this slave-trade?"—"I will simply add this: I have seen a good deal of the Arabs in the Comoro Islands, and other places, and I should certainly advise that we should deal with them with a strong hand in preference to any dallying with them; I would put the utmost pressure upon the Sultan of Zanzibar at once; I should show him that though we might be taking away from him shillings by stopping his slave-trade, yet that the vast increase in the legitimate trade that there must be in the course of a few years would be putting back pounds into his pocket. He is now a beggar set upon horseback; he is a man of enormous income; and from what General Rigby has said, he is a man with whom I think strong action would have more effect than any paper warfare in the way of treaties, and so forth."

961. "You have probably seen a great deal to enable you to form an opinion as to what would be the increase of commercial intercourse if the slave-trade were abolished?"—"I know most of the merchants connected with the trade on the east coast, and I get letters constantly from Dr. Kirk at Zanzibar; I also know Dr. Steere, who has resided there some time, and Mr. Alington who was there; I knew Mr.

Thornton, who was with Baron Van der Decken; and I have indirectly had very many opportunities of knowing how the trade of Zanzibar is increasing daily."

962. "Do you think that the merchants resident there are anxious to have the slave-trade put a stop to?"—"I think they are certainly. When the northern Arabs come down with the monsoon to carry away the slaves to Arabia and the Persian Gulf, there is no security for the life of Europeans in Zanzibar, and if a better state of things were established, if safety could be ensured, I am sure they would all be very glad. I cannot conceive that Europeans could have two opinions about it."

963. "They are not themselves at all connected with the slave-trade, are they?"—"Not at present. I cannot say that such was the case a few years ago. I know that a great commotion existed at Zanzibar, and also in the Comoro Islands, from the fact that Englishmen were very large employers of slave-labour, but that has been put a stop to by the Foreign Office."

964. "You think now there is a very general feeling among the merchants there that their interests would be promoted by the suppression of the slave-trade?"—"I am sorry I cannot back my opinion by evidence upon that point, but there are gentlemen in this country (one gentle-

man especially whose house is connected with Zanzibar, a member of the firm of Wiseman and Company, one of the leading merchants there) who, I am sure, could offer you better information on the subject than I can."

965. *Mr. Crum-Ewing.*] " Captain Fraser[1] had a large number of slaves, had he not?"—"Yes; the fact of Captain Fraser employing slaves led to everlasting murmuring on the part of the natives. One morning they would see us burning the dhows which were engaged in the slave-trade, and the next morning they would see an Englishman working factories and plantations with those slaves safely landed; it was a question which puzzled far more acute people than they were. The same thing existed at the Comoro Islands; it was a mere sham and delusion; the poor slaves were hired in gangs from their Arab master; the Arab master was called in by the English employer, who, merely as a matter of form, said, ' Now mind all these people are to be free labourers on my plantation. I will hand over their wages to you.' But, of course, they were not handed over. It was encouraging the slave-trade."

966. *Sir R. Anstruther.*] " As far as the slaves were concerned, they were as much slaves after the transaction as before?"—"Yes."

[1] A retired Indian officer.

967. *Mr. Crum-Ewing.*] "After they were manumitted, did not they remain with Colonel Fraser of their own accord?"—"I am not sure about that; I know at the time it was a great scandal."

970. *Sir R. Anstruther.*] "Independently of humane considerations, are not you of opinion that commercially it would be well worth our while to make an outlay for the purpose of suppressing the slave-trade, and putting a stop to this depopulation of large tracts of country which is now going on?"—"I cannot speak too strongly upon that point; a great part of the east coast of Africa is useless for any purposes of commerce at present. Of export you may say there is nothing except a few hides from the northern part, where the Somalis are in power, slaves, ivory, and a little gold-dust; nothing else comes from the interior. I have no doubt were the slave-trade stopped a very large trade with Europe might spring up at Zanzibar, because the produce from the eastern part of Africa must inevitably come through Zanzibar. Zanzibar would become a second Singapore or Kurrachee for that part of the world, more especially now the Suez Canal is opened; and, I think, it should be our policy on all considerations to try and get a stop put to this horrible loss of life; commercially it

would be of the greatest importance to us. According to the accounts of the recent discoveries of Dr. Livingstone and others, we have in the interior of that part of Africa a country equal in resources to any part of India, and I believe more healthy as a rule; the sea-board and the rivers are unhealthy, but when you get some distance from the coast you rise to a lovely table-land, and it is a country which, from what I saw, and from what I know from other men who have travelled there, is second in beauty to hardly any in the world, and it is also a most productive country. Iron abounds in all directions; in fact, the Portuguese get all their iron from there. Coal is to be found; lead I have seen myself in large quantities, and cotton can be grown to any extent. I have seen very large quantities of cotton there."

971. "In fact, apart from all humane considerations, you think it would be for our interest to make an outlay for the suppression of this trade?"—"Yes; but independently of our interest I think as Englishmen, as a people so blessed as we are, and as a people who profess to put down the slave-trade in different parts of the world, our foremost duty is to stop this frightful loss of life, particularly when we consider that there are only a few treaties, which have never been abided by, in our way. The

plainer we make things for the Arabs the better; hitherto there has been a vast amount of confusion; they do not know what we mean, and I candidly confess that such transactions as those I spoke of, in which Englishmen have had to do with the slave-trade, give them cause to complain of us, and give rise to complications. I have seen a French ship lying at the island of Johanna, crammed with slaves, with one of our men-of-war within a cable's length of her, and the poor creatures jumping overboard and swimming to us to protect them; and the Arabs would say to us, there is a Frenchman there full of slaves, if it was one of our ships you would burn her directly; why do not you go and take her? All these things lead to complications, and the sooner they are simplified by action *pur et simple* the better."

972. *Mr. Gilpin.*] " Have you yourself seen the dhows going down the river laden with slaves?" —" Not dhows, but canoes. I have seen twenty or more in a day, laden with slaves, going down the river Shiré into the Portuguese dominions."

973. *Sir R. Anstruther.*] " When was that?"— " In 1864."

974. " As to the healthiness of the coast, does not it depend principally upon the habits of the European settlers there; would not a man who was tolerably sober and correct in his habits

have a better chance of keeping himself in health than a man of intemperate habits?"—"It used to be said on the west coast that a stock of tombstones should be kept at Sierra Leone for the use of those that died there, and that one sentence would describe all their deaths, "brandy and water." That really has a good deal to do with it, but I must state this, that a man who lives in an unhealthy place very soon becomes demoralized in mind and body, and he is very likely to take to an unwholesome way of living. I think it would not be safe for a man to stay there long; but, in connexion with your question, I should like to state from information I have received from Dr. Kirk recently, that he is decidedly of opinion that a station might be found on the mainland near to Zanzibar, where Europeans could live in perfect health, and where, if it were necessary, liberated slaves could be sent to be kept under safe supervision."

978. *Mr. J. Talbot.*] "With regard to the depopulated country between the coast and Lake Nyassa, which you say is like a desert, you think it could be again made very productive?" —"Of course it must take some time for the remnants of those tribes which have been driven north, south, east, and west to come back to their old country."

979. "Do you think that there is still population sufficient in that part of Africa to reinhabit that country, and to recultivate it?"—"Without doubt there is population sufficient in the neighbourhood of the lakes. I may state this, as a peculiar feature of the depopulation going on in that part of the country, that when destruction and disturbance come, the natives are obliged to make for either a lake or a river, because, as I have stated, no corn can be sown except during the wet season in the highlands; but there is always a certain amount of swamp-land available in the neighbourhood of lakes and rivers, in which corn can be grown at all times of the year. When we were in the highlands, in 1863 and 1864, in the neighbourhood of the Shiré, all the population which was not swept off accumulated at the river; and it was a very frightful state of things there, because the people flocked to the river, perfectly famished and perfectly mad with hunger, and they risked their lives for the sake of a few heads of corn. The river all day long was carrying down the dead bodies of those who had been fighting amongst themselves, like starving dogs quarrelling over a bone. The population is very dense indeed on Lake Nyassa at present."

980. "Some of that population would, in the course of time, spread over the depopulated

district?"—"Yes, if there was anything like peace."

982. *Sir R. Anstruther.*] "With regard to the probability of the depopulated district becoming again inhabited, the fertility of the soil, and the salubrity of the climate, which induced people to go there, and cultivate the soil in time past, would operate as inducements to people to go there again, would they not?"—"Yes; this part of the country is full of little streams; in fact, it was some time before I knew what the native word for thirst was, though you may hear the word for hunger from morning to night. I never saw a better watered country in my life (when you get on the low lands, in fact, you have too much water), and where you have water, you are sure to have plenty of cultivation. We hear of African deserts, but that term only applies to the extreme south and the extreme north of Africa; there is not an approach to a desert in the interior at all, it is a very fertile country throughout."

983. *Mr. Kinnaird.*] "You referred just now to the suggestion that a European settlement might be established at some point near the coast?"—"I referred to a suggestion in a letter I recently received from Dr. Kirk; he found it necessary to make a journey for one or two days into the interior of the country to push on

c c

some of the porters who were conveying provisions to Dr. Livingstone, and he then passed through a part of the country, which he found exceedingly healthy and fertile, and which he thought could be very well inhabited by any Europeans."

934. "You have no suggestion to make to the Committee further than you have made, as to the policy of establishing a coast settlement for Europeans?"—"Seeing that it must be obvious to all of us, that it would help us out of a difficulty if we could provide for these liberated slaves, it would be a most important thing if a European settlement could be established near Zanzibar, where they could be carefully looked after; and I consider it most fortunate that Dr. Kirk has, in his opinion, discovered a place recently where such a settlement could be formed."

1352. *Chairman.*] "You have a letter from Dr. Livingstone, from which you wish to read some extracts to the Committee?"—"Yes; this letter is dated 1st February, 1867; he is writing from the country of the Chipéta, which he describes to be five days' march from Lake Nyassa on the east of it, and he says, 'I am a perfect bugbear to these coast Arab slave-traders. Party after party, on hearing that the English were coming along the road, skedaddled away through bush and brake and across pathless forests; one wise old party, who had about 800 slaves, and was just entering on a depopulated district of ten days' march with them, finding that I had lighted on him, came forward and presented an ox and big bag of flour. This man and brother added a dish of cooked meat on seeing that we were really famishing. We had pretty hard lines for 150 miles, could not get food for either love or money: and then the depopulated part! I accomplished it on the morning of the eighth day with four companions; our food was all expended on the sixth day, and it was in hard plight that this good Samaritan slave-trader became a friend indeed.' He afterwards says, 'Near the sea-coast the country is covered with dense forest. Farther inland the forest is more open, but you seldom see the horizon; then the country becomes undulating, and, from the crests of the earthen waves you may see mountains all about. The country about Mataka is Magomero magnified; a perfect rush of running rills flowing southwards and northwards, forming the Liendi and Rovuma, which unite at Ngomano. I counted fifteen of these burns in one day's march.' Farther on, speaking of the slave-traders, he says, 'Instead of a steamer, which I did my best to get on the lake, two Arab dhows ply their calling as slavers. The owner of one has swept a large tract on the western side of people; at least, so say his own people. They kept their craft out of my way lest I should burn them.' In another part of his letter, he says, 'Some Arabs were fleeing from the resentment of Manganja, who resented their bringing arms and ammunition into the country for their destruction.' He is there referring to the plan adopted by the slave-dealers of bringing arms and ammunition to set one tribe against the other. I can speak distinctly to the fact of its being the chief aim of the slave-traders to set one tribe against the other, in order that they may bring war and the consequent destruction into the country which produces just the state of things that makes slaves cheapest. Then farther on, speaking of travelling with the Africans, he says, 'With them we crossed Kirk's range, and got among Manganja in the primitive state, working in iron, and spinning buaze, and sowing grain extensively.' Buaze is a fibre used for nets. He is speaking there of a population which had not been visited by the slave-traders."

MADAGASCAR.

Inclosure 1 in No. 17.

The Chief Secretary of State to Consul Pakenham.
(Translation.)

"*Antananarivo, 6 Adizadza (March* 19, 1869).

"SIR,—I write this letter to tell you the words uttered by the Prime Minister.

"He has received a letter from the Governor of Mojanga, dated the 6th Adaoro (17th February), reporting two Arab dhows, with 194 Mozambiques. When the Governor saw these dhows with Mozambiques, they appeared suspicious, as they were not making for the port, but steering west, the other side of the forest. He therefore sent officers in a boat to reconnoitre. These officers, seeing the number of Mozambiques in the dhows, seized the Arabs and the whole of the Mozambiques, and took them before the Governor of Mojanga. When landing the 194 Mozambiques, fifteen died of starvation, there being no provisions on board the dhows. When the Governor and his officers inquired of the Arabs why they had those Mozambiques, the Arabs replied, that their King had sent them. The Governor then asked them, Who is the King who sent you, and from what place? The Arabs answered, We come from Sangazy, and the King who sent us is Imosohoanty, the Sovereign of Sangazy, at Mozambique. We were not coming here to Mojanga had the wind not driven us here. We did not enter the port, because we had heard that there was no dealing in Mozambiques here.

"In addition to the 194 Mozambiques, of whom fifteen died, there were forty-seven others in the dhows. The Governor having questioned the Arabs respecting these latter, they answered—

"Fifteen are free;

"Fifteen are slaves of King Mosakoanty;

"Two are slaves of Mohamady;

"Fifteen the wives of their masters.

"The Mozambiques and the Arabs who brought them are still detained at Mojanga by the Governor."

Extract of Annual Report from Commodore Heath to Secretary of the Admiralty, January, 22, 1870.

12. "On the 6th November, their Lordships issued 'Instructions for the Guidance of Naval

Officers employed in the Suppression of the Slave-trade.' Those instructions forbid the detaining of vessels having slaves on board, if there are attendant circumstances showing that the slaves are not being transported for the purpose of being sold as slaves; and there is added as an example of the nature of those circumstances:—'Where the slaves found on board are very few in number, are unconfined, and appear to be on board for the purpose of loading or working the ship or attending upon the master or the passengers, and there is no other evidence that the vessel is engaged in, or equipped for, the Slave-trade.'"

13. "I believe that, just as it is said a drunkard can only be cured by total abstinence, so the Slave-trade by sea can only be put down, if at all, by a rigid forbidding of the carrying to sea of any slaves of any description. As I have before remarked, even what is called a domestic slave is not only a salable article, but an article which is very often sold; and the return of those embarked to the port they originally left depends solely upon whether or no a good offer has been made for them at the ports they have visited in the interval. I attach (Inclosure No. 2) depositions made before me personally by some of the slaves captured by her Majesty's ship 'Forte,' as showing how numerous are the domestic slaves carried to sea for sale.

" LE TRAITÉ DES NÈGRES DE L'AFRIQUE CENTRALE.

" On sait tout le zèle humanitaire que déploie le gouvernement anglais contre le hideux commerce des noirs. Des croisières vigilantes sont organisées sur le littoral de l'Afrique orientale, et Zanzibar, ce grand marché de " chair noire," est très surveillé.

" D'un document récemment parvenu aux autorités britanniques, il résulterait que les marchands d'esclaves, évitant la surveillance des croiseurs, sont parvenus à se frayer une voie de transit facile et que le commerce des Africains capturés prend un grand développement.

"L'auteur du mémoire que nous analysons, le général Kirkham, auquel sa situation militaire auprès du souverain d'Abyssinie a permis de bien connaître la question qu'il croit de son devoir de soulever, pense que l'expédition annuelle des esclaves entre l'intérieur de l'Afrique et les possessions ottomanes varie entre 80 et 90,000 individus, ayant de 7 à 16 ans.

"Les caravanes viennent directement du centre de l'Afrique, passent par Bogos, se dirigent sur Massouah, d'où les malheureux captifs sont envoyés à Djeddah.

" Une belle esclave, de bonne apparence et

'bien cuivrée,' dit le général Kirkham, vaut jusqu'à 700 francs au premier marché de vente. En secondes et troisièmes mains, la 'marchandise' varie de valeur suivant la demande ou la fantaisie personnelle de l'acheteur.

"Les esclaves préférés sont celles qui sont originaires des tribus Shankeltos ou venant des Gallas; là, en effet, les sujets sont 'beaux et bien constitués.' Un garçon Shankeltos ou Gallas 'bien bâti,' suivant l'expression du général, vaut de 477 à 530 francs.

"Il résulterait de ces informations que les caravanes des marchands d'esclaves passent précisément dans cette partie du territoire abyssin (Bogos) que le khédive d'Egypte cherche à soumettre pour se l'annexer.

"L'expédition égyptienne, déjà si mystérieuse, et qui parait préoccuper le gouvernement anglais, emprunte aux renseignements qu'envoie le général Kirkham un intérêt nouveau." M.

Translation of the annexed Extract from the Moniteur Universel, of Paris, of the 10*th December,* 1872.

"THE SLAVE-TRADE IN CENTRAL AFRICA.

"The humane zeal employed by the English Government against the slave-trade is well-known. Vigilant cruisers are engaged on the coast of Eastern Africa, and Zanzibar, that great market for 'black flesh' is well watched.

"It appears from a document lately received by the British Government that the slave-dealers manage to avoid the cruisers, and that the trade in captured Africans assumes great proportions.

"The author of the memoir to which we refer, General Kirkman, whose military position, near the sovereign of Abyssinia, has enabled him to study the question which he thinks it his duty to discuss, believes that the annual transport of slaves from the interior of Africa to the Ottoman Empire varies from 80,000 to 90,000 individuals of from seven to sixteen years of age.

" The caravans come direct from the centre of Africa, passing by Bogos, to Massouah, whence the unhappy captives are sent to Djeddah.

" A good-looking, bright coloured negro girl, says General Kirkman, is worth as much as 28*l.* at first hand, and at the second and third market the price varies according to the demand and fancy of the purchasers.

"The slaves preferred are those of the Shankeltos or Gallas tribes, who are handsome and well made. A Shankeltos or Gallas boy, well built, according to the expression of the General, is worth 19*l.* to 21*l.* and upwards.

"It appears that the caravans of the slave-dealers pass precisely through that part of the Abyssinian territory (Bogos) which the Khedive is trying to annex.

"The Egyptian Expedition, already so mysterious, and which seems to occupy the attention of the English Government, gains additional interest from General Kirkman's despatch."

(Signed) M.

GERMANY.

No. 8.

Mr. Gordon to the Earl of Clarendon.—Received April 23.)

"*Stuttgardt, April* 15, 1869.

"My Lord,—I have the honour to transmit herewith a despatch from Mr. Cope, with its several inclosures, which reached me too late yesterday to be forwarded by the weekly messenger. Its object is to cover an interesting Memorandum on the East African Slave-trade to Egypt and Arabia, prepared by Dr. Wilhelm Schimpfer, a Baden naturalist, who seems to have resided long in the countries on both sides of the Red Sea, and to be well acquainted with the haunts and routes followed by the slave-traders, and with the various connivance and opposition which they meet with from the authorities of the different localities.

"The Memorandum has been communicated to Mr. Cope through Baron Freydorf, by the kindness of the Grand Duke of Baden, to whom it was addressed (in consequence of the absence of Mr. Munzinger, for whom it was originally intended, from Massowah), with the request that his Royal Highness would cause it to be forwarded to her Majesty's Government; and Mr. Cope has ably fulfilled the laborious task of translating the documents in question.

"I have, &c.
(Signed) "G. J. R. GORDON."

Inclosure 1 in No. 8.
Mr. Cope to Mr. Gordon.
"*Carlsruhe, April* 8, 1869.

"SIR,—I have the honour to transmit herewith, a translation of a letter and its inclosures, relating to the East African Slave-trade, which I have received from Baron von Freydorf.

"Dr. Wilhelm Schimpfer, the writer of the inclosed Memorandum, is, Baron Freydorf informs me, a naturalist who has spent several years in Abyssinia and Arabia.

"I have, &c.
(Signed) "EDMUND W. COPE."

Inclosure 2 in No. 8.

Baron von Freydorf to Mr. Cope.
(Translation.)

"*Carlsruhe, March* 27, 1869.

"SIR,—Through the assistance of the Consulate of the North German Confederation at Port Said, and of the Grand Ducal Consulate at Marseilles, a letter from Dr. Wilhelm Schimpfer, dated from Adoa in the province of Tigré, in Abyssinia, on the 10th November, 1868, addressed to his Royal Highness the Grand Duke, has lately come to hand, inclosed in which was a copy of a Memorandum, relative to the slave-trade in Abyssinia, which had been addressed to Mr. Munzinger, her Britannic Majesty's Vice-Consul in Massowah.

"Dr. Schimpfer had at the time sent the original of this Memorandum direct to the abovementioned British Vice-Consul, in order to give him useful information for the taking of effective measures against the slave-trade, but as Mr. Munzinger, when the letter addressed to him arrived, had already left his post, and so the Memorandum could not come into his possession, the writer of it sent a request to the Grand Duke, graciously to cause a copy of the said paper to be forwarded to her Majesty's Government, so that the British Government, if it thought fit to do so, might make use of the contents of it for the suppression of the slave-trade.

"As the Memorandum contains several remarks which show themselves to be the result of many years of observation, and as especially the minute description of the roads used by the slave-trade might afford ways and means for an effectual suppression of this traffic in human beings, I am instructed by my august Sovereign to forward, according to the wish of Dr. Wilhelm Schimpfer, a copy of the said Memorandum for her Britannic Majesty's Government.

"I have the honour therefore to forward to you the accompanying copy, certified in the Registry of the Department of the private correspondence of the Grand Duke, of the Memorandum by Dr. W. Schimpfer, together with two plans, with the request that you will kindly submit the same, with the proper explanations to her Majesty's Foreign Office; and I take the liberty of adding that the writer of the Memorandum hoped by the communication of the results of his many years of observation of the traffic in human beings in Abyssinia, that is to say, of the slave-markets, the roads taken by the slave caravans, and the shipping and landing places on the coast of the Red Sea, to place her Britannic Majesty's Vice-Consul in Massowah in a position to help the Commanders of the English ships of war, which cruise in the waters washing the East Coast of Africa, in the taking of effective measures for a complete suppression of the Slave-trade, as the accurate knowledge of the landing-places in Arabia, where the cargoes of slaves are received by the purchasers seemed to be of great importance for the capture of the slave-ships.

" Accept, &c.
(Signed) " VON FREYDORF."

Inclosure 3 in No. 8.

Memorandum by Dr. W. Schimpfer relative to the East African Slave-trade.
(Translation.)

" Dedschasmadsch Kassai, as Regent of Tigré, forwards to you a letter addressed to her Majesty the Queen of England, in which he expresses his determination to abolish the slave-trade, and with this view he prays the help of the English officials, and particularly your own. As to the way in which your assistance will probably be required, experience must decide, as many conflicting interests will have to be combated, and particularly dissensions with the Turkish officials, as it is the Turkish Governors on the frontier, who, in spite of the prohibition, secretly support this traffic.

"To begin with, a definite course is necessary, and is at the same time in some measure difficult, because, as you well know, the greater part of the high land of Abyssinia, inhabited by Christians, is surrounded by a kind of desert, scantily peopled by uncivilized races—half Mohammedan, half nomad—which district is in every way favourable to smuggling, there being several hiding-places which are difficult to watch, and it is especially people belonging to these different, almost independent tribes, who occupy themselves with buying and selling of Abyssinian children, as well as stealing them, and who give profitable help to the smugglers who are engaged in the trade of Galla and negro slaves.

"These districts are on the north-western slopes of Wolhait, belonging to Addi Abo, of Schire, and to Kohaim, of Hamasjèn; in the other direction, on the north-eastern slopes of Akullogussay and Agame. The tribes of (or beyond) Wolkaih and Addi Abo, called Schamgallas, are a mixture of old Ethiopian, Arabian, and negro elements. At Hamasjèn the Abyssinian inhabitants on the frontier partially engage in this infamous traffic, as do the Hall-hall and the Bogos, and also branches of the Habab tribe. The inhabitants of the frontier of the highland of Akullogussay, that is Abyssinian mixed with Schoho, willingly encourage the slave-trade. The Schoho and Taltal tribes, who dwell in the mountainous districts near the Red Sea, beyond Akullogussay and Agamé, in the greatest uncivilization, occupy themselves at the present moment with stealing human beings and with secretly forwarding the slaves, which are brought through their barren territory by Mohammedans.

"It appears that from Lasta, or rather, by way of Lasta, Ayeba-Galla and Eudärte, with the help of the frontier inhabitants of Agamé and of Schumat-Sana, and the assistance of the Schoho and Taltal tribes, slaves are brought to the inhabitants of the sea-coast in the district of Adulis, and south-east of that place. The inhabitants of the sea-coast are Dannakils, a small remnant undoubtedly of a tribe of Gallas, strongly mixed with Arabian elements. These people are sailors and fishermen, who carry on a small trade with Confuda, Hodaida, and Mocha, where they deposit a few slaves, a fact I noticed at the time at these three places.

"It is possible that the Turkish Governor of Massowah is not aware of this, but it cannot escape the notice of the Naib (Governor of the mainland). The Turkish Governors, as well as the troops in Massowah, are so often changed, that they cannot attain a correct knowledge of the country. The Naib, however, who is in a measure dependent on these Governors, but who deceives them, is an hereditary appointment, going from father to son, and from family connexion he must be well aware of the trade of the Dannakils and other tribes on the coast.

"Among the Dannakils I found Abyssinian children as slaves, who had openly been brought there by theft, and about whom I gained some information in Addigrat (Agamé) through a convicted thief, whose hands had been cut off by order of Dedsch-Kassai, son of Sohagadis (Feuer Kassai is dead; not, however, the present Regent of Tigré of the same name).

"Slaves are secretly brought to Harkiko (the residence of the Naib on the mainland) from Halai and the neighbourhood; apparently owing to the prohibition they are not brought to Massowah, but secretly from there to the district of Habab, from whence they are taken from one to three at a time, unnoticed, to Hadaida, Lidd, or Gedda, by fishermen from the sea-coast of Arabia. Fishing is carried on by the Arabians more on the African than on the Arabian coast, on account of the coral reefs, as it is amongst those that the fish are mostly to be found. The fish are salted and dried on the spot, and are then sold in the seaport towns of Arabia. The Naib and Governor of Massowah are secret protectors of the slave-trade in Harkiko, and they are also accessories, who derive advantage from this traffic.

"Wora, a not unimportant place between Hamasjèn and the highland of Bogos, is one of the principal scenes of the slave-trade. It has a position well hidden, on the confines of a wooded desert, and is some distance from the Christianized village of Hamasjèn, and inhabited only by Mohammedans who carry on farming and cattle-breeding operations, but trade especially in slaves, has for these purposes allies among the Mohammedans of the inner Christian highlands of Tigré. In Adoa and its neighbourhood, the places chiefly to be counted on are,—the village of Mai Sigamo, in the district of Addi Abum (Memsach), and farther on; the whole district of Mosba (with the sovereignty of which the Naib of Harkiko is temporarily and most curiously invested, a most impolitic proceeding, as the Naib (1845) is actually the servant of Turkey). In the year 1836, the Naib, in consideration of a monthly payment of 1500 thalers (225*l*.), was the Protector of Turkish interests in Massowah, and the Turkish Governor paid an official visit to the Naib, who, till then, had been officially in the service of Abyssinia (Agamé-Tigré).

"Members of the confederation of the towns of

Bellan and Molochseto, in the district of Zewan-Quilla, and not less in the villages of Maibesso and Endarharat in the province of Antitscho, bring single slaves secretly to Wora, particularly children stolen from the Christian population of Tigré, of which fact I was convinced by what I saw in Wora; and also, near this village, I released a child who had been stolen from one of my own people; the thief, whom I knew, was hung by order of Prince Ubye.

" From Wora the slaves are conducted to the country of Habab, on which coast are several harbour-like places which are frequented by Arabian fishermen, who take single slaves to the Arabian Coast in their small barks, from whence they go to Mecca and the neighbourhood.

" The spot on the northern frontier of Habab's country which coral reefs make into a kind of harbour, and where more particularly the shipment of single slaves takes place, is called Mersa Mandele.

" In the Haseri country, north of Nabab's territory, slaves are also shipped in the same way, that is, to Mersa Abid.

" The large bay of Agik is one of the principal places for smuggling, and slaves are embarked there, singly and also in hundreds. On a small island in this bay, bearing the same name is a

Turkish garrison of twelve men, who make great gains by this traffic.

"The mainland is thickly populated, and is called Scheaura.

"The Island of Agik is scantily peopled, and contains about twenty miserable huts; is a place of transport trade in butter, honey, and goats. It is flat, being but little above the level of the sea, and not healthy.

"Farther north, about six hours south-west of Souakin, is Mersa Hadub, a place of exportation of single slaves.

"The Turks have certainly forbidden the traffic in slaves, but, notwithstanding, it is carried on with very little secrecy, only that those people who conduct slaves do not unload their vessels at Gedda where European Consuls reside, but at Lidd, a day's journey only, to the south-east of Gedda.

"North-west of Souakin is the large bay of Mersa Derur. The monument of the Marabut Schech Bergut is on a promontory stretching far out to sea, and owing to the glittering white of the building it acts as a beacon to the fishermen, who see it from a great distance. Some of the elevated coral reefs in this large irregular bay are inhabited, and occasionally favoured with a small Turkish garrison of from five to ten men strong, placed there to prevent smuggling; but these guardians of order, instead of preventing, encourage smuggling, as well as the shipment of slaves, receiving bribes in the most unprincipled manner.

"Skins, honey, butter, and slaves are exported from here to Suez and Gedda. The slaves are disembarked on the African Coast at the entrance of a wide valley opposite El Tor, and are probably taken from there to Cairo. The mainland near Mersa Derur, Marabut Schech Bergut, is thickly peopled by the shepherd tribe of Amaret or Amma Erret, who border on Bischarieh on the north.

"About forty hours (to walk) north-west of Souakin is the useful deep bay Sellak-sereir, another principal place for the export of slaves. I found here, in 1857, about 200 slaves, in two large vessels, who probably had been embarked at the above-mentioned bay of Agik, and who were being taken to Lidd and from there with the secret official help of the Governor of Gedda, some to Gedda itself, but the greater part to Mecca. I found it impossible to ascertain the birth-place of these slaves; although they had black faces their bodies were more of the Galla than of the negro type.

"There is no doubt that the Turkish Governor of Kassala (as well as the Governors of Souakin and Massowah) are well aware of the trade in all these places. All these Governors enrich themselves by the official prohibition of the slave-trade because they secretly encourage it and retain, for themselves, the duty which ought to be levied." (The vessels from the coast seldom go from Souakin direct to Gedda, but generally make for the African coast far north, in order to sail from there over the high seas and benefit by the north wind.)

" The slaves from Lidd do not all go to Mecca, they come from Lidd along a part of Wadi Bahàra to the mud village of Adda, inhabited by freed negro slaves, who look after and lodge them; it is only a few hours from Mecca on the much frequented road which leads from Gedda to this holy city. Owing to the proximity of Mecca it is free from any surveillance of European Consuls, and owing to the extreme religious fanaticism of the Mahometans it is also free from surveillance of any Mahometan officials. But European surveillance is quite possible in Lidd. The caravans of slaves are generally divided in the negro village of Adda, a portion going by way of Wadifatme, one to one and a half hour north of Mecca, and Madora to the town of Saima, inhabited by a thieving rabble. Saima, like Mecca, is in a kettle-like valley, surrounded on all sides by hills, and here a trade of a few slaves is carried on. The remainder of the caravan goes across the sandy valley of Wadi Sehl, and over a lower ridge of the mountain of Karra to Tayf. Another portion of the caravan goes to the east, along the beautiful cistern road of Wadi Soci to a western suburb of Mecca, where it is again divided; part entering the town, and part turning off to the south and south-east beyond the citadel of Mecca, past the southern suburb of Samieh, which is busied with all kinds of trade, and where it remains some time for some unaccountable reason, as no steps seem to be taken to dispose of the slaves. From Samieh the further route of the slaves is to the east, along the broad district of Naaman and past an Abdia Bel el Scherif, where beautiful gardens are sheltered by palm date-trees, and then passing the sacred Gebel Arafat to the beginning of the valley of Naaman, where slaves are often sold. Near Arafat the valley becomes narrower with singular turns and twists, and is then called Wadi Thama, where two hamlets are: one stationary and the other temporary. A fine artificial road leads zig-zag over the high mountain of Karra to a smooth well-formed plateau (gneis), about 8000 (7500) feet above the level of the sea; here there is the large but ill-built village of Hadda, where barley is cultivated, and fruit culture carried on. In spite of there occasionally being snow in the months of December and January, and with the thermometer at +2 to +10 degrees Reaumur, figs, almonds, lemons, apples, pears, plums, apricots, peaches, thrive here. The inhabitants are red Arabians of fine form. But few slaves are brought here for agricultural purposes, for even if the Arab of the country farms, he is still more or less of a nomad, and does not willingly have strangers about him.

"From Hada the route lies in a south-easterly direction, ascending for 2000 feet to the village of Geru, where some slaves are generally sold.

"An hour from Geru is Tayf, where slaves, and also beautiful female slaves from Abyssinia and the Galla countries, are to be met with. Tayf is one of the most beautiful, as well as one of the pleasantest towns of Arabia, and has about 5000 inhabitants, who carry on farming to a large extent, as well as cultivation of the vine. Here, as in Rhenish Bavaria, the vines are kept low. Barley, wheat, durra (that is, sorgheim), are here cultivated in a temperature which, in the course of the year, varies from + 7 to 23 degrees of Reaumur.

"Tayf is perhaps rather more than 4000 feet above the level of the sea, and it is one of the cleanest of all the towns that I saw in the

East; in fact, such cleanliness as is to be found there in the houses and streets, is seldom met with even in Europe. The streets are wide, and very much in straight lines. The private houses of the native citizens have only one story, but are cheerful, light, and most carefully looked after in every way, although the owners are only farmers who keep oxen, sheep, and goats. This town is very striking from the number of watch-towers in the walls which surround its many palatial houses; also many houses with two and three stories built by rich Arabians of the higher classes who reside at Mecca, but who here spend, very agreeably, the hot months, which would be unbearable in Mecca: it is these richer classes who purchase slaves to look after their gardens, and who attract the dealers. This seems to be the last point where Abyssinian slaves, i. e. those who come from Abyssinia, are sold.

"Tayf is about 100 English miles from Gedda. There I found slaves who were stolen, Abyssinian Christians converted to Mohammedanism. In Wadi Thama I found a small nomad race, old Ethiopians, or are they freed Abyssinian slaves of past generations? The root of their dialect is Gees.

"Tayf lies at the beginning, or rather the end of the paradise-like portion of Arabia. Immediately outside the northern gate of the town, begin the vast barren deserts, where there is no water (tertiary limestone and chalk formation), which lie to the south of the district of Wohabi, and where constant and lasting simooms come, transforming the passing traveller into a kind of mummy, and leaving him half-conscious, and in many cases lifeless, and dries up the entire system. Tayf is reckoned to be twelve or fourteen days' journey from the northern end of the desert, i. e. to the beginning of the district of Nedsch. There are but few oases in the midst of this vast barren tract. Immediately beyond the southern gate of the city of Tayf begin the cultivated land, high mountains, and rich grass valleys, resembling in many respects some of the districts of Abyssinia; and from one to one and a half day's journey farther south, are the mountains (10,000 feet high) of Gurnads, the highest peak of which is sometimes covered with snow and hail, the valleys being perpetually green. The powerful tribe of Beni Sephian carries on farming to a large extent. This is the northern frontier of Asiatic Arabians. I did not find any actual slaves there: but in the inner uninhabited valley of Gurnads, half desert, half steppe, I again found some of the same small nomad tribe of Ethiopian extraction, which I had seen in Wadi Thama. The fact of this race being found in many parts of this portion of Arabia, gives rise to the conjecture that, according to the saying, the Ethiopians must at one time have forced themselves into Arabia for a short period. (Here belongs the remark, that the present inhabitants of the highland of Tigré, Lassa, and Wolkaih, and the greater part of Abyssinia, have many elements in common with the Arabians of Hadrament.) I found no one in this small wandering tribe who could give any information as to their origin; and I could not question other better-informed Arabians, for the condition of this country is such, that I deemed it expedient to avoid much intercourse with men; and by choosing unfrequented roads, to be as little seen as possible. The features, colour, and hair of these solitary wandering tribes, and their bodily form and character are identical with the Abyssinians of the present day, near Hamasjèn. Their dialect resembles that spoken in the district of Modat.

"The mountains and vegetation strongly recall that of Abyssinia, particularly the towns and grouping of the trees. The meteorological relations and the elevation of the land are very similar to the high land of Bogos, near Hamásjèn in Abyssinia (the formations there, as in Abyssinia, is chiefly granite, syenite, gneis, clay, dolomite, trachyte, and *larage bilde*.) The shape of the mountains resembles those of Adoa, but there, the transition limestone formation shows itself by petrifactions (gonialites, trilobites, and delthyris), chiefly, however, secondary limestone, which shows itself by ammonites, lithographical stone, and *Terebratula vulgaris* (near Antalo the same terebratula kind is also found, which points to the fact that the period of the formation of Arabia must have been identical with that of Abyssinia). These limestone deposits at the foot of the higher mountains are only found partially and in small quantities in the high land of Arabia-Asin, and they are generally mixed with clay, precisely in the same way as in many districts of Abyssinia. The larger limestone formations, containing clay in larger quantities, has been transformed in many places into dolomite by volcanic power, and by the same process the limestone has become separated from the clay (there have also been gentle volcanic eruptions), and by the change scattered on the surface as kidney-shaped limestone, or also impressed with dammerde, which can be recognized, as it is constantly found in ploughing.

"Excuse me for thus writing about things irrelevant to the slave-trade, the cause of my loquacity is the great need of conversation, which I cannot enjoy here, as there is no one with whom I can converse, and there are times when talking is almost a necessity, at any rate, it can injure no one if I make some remarks on countries which are but little frequented.

"I have brought before you the slave-trade to the Red Sea, and from there to Arabia, without being able to give any exact account as to the number of slaves who pass through this portion of Abyssinia, it must, however, be considerable, for, notwithstanding the export by routes not under inspection, the Customs of Tigré, Eudarte, Wolkeit, and Wogara, as also from Halai to Gondar, and to there from Wolkait and Eudarte, from the year 1836 to 1855, have brought in the yearly receipt of from 8000 to 10,000 thalers (and there is but little doubt that a like sum is lost to the Regent by the fraud of his employés). The above calculations do not include the Customs receipts on ordinary articles of commerce. Some slaves go from Godscham and its neighbourhood by Matemma to the Sennaar, and from there to Egypt. In Khartoom, the sale of slaves is encouraged by some ill-conditioned, avaricious Europeans. And in Matemma there is actually a European to be found who deals in slaves (?). Formerly some slaves went from Schoo and the Adal to the Arabian seaport of Mocca (Mokka).

"I have given two instances above of punishment to slave-traders, the public execution of which takes place in the market-place. It is to be remarked that these punishments are not on account of the slave-trade, but on account of the theft of Christian children, which perhaps would not take place without the presence of a European friendly to the Abyssinians. The Abyssinian chiefs feel the bitter shame which attaches to the slave-trade, but the demon of avarice makes them put up with what is evil.

"The traffic in slaves from the Galla and negro countries has been permitted up to the present time, and was (is ?) allowed because the chiefs willingly saw large sums pour into their treasury. For some years the open trade in slaves has visibly decreased, because guards are placed on the frontier by order of the English Consulate.

"The Emperor Theodore—now no longer, very fortunately—forbade the sale of slaves, but this prohibition was only a feigned one to deceive Europe (England?); he not only countenanced it without any feeling of shame, but constantly levied the tax on passing slaves after the issue of this prohibition, and even went so far as himself to point out to caravans of slaves the best bye-roads. One reason of the diminution of the traffic is, that many purchasers will no longer risk their money on account of the prohibitions of other countries, preferring to use it in other equally profitable ways.

"Owing to the changeableness of the Abyssinian character, the question naturally arises as to whether the written and uttered intention of the Dedschasmadsch Kassai, of abolishing slavery, will be honestly carried out? Although I can answer for it that this chief will unwillingly see a diminution of his revenue, I firmly believe he will willingly forego this pecuniary advantage, as he has come to the conclusion that an alliance with England will be of far greater importance to him than anything he can gain by countenancing this miserable traffic.

"Another question arises as to whether the Dedschasmadsch Kassai can depend on his Government in this matter? Public opinion differs very much on this point. At the present moment all the chiefs subject to the Dedschasmadsch Kassai are persons totally inexperienced in all matters of business; many have the option to act as they like, in consequence of which many districts become barren and desert, with few or no inhabitants. These drawbacks on all sides must be very intimidating. In justice to Kassai, it must be borne in mind that by the singular formation of his Government he was, in a way, obliged to attract people towards him, and to give way to their covetous desire until the time came when he could tighten the reins of Government. He appears now to be really dissatisfied with the savage barbarism of his subjects, and would willingly do everything to promote the welfare of the country. He has privately confided to me his scheme for issuing stringent orders—verily a pleasant expressing of a most praiseworthy idea.

"If, after the issue of such an order, the observance of it is not injudiciously enforced, and if it does not appear too late, the arrogance of his subject chiefs can be suppressed, and all threatening danger from that quarter diminished: much good can then be attained in case he is not attacked by Dedschasmadsch Gobasie, who reigns at present throughout Amhaaraland.

"It is the opinion of the public generally, as well as of many capable chiefs, that he, Kassai, is not a favourite with Gobasie, but I have reason to suppose that Dedschasmadsch Gobasie has so much to do in looking after his over-expanding kingdom that, if he is wise, he would not think of attacking Tigré at once; and General Sir Robert Napier exhorted him, as well as other chiefs, to preserve a peaceful demeanour.

"You will blame me for my many queries, but perhaps you will allow that they are not without reason, as the condition of the country and the discretion of the Regent of Abyssinia, are all most doubtful.

"The expressed opinion of the Dedschasmadsch Kassai, who is at present acting as Regent of Tigris, is so good that it must be respected and honoured, and from the anticipation of his strengthening in good and in the necessary knowledge, we must wish for the security of his position as Regent.

"*Two more Remarks.*—There is a great demand for Galla-Abyssinian slaves in Arabia, and for this reason, the greater part of those stolen from Abyssinia are taken to Mecca and the neighbourhood. I found sixty-three stolen Tigréan boys and girls there in the space of thirty by twelve square miles. These slaves find ample employment in the service of the richer inhabitants of Mecca, Tayf, and the neighbourhood. Negro slaves are to be found in rather large numbers in the service of the middle-classes there, as well as the farmers or yeomen of the rich land-owners. I have never entered the city of Mecca, as I travelled openly as a Christian, but I have bivouacked for several months in Wadi-fatime, the garden of that city, in the partial shade of date-trees (*Pfönix dactilifera*), where all kinds of vegetables are cultivated by means of artificial irrigation. I have also been in Sannich and other towns in the neighbourhood of Mecca.

"No Christian is permitted to set foot in Tayf, it being held as a sacred city and the residence of the second Scherif, and containing the mausoleum of near relations of Mahomed, but I was allowed to live there because my botanizing occupations gave rise to the supposition that I should be useful as a medical man! Those inhabitants of Tayf who do not belong to Mecca, that is to say, the native townspeople of pure Arabian origin, have much less religious fanaticism than the Mohammedan mixture of many nationalities in and near Mecca. Here I had the opportunity of gaining a great deal of accurate information as to the state of affairs as regards slavery, and also learned much from my own observation.

"It is an error to suppose that the actual Arabians keep slaves; they are only to be found in Mecca, Tayf, and the neighbourhood, and also in the seaport towns, where there is a conflux of many different nationalities of Islam. In the interior of Arabia, from north to south, I saw no slaves, not even in the densely-populated district of Nedsch (956,000 inhabitants); in the country of Wohabi, with the exception of

Read (population 50,000), the residence of the Amir, where equally the population is partly mixed with Persian. In this town there are female Circassian slaves, also several white men as slaves, and but few negroes or Nubians. In other towns of Nedsch, single slaves are to be found here and there, but none at all among the Bedouin Arabs, who number 200,000. The former capital, Deraya, was partially destroyed by order of Ibrahim Pasha (adopted son of Mahommed Ali), and now numbers but few inhabitants.

"In Asia, where I travelled by bye-roads and saw no actual towns, the Arabians carry on farming and cattle-breeding, employing their own people; and they do not use any strangers. They have camels, goats, and sheep, also cows —the latter of a very small breed. It is a singular fact that here, as in Tayf, I remarked it was looked upon as a sin to sell cow's milk, so that strangers are supplied with it gratis, but most liberally.

"*Remark No. 2.*—To abolish the slave-trade entirely in Abyssinia will be a great undertaking. The opinion of the Abyssinian Regent is liable to change, and all kind of smuggling is facilitated by the fact of there being so many different tribes on the frontier who live in comparatively independent wildness, and by there being so many secret roads through deserts difficult to be traversed, and there are also tribes of Mohammedans or heathens of a Mohammedan character, who willingly give the slave-trade every assistance.

"Then, on the Red Sea, owing to the coral reefs, there are a number of harbour-like places near the coast, which admit of secret export of slaves, not the less because this contraband and criminal trade enjoys the official countenance of the Turkish Governors. In the matter, the only secret is the official protection, which enriches the Governors.

"In order to put a stop at once to the export of slaves on the African coast, it would be necessary to establish a blockade from Bab-el-Mandeb to Cosseir, but it would be much less difficult to keep a watch over the import of slaves on the Arabian coast in order to stop the sale. If the buyers disappear, the sellers will soon follow. With this view I have entered into all details with reference to the slave-trade in Arabia.

"Attention ought also to be given to diminish the export of slaves on the African coast, and this can be done by united action on the part of the officials, as for instance if you were to give timely information to Dedschasmadsch Kassai of the approach of Abyssinian slave-dealers on the coast. I can then communicate to you the result of your announcement to Kassai, if you also give me notice when you communicate with him.

"*Adoa, August* 25, 1868."

No. 9.

The Earl of Clarendon to Mr. Gordon.

"*Foreign Office, April* 27, 1869.

Sir,—" I have received your despatch of the 15th instant, inclosing a Memorandum on the East African Slave-trade, drawn up by Dr. Schimpfer and communicated to you by desire of the Grand Duke of Baden, to whom it was addressed; and I have to instruct you to convey to his Highness the best thanks of her Majesty's Government for the communication of so interesting a paper.

" I have, &c.
(Signed)   " CLARENDON."

INTERIOR OF AFRICA.

No. 10.

Dr. Livingstone to the Earl of Clarendon.—
(*Received November* 6.)

" *Near Lake Bangweolo, South Central Africa,*
" *July*, 1868.

"My Lord,—When I had the honour of writing

to you in February, 1867, I had the impression that I was then on the watershed between the Zambesi and either the Congo or the Nile. More extended observation has since convinced me of the essential correctness of that impression; and from what I have seen, together with what I have learned from intelligent natives, I think that I may safely assert that the chief sources of the Nile, arise between 10° and 12° south latitude, or nearly in the position assigned to them by Ptolemy, whose river Rhapta is probably the Rovuma. Aware that others have been mistaken, and laying no claim to infallibility, I do not yet speak very positively, particularly of the parts west and north-north-west of Tanganyika, because these have not yet come under my observation; but if your Lordship will read the following short sketch of my discoveries, you will perceive that the springs of the Nile have hitherto been searched for very much too far to the north. They rise some 400 miles south of the most southerly portion of the Victoria Nyanza, and, indeed, south of all the lakes except Bangweolo.

"Leaving the valley of the Loangwa, which enters the Zambesi at Zumbo, we climbed up what seemed to be a great mountain mass, but it turned out to be only the southern edge of an elevated region, which is from 3000 to 6000 feet above the level of the sea. This upland may roughly be said to cover a space south of Lake Tanganyika, of some 350 miles square. It is generally covered with dense or open forest, has an undulating, sometimes hilly, surface; a rich soil; is well watered by numerous rivulets, and, for Africa, is cold. It slopes towards the north and west, but I have found no part of it under 3000 feet of altitude. The country of Usango, situated east of the space indicated, is also an upland, and affords pasturage to the immense herds of cattle of the Basango, a remarkably light-coloured race, very friendly to strangers. Usango forms the eastern side of a great but still elevated valley. The other or western side is formed by what are called the Kone Mountains, beyond the copper mines of Katanga. Still farther west, and beyond the Kone range or plateau, our old acquaintance the Zambesi, under the name Jambaji, is said to rise. The southern end of the great valley inclosed between Usango and the Kone range is between 11° and 12° south. It was rarely possible there to see a star, but accidentally awaking one morning between two and three o'clock, I found one which showed latitude 11° 56′ south, and we were then fairly on the upland. Next day we passed two rivulets running north. As we advanced, brooks evidently perennial became numerous. Some went eastwards to fall into the Loangwa; others went north-west to join the river Chambeze. Misled by a map calling this river in an offhand manner "Zambesi, eastern branch," I took it to be the southern river of that name; but the Chambeze, with all its branches, flows from the eastern side into the centre of the great upland valley mentioned, which is probably the valley of the Nile. It is an interesting river, as helping to form three lakes, and changing its name three times in the 500 or 600 miles of its course. It was first crossed by the Portuguese, who always inquired for ivory and slaves, and heard of nothing else. A person who collected all, even the hearsay geography of the Portuguese, knew so little actually of the country that he put a large river here running 3000 feet uphill, and called it the New Zambesi.

"I crossed the Chambeze in 10° 34' south, and several of its confluents south and north, quite as large as the Isis at Oxford, but running faster, and having hippopotami in them. I mention these animals because in navigating the Zambesi I could always steer the steamer boldly to where they lay, sure of finding not less than eight feet of water. The Chambeze runs into Lake Bangweolo, and on coming out of it assumes the name Luapula. The Luapula flows down north past the town of Cazembe, and twelve miles below it enters Lake Moero. On leaving Moero at its northern end by a rent in the mountains of Rua, it takes the name Lualaba, and passing on north-north-west, forms Ulenge in the country west of Tanganyika. I have seen it only where it leaves Moero, and where it comes out of the crack in the mountains of Rua, but am quite satisfied that even before it receives the river Sofunso from Marungu, and the Soburi from the Baloba country, it is quite sufficient to form Ulenge, whether that is a lake with many islands, as some assert, or a sort of Punjaub—a division into several branches, as is maintained by others. These branches are all gathered up by the Lufira—a large river, which by many confluents drains the western side of the great valley. I have not seen the Lufira, but pointed out west of 11° south, it is there asserted always to require canoes. This is purely native information. Some intelligent men assert that when Lufira takes up the water of Ulenge, it flows north-north-west into Lake Chowambe, which I conjecture to be that discovered by Mr. Baker. Others think that it goes into Lake Tanganyika at Uvira, and still passes northward into Chowambe by a river named Loanda. These are the parts regarding which I suspend my judgment. If I am in error there and live through it, I shall correct myself. My opinion at present is, if the large amount of water I have seen going north does not flow past Tanganyika on the west, it must have an exit from the Lake, and in all likelihood by the Loanda.

"Looking back again to the upland, it is well divided into districts, Lobisa, Lobemba, Ubengu, Itawa, Lopere, Kabuire, Marungu, Lunda or Londa, and Rua; the people are known by the initial 'Ba' instead of the initial 'Lo' or 'U' for country. The Arabs soften 'Ba' into 'Wa' in accordance with their Suaheli dialect; the natives never do. On the northern slope of the upland, and on the 2nd April, 1867, I discovered Lake Liemba; it lies in a hollow with precipitous sides 2000 feet down; it is extremely beautiful, sides, top, and bottom being covered with trees and other vegetation. Elephants, buffaloes, and antelopes feed on the steep slopes, while hippopotami, crocodiles, and fish swarm in the waters. Guns being unknown, the elephants, unless sometimes deceived into a pitfall, have it all their own way. It is as perfect a natural paradise as Xenophon could have desired. On two rocky islands men till the land, rear goats, and catch fish; the villages ashore are embowered in the palm-oil palms of the West Coast of Africa. Four considerable streams flow into Liemba, and a number of brooks (*Scottice*, 'trout-burns'), from twelve to fifteen feet broad, leap down the steep bright red clay schist rocks, and form splendid cascades, that made the dullest of my attendants pause and remark with wonder. I measured one of the streams, the Lofu, fifty miles from its confluence, and found it at a ford 294 feet, say 100 yards broad, thigh and waist deep and flowing fast over hardened sandstone flag in September—the last rain had fallen on the 12th of May. Elsewhere the Lofu requires canoes. The Louzua drives a large body of smooth water into Liemba, bearing on its surface duckweed and grassy islands; this body of water was ten fathoms deep. Another of the four streams is said to be larger than the Lofu, but an over-officious headman prevented my seeing more of it and another, than their mouths. The lake is not large, from eighteen to twenty miles broad, and from thirty-five to forty long; it goes off north-north-west in a river-like prolongation two miles wide, it is said, to Tanganyika; I would have set it down as an arm of that lake, but that its surface is 2800 feet above the level of the sea, while Speke makes that 1844 feet only. I tried to follow the river-like portion, but was prevented by a war which had broken out between the Chief of Itawa and a party of ivory traders from Zanzibar. I then set off to go 150 miles south, then west, till past the disturbed district, and explore the west of Tanganyika, but on going eighty miles I found the Arab party, showed them a letter from the Sultan of Zanzibar, which I owe to the kind offices of his Excellency Sir Bartle Frere, Governor of Bombay, and was at once supplied with provisions, cloth, and beads; they showed the greatest kindness and anxiety for my safety and success. The heads of the party readily perceived that a continuance of hostilities meant shutting up the ivory market, but the peacemaking was a tedious process, requiring three and a half months; I was glad to see the mode of ivory and slave-trading of these men, it formed such a perfect contrast to that of the ruffians from Kilwa, and to the ways of the Portuguese from Tette.

"After peace was made I visited Msama, the chief of Itawa, and having left the Arabs, went on to Lake Moero, which I reached on the 8th September, 1867. In the northern part Moero is from twenty to thirty-three miles broad. Farther south it is at least sixty miles wide, and it is fifty miles long. Ranges of tree-covered mountains flank it on both sides, but at the broad part the western mountains dwindle out of sight. Passing up the eastern side of Moero we came to Cazembe, whose predecessors have been three times visited by Portuguese. His town stands on the north-east bank of the lakelet Mofwe; this is from two to three miles broad and nearly four long. It has several low, reedy islets, and yields plenty of fish—a species of perch. It is not connected with either the Luapula or Moero. I was forty days at Cazembe's, and might then have gone on to Bangweolo, which is larger than either of the other lakes; but the rains had set in, and this lake was reported to be very unhealthy. Not having a grain of any kind of medicine, and, as fever, without treatment, produced very disagreeable symptoms, I thought that it would be unwise to venture where swelled thyroid gland, known among us as Derbyshire-neck, and elephantiasis (scroti) prevail. I then went north for Ujiji, where I have goods, and, I hope, letters; for I have heard nothing from the world for more than two years: but when I got within thirteen days of Tanganyika, I was brought to a standstill by the superabundance of water in the country in front. A native party came through, and described the country as inundated so as often to be thigh and waist deep, with dry sleeping places difficult to find. This flood lasts till May or June. At last I became so tired of inactivity that I doubled back on my course to Cazembe.

"To give an idea of the inundation which, in a small way, enacts the part of the Nile lower down, I had to cross two rivulets which flow into the north end of the Moero; one was thirty, the other forty yards broad, crossed by bridges; one had a quarter, the other, half a mile of flood on each side. Moreover, one, the Luao, had covered a plain abreast of Moero, so that the water on a great part reached from the knees to the upper part of the chest. The plain was of black mud, with grass higher than our heads. We had to follow the path which in places the feet of pasengers had worn into deep ruts. Into these we every now and then plunged and fell, over the ancles in soft mud, while hundreds of bubbles rushed up, and, bursting, emitted a frightful odour. We had four hours of this wading and plunging—the last mile was the worst; and right glad we were to get out of it and bathe in the clear tepid waters and sandy beach of Moero. In going up the bank of the lake, we first of all forded four torrents, thigh deep; then a river 80 yards wide, with 300 yards of flood on its west bank, so deep we had to keep to the canoes till within fifty yards of the higher ground; then four brooks from five to fifteen yards broad. One of them, the Chungu, possesses a somewhat melancholy interest, as that on which poor Dr. Lacerda died. He was the only Portuguese visitor who had any scientific education, and his latitude of Cazembe's town on the Chungu being fifty miles wrong, probably reveals that his mind was clouded with fever when he last observed, and any one who knows what that implies will look on his error with compassion. The Chungu went high on the chest, and one had to walk on tiptoe to avoid swimming. As I crossed all these brooks at both high and low water, I observed the difference to be from fifteen to eighteen inches, and from all the perennial streams the flood is a clear water. The state of the rivers and country made me go in the very lightest marching-order; took nothing but the most necessary instruments, and no paper except a couple of note-books and the Bible. On unexpectedly finding a party going to the coast, I borrowed a piece of paper from an Arab, and the defects unavoidable in the circumstances you will kindly excuse. Only four of my attendants would come here; the others, on various pretences, absconded. The fact is, they are all tired of this everlasting tramping, and so verily am I. Were it not for an inveterate dislike to give in to difficulties, without doing my utmost to overcome them, I would abscond too. I comfort myself by the hope that by making the country and people better known I am doing good; and by imparting a little knowledge occasionally, I may be working in accordance with the plans of an all-embracing Providence which now forms part of the belief of all the more intelligent of our race: my efforts may be appreciated in the good time coming yet.

"I was in the habit of sending my observations to the Cape Observatory, where Sir Thomas Maclean, the Astronomer Royal, and the Assistant Astronomer, Mr. Mann, bestowed a great deal of gratuitous labour on them in addition to the regular duties of the Observatory. They tested their accuracy in a variety of ways, which those only who are versed in the higher mathematics can understand or appreciate. The late Earl of Ellesmere publicly said of a single sheet of these most carefully-tested geographical positions, that they contained more true geography than many large volumes. While the mass of observations which went to the Royal Observatory at the Cape required much time for calculation, I worked out a number in a rough way, leaving out many minute corrections, such as for the height of the thermometer and barometer, the horizontal parallax and semi-diameter of planets, using but one moon's semi-diameter and horizontal parallax for a set of distances, though of several hours' duration; corrections for the differences of proportional logarithms, &c., and with these confessedly imperfect longitudes made and sent home sketch-maps to give

F f

general ideas of the countries explored. They were imperfect, as calculated and made in the confusion of the multitude of matters that crowd on the mind of an explorer, but infinitely better than many of the published maps. Sir Thomas Maclean, for instance, says that short of a trigonometric survey, no river has been laid down so accurately as the Zambesi; and Mr. Mann, after most careful examination of the series of chronometric observations which more than once ran from the sea and Tette up to Lake Nyassa, says that any error in the longitude cannot possibly amount to four minutes. Well, after all my care and risk of health, and even of life, it is not very inspiriting to find 200 miles of lake tacked on to the north-west end of Nyassa—and these 200 miles perched up on the upland region and passed over some 3000 feet higher than the rest of the lakes!

"We shall probably hear that the author of this feat in fancyography claims therefrom to be considered a theoretical discoverer of the sources of the Nile. My imperfect longitudes and sketches led some to desecrate the perfect ones from the Observatory. Thus, Golungo Alto, in Angola, was fixed by seven sets of lunar distances; that is, at least sixty-three distances between the moon and stars, and probably a hundred altitudes of sun or stars all made in risk of, and sometimes actually suffering from, African fever. Six sets showed from one to three minutes on each side of longitude 14 degrees east; but the seventh showed a few minutes to the west. The six were thrown aside, and the seventh adopted, because a Portuguese said to me that he thought that spot might be about midway between Ambaca and the sea. Ambaca, he had never seen; and the folly of the intermeddling is apparent from the change not making the spot perceptibly nearer the imaginary midway, and no one had ever observed them before, nor in our day will observe again. Other freaks, and one specially immoral, were performed, and to my gentle remonstrance I received only a giggle. The desecration my positions have suffered is probably unknown to the Council, but that is all the more reason why I should adhere to my resolution to be the guardian of my own observations till publication. I regret this, because the upsetting of a canoe, or anything happening to me, might lead to the entire loss of the discoveries.

"My borrowed paper is done, or I should have given a summary of the streams which, flowing into Chambeze, Luapula, Lualaba, and the lakes, may be called sources. Thirteen, all larger than the Isis at Oxford, or Avon at Hamilton, run into one line of drainage, five into another, and five into a third receptacle—twenty-three in all. Not having seen the Nile in the north, I forbear any comparison of volume. I trust that my labours, though much longer than I intended, may meet with your Lordship's approbation.

"I have, &c.

(Signed) "DAVID LIVINGSTONE."

"P.S.—Always something new from Africa: a large tribe lives in underground houses in Rua. Some excavations are said to be thirty miles long, and have running rills in them—a whole district can stand a siege in them. The "writings" therein I have been told by some of the people are drawings of animals, and not letters, otherwise I should have gone to see them. People very dark, well made, and outer angle of eyes slanting inwards."

No. 11.

Extract of Letter from Dr. Livingstone to Dr. Kirk.

"*Ujiji, May* 30, 1869.

"As to the work to be done by me it is only to connect the sources which I have discovered from 500 to 700 miles south of Speke and Baker's with the Nile. The volume of water which flows north from latitude 12° south is so large, I suspect I have been working at the sources of the Congo as well as of the Nile.

"I have to go down the eastern line of drainage

to Baker's turning-point; Tanganyika, Uzige, Chowambe (Baker's) are one water, and the head of it is 300 miles south of this. The western and central lines of drainage converge into an unvisited lake, west or south-west of this. The outflow of this, whether to Congo or Nile, I have to ascertain.

"I have, &c.
(Signed) "DAVID LIVINGSTONE."

THE SLAVE-TRADE ON THE EAST COAST OF AFRICA.

The *Times of India* gives a stirring account of the capture of a slave dhow, near Ras-el-Had, in the Gulf of Persia, by the boats of her Majesty's ship "Vulture." When the capture was completed, it was found that the crew and passengers, including the slave-merchants, comprised 36 Arabs, all heavily armed:—"The number of slaves it was impossible at the time to estimate. So crowded on deck, and in the hold below was the dhow, that it seemed, but for the aspect of misery, a very nest of ants. The hold, from which an intolerable stench proceeded, was several inches deep in the foulest bilge-water and refuse. Down below, there were numbers of children and wretched beings in the most loathsome stages of small-pox and scrofula of every description. A more disgusting and degrading spectacle of humanity could hardly be seen, whilst the foulness of the dhow, was such that the sailors could hardly endure it. When the slaves were transferred to the 'Vulture,' the poor wretched creatures were so dreadfully emaciated and weak, that many had to be carried on board, and lifted for every movement. How it was that so many had survived such hardships was a source of wonder to all that belonged to the 'Vulture.' On examination by the surgeon, it was found that there were no less than 35 cases of small-pox in various stages; and from the time of the first taking of the dhow to their landing at Butcher's Island, Bombay, 15 died out of the whole number of 169, and since then there have been more deaths amongst them. But perhaps the most atrocious piece of cruelty of the Arabs was heard afterwards from the slaves themselves—viz. that at the first discovery of small-pox amongst them by the Arabs, all the infected slaves were at once thrown overboard, and this was continued day by day, until, they said, forty had perished in this manner. When they found the disease could not be checked, they simply left them to take their chance, and to die. Many of the children were of the tenderest years, scarcely more than three years old, and most of them bearing marks of the brutality of the Arabs in half-healed scars, and bruises inflicted from the lash and stick."—Quoted from "*Indian Times*," October, 1872.

REPORT.

THE SELECT COMMITTEE appointed to inquire into the whole question of the SLAVE-TRADE on the EAST COAST of AFRICA, into the increased and increasing amount of that Traffic, the Particulars of existing Treaties and Agreements with the Sultan of Zanzibar upon the subject, and the possibility of putting an end entirely to the Traffic in Slaves by Sea;—Have considered the matters to them referred, and have agreed to the following REPORT :—

"THAT the Slave-trade in negroes on the East Coast of Africa is now almost entirely confined to a trade between the dominions of Zanzibar on the one hand, and the coast of Arabia and Persia and the island of Madagascar on the other hand, the principal and by far the largest portion of the traffic being in the former direction. The dominions of Zanzibar extend along the eastern coast of Africa for about 350 miles, and lie between the Equator and ten degrees south latitude, and include the islands of Zanzibar, Pemba, and Momfia, the head-quarter of government being the island of Zanzibar, which lies opposite the centre of the coast-line, and about twenty-five miles from the mainland. The town of Zanzibar is rapidly growing in importance, as is evidenced by the progressive increase of ·imports at the Custom-house there, from 245,981*l.* in 1861-62, to 433,693*l.* in 1867-68, of which trade about one-half is in the hands of British-Indian subjects. It was reported in 1867 by General Rigby to be the chief market of the world for the supply of ivory, gum, and copal, and to have a rapidly increasing trade in hides, oils, seeds, and dyes, while sugar and cotton promise to figure largely amongst its future exports. The country in the interior of that part of Africa, and of which Zanzibar is the outlet, is said, according to the recent accounts of Livingstone and others, to be equal in resources to any part of India, and to be, as a rule, more healthy. Iron abounds in all directions, coal is to be found, and cotton can be grown to any extent.

"The negro slave in general passes through three stages ere he reaches his final destination.

"These are, (1) the land journey from his

home to the coast, (2) a short sea voyage to the island of Zanzibar, where is the open slave-market, and (3) the final sea passage from Zanzibar to Arabia, Persia, or Madagascar.

"From the evidence laid before the Committee it appears that the large majority of the slaves are now brought from the western side of the Lake Nyassa (a distance of nearly 500 miles from the coast) to Kilwa, which is the principal port of shipment for Zanzibar, and is near the southern limit of the Zanzibar dominions.

"Your Committee had before them extracts from despatches of Dr. Livingstone, addressed to the Earl of Clarendon, when her Majesty's Secretary of State for Foreign Affairs, and his testimony as to the methods resorted to by the slave hunters; and the cruelties and horrors of the trade is fully supported by the evidence of witnesses who had travelled in the interior. This evidence is well summed up in the Report of the Committee on the East African Slave Trade, addressed to the Earl of Clarendon, a quotation from which is as follows:—

"'The persons by whom this traffic is carried on are for the most part Arabs, subjects of the Sultan of Zanzibar. These slave dealers start for the interior, well armed, and provided with articles for the barter of slaves, such as beads and cotton cloth. On arriving at the scene of their operations, they incite and sometimes help the natives of one tribe to make war upon another. Their assistance almost invariably secures victory to the side which they support, and the captives become their property, either by right or by purchase, the price in the latter case being only a few yards of cotton cloth. In the course of these operations, thousands are killed, or die subsequently of their wounds or of starvation, villages are burnt, and the women and children carried away as slaves. The complete depopulation of the country between the coast and the present field of the slave dealers' operations attests the fearful character of these raids.

"' Having by these and other means obtained a sufficient number of slaves to allow for the heavy losses on the road, the slave dealers start with them for the coast. The horrors attending this long journey have been fully described by Dr. Livingstone and others. The slaves are marched in gangs, the males with their necks yoked in heavy forked sticks, which at night are fastened to the ground, or lashed together so as to make escape impossible. The women and children are bound with thongs. Any attempt at escape or to untie their bonds, or any wavering or lagging on the journey, has but one punishment—immediate death. The sick are left behind, and the route of a slave caravan can be tracked by the dying and the dead. The Arabs only value these poor creatures at the price which they will fetch in the market, and if they are not likely to pay the cost of their conveyance they are got rid of. The result is, that a large number of the slaves die or are murdered on the journey, and the survivors arrive at their destination in a state of the greatest misery and emaciation.'

"From Kilwa the main body of the slaves are shipped to Zanzibar, but some are carried direct from Kilwa to the northern ports.

"At Zanzibar the slaves are sold either in open market or direct to the dealer, and they are then shipped in Arab dhows for Arabia and Persia; the numbers of each cargo vary from one or two slaves to between three and four hundred.

"The whole slave-trade by sea, whether for the supply of the Sultan's African dominions or the markets in Arabia and Persia, is carried on by Arabs from Muscat and other ports on the Arabian coast. They are not subjects of Zanzibar, but chiefly belong to tribes of roving and predatory habits.

"The sea passage exposes the slave to much

suffering; and, in addition to the danger from overcrowding and insufficient food and water, the loss of life connected with the attempt to escape her Majesty's cruisers is very considerable, it being the practice to use any means to get rid of the slaves in order to escape condemnation, should the dhow be captured. Between Kilwa and Zanzibar a dhow lately lost a third of the slaves; there were ninety thrown overboard, dead or dying, many of them in a terribly emaciated state.

"The ready market found for the slave in Arabia and Persia, and the large profit upon the sale, are quite sufficient inducements for the continuance of the traffic.

"It seems impossible to arrive at an exact conclusion as to the actual number of slaves who leave the African coast in one year, but from the returns laid before the Committee an estimate may be formed. At the port of Kilwa is the Custom-house of the Sultan of Zanzibar, through which pass all slaves that are not smuggled, and there a tax is levied on all that pass the Custom-house.

"The following is a Return of the number of slaves exported through the Custom-house at Kilwa between 1862 and 1867, distinguishing those sent to Zanzibar from those shipped to other places:—

Year.	Zanzibar.	Elsewhere.
1862-63	13,000	5,500
1863-64	14,000	3,500
1864-65	13,821	3,000
1865-66	18,344	4,000
1866-67	17,538	4,500
	76,703	20,500
	20,500	

Total Exports from Kilwa in five years } 97,203

"From a despatch of Dr. Kirk, dated 1st February, 1870, it appears that 14,944 were exported from Kilwa in the year ending 23rd August, 1869. But besides those passed through the Custom-house at Kilwa, numbers are exported from other places on the coast.

"Such is the extent to which the exportation of slaves takes place from the Zanzibar territory on the East Coast of Africa. It has also been shown that there the slave-trade still exists from the Portuguese territory to the island of Madagascar, and that slaves are still imported into Turkish ports in the Red Sea, General Rigby having recently seen fresh importations even in the civilized port of Suez. It must not, however, be thought that those who are taken captive, great as the numbers are, represent in any degree the total number of the sufferers from this iniquitous traffic. Such is the fearful loss of life resulting from this traffic, such the miseries which attend it, that, according to Dr. Livingstone and others, not one in five, in some cases not one in ten, of the victims of the slave hunters ever reach the coast alive.

"The slaves, when liberated from the dhows, have been sent of late years to Aden and Bombay, being maintained there at a heavy cost to the Imperial Exchequer. In time past some have been landed at the Seychelles, a dependency of the Mauritius. The climate in these islands is said to suit them exactly, and the inhabitants to be anxious for emancipated slave labour. Every variety of tropical product grows there in the greatest abundance.

"Measures have at various times been adopted by the Government of this country to control and check the trade, but hitherto with but partial success. To control the trade, treaties have been made with the Sultan of Muscat, with the friendly Arab chiefs on the Arabian coast, and with the Shah of Persia. The treaties with the Sultan of Muscat are acknowledged to be binding upon the Sultan of Zanzibar, who has issued orders accordingly, and they prohibit the export of slaves from Africa, as well as their import from Africa into Asia,

Arabia, the Red Sea, or Persian Gulf, but permit the transport of slaves to and fro between Kilwa, Zanzibar, and any coast port up to Lamoo, which is the northern limit of the Sultan of Zanzibar's dominions.

"The result of the treaties, as far as the Sultan of Zanzibar is concerned, is, that not only are the slave traders enabled to rendezvous in great numbers at Zanzibar, but the dhows, often so laden that the deck is entirely covered with slaves, squatting side by side, and so closely packed that it is impossible for them to move, come up openly from Kilwa, to Zanzibar, and then starting afresh, and provided with proper clearances for Lamoo, are enabled to make the first half of the journey north unmolested by British cruisers.

"The object of the British Government in assenting to these treaty provisions was to avoid interference with the status of domestic slavery in the dominions of the Sultan of Zanzibar, as appears by a Despatch from the Right Honourable Earl Russell, dated 14th March, 1864, in which it is stated 'that her Majesty's Government do not claim the right to interfere in the status of domestic slavery in Zanzibar, nor with the *bonâ fide* transport of slaves from one part of the Sultan's territory to another. So long as this traffic shall not be made a cloak to cover the foreign slave-trade, which his Highness is bound by treaty to prevent, and which her Majesty's Government are also determined to suppress.'

"It appears from the evidence that the transport of slaves between the island and coast dominions of the Sultan of Zanzibar has afforded a cover for the foreign slave-trade, as the traders procure at Zanzibar or Kilwa the requisite port clearances and passes for Lamoo, and thence run northwards, taking their chance of escaping the British cruisers.

"There are no means of ascertaining the exact numbers intended for the foreign market, but different witnesses have estimated the numbers annually needed to maintain the supply of slave labour in the dominion of Zanzibar, at from 1700 to 4000, which would leave at least 16,000 as the number destined for the foreign slave-market. The treaty stipulations and agreements with the Sultans of Muscat and Zanzibar have been carried into effect by various Acts of Parliament and Orders in Council, which contain provision for the establishment of courts of adjudication for the trial of vessels captured as slavers at Zanzibar,

"The carrying out of these measures has been committed to the Political Agent of the Government of India, who also holds the appointment of British Consul at Zanzibar, and, in addition to the ordinary duties of a Political Agent and Consul, is Judge of the Vice Admiralty Court. The expenses of this Establishment are borne by the Indian Government.

"The Government have proposed to enter into a new treaty with the Sultan of Zanzibar to the following effect:—

"'1. To limit the shipment of slaves from the mainland to one point only on the African coast, namely, Darra Salaam, and to prohibit entirely their export from any other places.

"'2. To make Zanzibar the only port for the reception of slaves shipped from Darra Salaam, but with liberty to transport from thence to Pemba and Mombaza only; imports of slaves to any other place, or which have not come through Zanzibar, should be declared illegal, and liable to seizure.

"'3 That the number of slaves exported from Darra Salaam to Zanzibar, and thence to Pemba and Mombaza, shall be strictly limited to the actual requirements of the inhabitants of those places, to be annually settled by mutual consent between the Sultan and the British Agent, such number to be gradually decreased so as to cease altogether within a certain time.

"'4. That every vessel engaged in the transport of slaves shall be liable to capture, unless she is provided with a proper pass from the Sultan, which shall be valid only for one voyage, and with distinctive marks on her hull and sails; a heavy penalty being attached to any piracy of these passes or marks.

"'5. That the public slave-markets at Zanzibar shall be closed.

"'6. That the Sultan shall engage from the date of the treaty to punish severely any of his subjects who may be proved to be concerned, directly or indirectly, in the slave-trade, and especially any attempt to molest or interfere with a liberated slave.

"'7. That the Kutchees, and other natives of Indian states under British protection, shall be forbidden, after a date to be fixed by the Government of India to possess slaves, and that in the meantime they shall be prevented from acquiring any fresh slaves.

"'Lastly, The treaty shall contain a stipulation providing for the eventual entire prohibition of the export of slaves from the mainland.'

"The Government have sent out instructions to press this proposed treaty upon the present Sultan; but pending the inquiry of this Committee nothing more has been done.

"It has been stated to the Committee that for the performance of the additional duties which would devolve upon the Consul, should the proposed treaty be carried into effect, some increase in the present small staff would be required, and it was recommended by witnesses that an officer be appointed at Zanzibar to assist the Consul and Judge of the Vice Admiralty Court in all matters connected with the slave-trade, with the title of Assistant Political Agent and Vice-Consul at Zanzibar, and to act for him in his absence; that a Consular Officer should also be appointed at Darra Salaam, under the superintendence of her Majesty's Consul, to whom he should report upon all matters connected with the slave-trade, the number of slaves exported, and whether the Sultan's engagements with her Majesty's Government are strictly observed. This officer would be required to visit, from time to time, the various points on the coast, and to report whether any irregularities exist, or any illegal exports are carried on; and as it is probable that for some time the slave traders would attempt to continue the exportation of slaves from Kilwa, the distance of which from Zanzibar and Darra Salaam would prevent the British authorities at those places from watching and checking such practices, it might be necessary, at first, to station a consular officer at that port also.

"It was also stated to the Committee that this proposal was concurred in by the Secretary of

State for Foreign Affairs and the Secretary of State for India in Council, who recommended that, as the duties of the agency and consulate at Zanzibar were of a twofold character—one part concerning the Indian, and the other the Imperial Government—that the cost of maintenance should be equally divided between the Imperial and Indian Governments.

"This proposal was negatived by the Lords Commissioners of the Treasury, and it was stated in evidence that, in consequence of this refusal and of the representation of the Indian Government, her Majesty's Secretary of State for India in Council had informed the Secretary of State for Foreign Affairs that the Foreign Office would no longer be privileged to send any instructions to the Zanzibar agent; and the whole matter, therefore, was brought to a dead-lock.

"The principal means used to check the trade have been the employment of some vessels of her Majesty's Navy upon the East Indian station as cruisers to watch the East African Coast during the slaving season, which, depending upon the monsoon, is from April to the end of June, and from September to the beginning of November. It was stated in evidence that during the years 1867, 1868, and 1869, there were captured by the squadron

116 dhows, containing 2645 slaves; while, according to the returns of slaves exported from Zanzibar and Kilwa during those years, dhows carrying 37,000 slaves must have evaded capture, making the captures about 6·6 per cent. only.

"These figures are sufficient to show the insufficiency of the present squadron to check, much less to stop the trade; and the reasons assigned are that the existing treaties and the instructions as to domestic slaves render it impossible to seize a dhow south of Lamoo, and during the south-west monsoon it is very difficult to keep the cruisers sufficiently near the coast to intercept the dhows as they run northward before the wind, while there appears a general concurrence of testimony that the present number of the squadron is insufficient for the work to be performed, and that the efficiency of the squadron would be materially increased by an additional supply of steam launches for the arduous boat service on that coast. The traffic in slaves was, on the 31st of May, 1871, as reported by the Admiral Commanding in Chief on the station to be, 'without doubt, as busy and profitable as ever.'

" In connexion with the failure of the measures hitherto adopted, it was given in evidence that much was owing to the want of recorded information, and the necessarily frequent change of commanders, who, moreover, are not supplied with the official reports of those who have preceded them, as well as to the inefficiency and untrustworthiness of the interpreters employed, who not unfrequently are in league with the traders, and mislead the commanders of the squadron.

"Evidence given before your Committee shows the very great inconvenience and loss resulting to British residents, and a frequent diversion of trade into foreign bottoms from the want of any regular postal communication with Zanzibar; the mails lying sometimes at Seychelles for months together, waiting for a chance vessel. It has been stated to them that a very small subsidy would suffice to start monthly steam communication, either with the Seychelles, distant about 800 miles, in correspondence with French steamers running from Aden, or from the latter port direct.

"Your Committee having heard the evidence, are strongly of opinion that all legitimate means should be used to put an end altogether to the East African slave-trade.

"They believe that any attempt to supply slaves for domestic use in Zanzibar, will always be a pretext and cloak for a foreign trade, while the loss of life and the injury caused to maintain even the limited supply of slaves required for this purpose, must of necessity be so great as to forbid this country continuing to recognize any such traffic in slaves.

"It has been stated by some of the witnesses, that should the Sultan consent to relinquish the slave-trade a revolution would follow, and that a sudden stoppage of the importation of slaves into Zanzibar would seriously affect the industrial position of the island; but on the other hand, a witness of great experience has given it in evidence, that the Zanzibar Arabs are fully aware that the trade will be stopped, and are beginning to understand that more profit can be made by retaining the labourers to cultivate their own country, than by selling them away as slaves, while the abolition of the trade would encourage free labourers from all parts to reside at Zanzibar, so ensuring a larger and better supply of labourers than exists at present.

"It appears from the evidence, that the parties from whom serious opposition may be expected are the northern Arabs, but the presence of an English naval force at Zanzibar would afford sufficient protection.

" Your Committee therefore recommend that it be notified to the Sultan of Zanzibar, that the existing treaty provisions having been systematically evaded, and having been found not only insufficient to protect the negro tribes in the interior of Africa from destruction, but rather to foster and encourage the foreign trade in slaves, her Majesty's Government, unless further securities can be obtained for the entire prohibition of the foreign slave-trade, will feel itself compelled to abrogate the treaty, and to take such further legitimate measures as it may find necessary to put an end to all slave-trade whatever, whether foreign or coasting.

" Further, that should the Sultan be willing to enter into a new treaty, having for its object the entire abolition of the slave-trade, her Majesty's Government would agree to settle at Zanzibar a proportion of adult negroes, who might thereafter be captured by her Majesty's cruisers, provided the Sultan agreed to such measures for their protection and freedom as might be deemed necessary.

" It has been represented to the Committee by some of the witnesses, that as the Sultan derives a considerable part of his revenues from the slave-trade, it would be necessary to make him some compensation for the loss he would sustain by the abolition of the trade.

"It appears, from the evidence, that the Sultan of Zanzibar levies a tax of two dollars upon all slaves shipped from Kilwa for Zanzibar, and four dollars upon those shipped for Lamoo, and a further tax of two dollars upon all slaves shipped from Zanzibar. The witnesses have estimated the proceeds of this tax at various amounts, some putting it as high as 15,000*l.* or 20,000*l.*; others as low as 5000*l.*; but whatever the amount may be, the prospect of compensation has been suggested in the negotiations for a new treaty with the Sultan, already alluded to in this Report.

"It has been suggested that, as an equivalent for the supposed loss to his revenue, the Sultan should be released from the payment of an annual subsidy of 40,000 crowns to the Sultan of Muscat, which was arranged upon the partition of the dominion of the Imaum of Muscat, between his two sons, by the Indian Government as arbitrators; but it now appears that the circumstances under which it was supposed this release might be effected have altered.

"It has been given in evidence that from 1700 to about 4000 slaves is probably sufficient to supply the requirements of the island and dominions of Zanzibar, and this, therefore, is the extent of the legalized trade, and the value to the Sultan of Zanzibar at the present rate of tax would not exceed 4000*l.* annually.

"Your Committee, however, do not believe that the Sultan of Zanzibar would be ultimately a loser by the abolition of the trade; on the contrary, it was given in evidence that already the revenues of the Sultan, derived from the rapidly increasing trade of Zanzibar, and from his private estates in India are ample to maintain the government of his state, independently of the sum received from the slave-trade; while the witnesses generally concur in stating that were the slave-trade abolished, and a more ready means of communication afforded between Bombay, Aden, and Zanzibar, the already flourishing trade of that state would be rapidly developed. Material assistance to this development might be afforded by a line of mail steamers to Zanzibar. Should the Sultan be willing to enter into a new treaty, the Committee recommend that it contain provisions for the entire abandonment of the slave-trade, the closing of the Zanzibar and Kilwa slave-markets, the punishment of any of the subjects of Zanzibar in any way engaged in the slave-trade, permission to the British Government to station Vice-Consuls at Kilwa, Darra Salaam, and Lamoo; and on the part of the British Government an agreement to settle, under full and stringent measures for their protection, a certain number of negroes released from slavery by her Majesty's cruisers.

"The Committee concur in the opinion expressed by the witnesses as to the necessity of an increase in the consular establishment; and, inasmuch as the staff of that establishment would be largely employed in the suppression of the slave-trade, they think that the expense should be equally shared by the Indian and Imperial Government.

"The Committee are of opinion that there should be for a time an increase, as recommended in the Report of the Committee on the Slave-Trade, addressed to the Earl of Clarendon, as well as by the evidence of the naval officers, in the strength of the naval squadron; and that it should be well supplied with steam launches to perform the in-shore duties, which necessarily must be conducted in boats.

"The Committee feel that the disposal of the squadron must be left to the discretion of the commanding officers, and they would recommend that advantage should be taken of their experience as to the class of vessels to be employed; and that they should be provided, as far as possible, with all recorded information on the subject.

"The Committee also recommend that some effort be made to provide the squadron with efficient and trustworthy interpreters.

"It has been stated in evidence, that some time must elapse after the measures above referred to have been put in force before the slave-trade could be stopped; and assuming that an efficient squadron is maintained, the Committee see that the disposal of the liberated slaves becomes a matter of large importance. They have recommended the liberation at Zanzibar of adult slaves on the assumption that the Sultan would enter into a new treaty: should he, however, oppose the formation of a depôt there, it will be necessary to seek some other locality for that purpose, and no other place combines the advantages possessed by the Seychelles Islands.

"It was given in evidence that the Church Missionary Society are willing to enter into an arrangement for the superintendence and education of the children at the Seychelles, similar to that entered into with the Government with respect to liberated children at Sierra Leone, the Mauritius, and at Nassuck in Bombay.

"In urging the necessity of retaining in this service trained and experienced men, the Committee consider that this principle most strongly applies to the Political Agency at Zanzibar. So complicated are our political relations at present with the Sultan, and so difficult will be the task of dealing with him, that they do not hesitate to advise that the services should be retained of the present acting Political Agent;[1]

[1] Dr. Kirk.

bearing in mind his long and tried experience of Africa, its climate, its slave-trade difficulties, his knowledge of the Sultan, and his activity in conducting the greater part of the work of the department for some years, they would recommend that no technical rules of the service be allowed to interfere with his appointment as Political Agent at Zanzibar.

"In view of the considerable commercial interests which Germany, France, America, and Portugal possess in commerce with Zanzibar and the surroundings, your Committee suggest that her Majesty's Government invite the co-operation of these several Governments in the suppression of a traffic so subversive of these interests. There is reason to believe that such an overture would be responded to, especially by the Government at Berlin, in virtue of the preponderance of German trade at the port of Zanzibar.

"It would be also desirable to enter into negotiations with the Government of Persia, to secure, if possible, for her Majesty's officers greater facilities of search in vessels suspected of carrying slaves."

August 4, 1871.

THE END.

LONDON:
GILBERT AND RIVINGTON, PRINTERS,
ST. JOHN'S SQUARE.

Crown Buildings, 188, *Fleet Street,*
London, October, 1871.

A List of Books

PUBLISHING BY

SAMPSON LOW, MARSTON, LOW, & SEARLE.

NEW ILLUSTRATED AND OTHER WORKS FOR

THE SEASON 1871-2.

In super royal quarto, handsomely bound, 25s.

FAIRY TALES.

By HANS CHRISTIAN ANDERSEN. Illustrated by TWELVE LARGE DESIGNS IN COLOUR,

AFTER ORIGINAL DRAWINGS BY E. V. B.

The Text newly translated by H. L. D. WARD and AUGUSTA PLESNER. The following are the Tales selected, and the subjects chosen for illustration:—

The Ugly Duckling.
　The Old Woman, with Cuckoo Shortlegs and the Cat, who wouldn't associate with the Ugly Duckling.

The Wild Swans.
　The Dumb Maiden attired gorgeously and shown to the People.
　The King riding off with the Dumb Maiden.
　The Dumb Maiden's funeral pyre.

The Fellow Traveller.
　The Old King pointing out to the Student the Wicked Princess's Garden.
　The Wicked Princess in her Garden.

The Snow Queen.
　The Witch in the Cherry Garden drawing in Gerda's boat with her crutch.
　The Old Witch combing Gerda's hair with a golden comb to cause her to forget her friend.

The Little Mermaid.
　Children playing in the water and alarmed by one of the Mermaids approaching the shore.

Thumbkinetta.
　Thumbkinetta very desolate on the water lily-leaf.
　Thumbkinetta borne on the swallow's back to the south, where she sees the Fairy-flower Prince.

The Angel.
　The Child after death in the Angel's arms pities the poor Rose-tree with its buds and flowers crushed down and broken.

The Garden of Paradise

Price complete, with Texts Imp. folio, £3 10s.

CARL WERNER'S NILE SKETCHES.

Painted from Nature during his travels through Egypt. The first of a series of Water-colour Drawings in perfect fac-simile of the originals, mounted on strong English cardboard, large folio, 23 inches by 17½ inches, with Preface and descriptive Text by Dr. A. E. BREHM and Dr. DUMICHEN. The subjects comprise—

PYRAMIDS OF GIZEH AT SUNRISE.	TOMB OF SHEIK ABABDE.
MEMNON IN MOONLIGHT.	NUBIAN CHILD.
TEMPLE OF ISIS.	BARBER'S SHOP IN ACHMIM.

*** The Pictures are equally suitable for portfolio or for wall adornment.

Royal 8vo. cloth extra, 10s. 6d.

ILLUSTRATIONS TO GOETHE'S FAUST.

By PAUL KONEWKA, Author of Illustrations to Shakespeare's "Midsummer Night's Dream," "Falstaff and his Companions," &c. The English Text from Bayard Taylor's Translation.

The Illustrations are very finely finished *Silhouettes*.

Imperial 4to., cloth extra, 63s.

SAINT GEORGE'S CHAPEL, WINDSOR.

Eighteen Views printed in permanent pigments by the Woodbury process, with descriptive letterpress by JOHN HARRINGTON, author of "The Abbey and Palace of Westminster," dedicated by special permission to the Hon. and Very Rev. the Dean of Windsor. The following are the views selected:—

1. The South Front.
2. The West Front.
3. The Nave, looking east.
4. The Nave, looking south-west.
5. The Choir, east.
6. The Choir, west.
7. The Reredos below the great east window.
8. The Royal Closet.
9. Cross View from South Transept.
10. The Rutland Chapel.
11. The Bray Chapel.
12. The Beaufort Chapel.
13. Oliver King's Chapel.
14. The Monument of the Duchess of Gloucester.
15. The Cenotaph of H.R.H. the Princess Charlotte.
16. The Oxenbridge Chapel.
17. Oak Panel Paintings.
18. The Aldworth Chapel.

Super royal 4to., cloth extra, 25s.

GEMS OF DUTCH ART.

Twelve Photographs from the finest Engravings in the British Museum, by Stephen Thompson, with descriptive letterpress by G. W. REID, Keeper of the Prints, British Museum. The following are the subjects—

The Drinker. By Frans Van Mieris.	The Bunch of Grapes. By Gabriel Metzu.
The Cottage Door. By Isaac Van Ostade.	The Village Ale House. By Adrian Van Ostade.
The Smoker. By Adrian Van Ostade.	The Jocund Peasants. By Cornelis Dusart.
The Dutch Ale House. By Adrian Van Ostade.	The Happy Cottagers. By Cornelis Dusart.
The Spinner. By Gaspar Netscher.	A Country Gathering. By Isaac Van Ostade.
The Trumpeter. By Gerard Terburg.	
A Conversation. By Jan Steen.	

GIRLS' BOOKS. A Series Written, Edited, or Translated by the Author of "John Halifax, Gentleman."

Small Post 8vo. Cloth Extra, Gilt Edges. Price of each Volume, 4s.

1. LITTLE SUNSHINE'S HOLIDAY:

A Picture from Life. By the author of "John Halifax, Gentleman." (Forming Vol. I. of the "'John Halifax' Series of Girls' Books."
"This is a pretty narrative of baby life, describing the simple doings sayings of a very charming and rather precocious child nearly three years —*Pall Mall Gazette.*
"Will be delightful to those who have nurseries peopled by 'Little Sunshines' of their own."—*Athenæum.*

2. THE COUSIN FROM INDIA.

By GEORGIANA M. CRAIK.

"The tale is a clever and interesting one."—*Athenæum.*
"The authoress is equally skilful in the humourous and in the pathetic. . . . Few very few, one may hope, could read with dry eyes of Little David's accident, and quite as few could listen without laughing, to Effie's attempt at a funny tale."—*Guardian.*

3. TWENTY YEARS AGO.

From the Journal of a Girl in her Teens. Edited by the author of "John Halifax, Gentleman." With Illustrations by Sydney Hall.

** Other volumes are in preparation.

The ADVENTURES of a YOUNG NATURALIST.

By LUCIEN BIART. With 117 beautiful Illustrations on Wood. Edited and Adapted by PARKER GILLMORE, Author of "All Round the World," &c. Post 8vo. cloth extra, gilt edges, new edition, price 7s. 6d.
"We can strongly recommend this most attractive boy's book."—*Graphic.*
"The adventures are charmingly narrated, and information is given about all the trees, plants, and native productions that are met with."—*Athenæum.*

BLACKMORE (R. D.) CRADOCK NOWELL.

New Edition, small post 8vo. cloth; uniform with the 6s. Edition of Lorna Doone," by the same Author. [*In the press.*

Also Uniform.

BLACKMORE (R. D.) CLARA VAUGHAN.

[*In the press.*

FRISWELL, J. H. A NEW VOLUME OF ESSAYS.
Uniform with the "Gentle Life."

Small Post 8vo., cloth extra, gilt edges, 3s. 6d.
HEALY (MARY). THE HOME THEATRE.

Numerous Illustrations, small post 8vo., cloth extra, 3s. 6d.
TROWBRIDGE (J. T.) JACK HAZARD AND HIS FORTUNES.
A Story of Adventure.

2 Volumes, Crown 8vo., 21s.
KAVANAGH (MORGAN). THE ORIGIN OF LANGUAGE AND OF MYTHS.

Small Post 8vo., cloth extra, 3s. 6d.
KINGSTON (W. H. G.) BEN BURTON,
Or, Born and Bred at Sea. With Illustrations by SYDNEY HALL.

8vo., cloth.
KENNAN (G.) JOURNEY ACROSS THE CAUCASIAN MOUNTAINS.

Small Post, 8vo., cloth extra, 7s. 6d.
MACKAY (Dr.). UNDER THE BLUE SKY.
Open air Studies of Men and Nature. By CHARLES MACKAY, author of "Studies from the Antique," "Voices of the Crowd," &c.

2 Volumes, Crown 8vo., 15s.
MERCIER (Rev. L.) OUTLINES OF THE LIFE OF THE LORD JESUS CHRIST.

Square 8vo., cloth extra.
MOTHER GOOSE'S MELODIES FOR CHILDREN;
Or, Songs for the Nursery. With Notes, Music, and an Account of the Goose or Vergoose Family, and with Illustrations by HENRY L. STEPHENS and GASTON FAY.

List of Publications.

In one Vol., medium 8vo., half mor. gilt top, 100,000 Names, occupying 1032 pp., 31s. 6d.

PHILLIPS (L. B.) THE DICTIONARY OF BIOGRAPHICAL REFERENCE.

The value and importance of this Dictionary will be best perceived when it is stated that it contains one hundred thousand names, a number which exceeds by many thousands those contained in the most voluminous existing works upon the subject, and upwards of a quarter of a million of references. The chief letters run as follows:—In B, 12,600 names; C, 9,397; G, 5,640; L, 5,481; M, 6,816; S, 7,800.

Thus work also contains as an addendum, a Classed Index of the principal works on biography, published in Europe and America to the present day, arranged under three divisions, viz:—General, or those which contain the accounts of individuals of all nations; National, or those which relate to the celebrities of particular countries; and Class, which treat only of the members of respective bodies or professions, &c.

⁎⁎ Prospectuses, containing sixteen pages of Preface, Explanatory Matter, and Specimen Pages, may be had on application.

Square, cloth, Illustrated, 2s. 6d.

PREW (M. T.) GERMAN PRIMER.

Being an Introduction to First Steps in German.

Small Post 8vo., cloth,

RICHARDSON (ABBY SAGE). STORIES FROM OLD ENGLISH POETRY

Fcap. 8vo. cloth, 5s.

STEELE (THOS.) UNDER THE PALMS.

A volume of Verse. By THOMAS STEELE, Ceylon Civil Service, Translator of "An Eastern Love Story," &c.

Flexible cloth, extra gilt, 2s. 6d.

ROCHEFOUCAULD'S REFLECTIONS:

Or Moral Sentences and Maxims. (New volume of the Bayard Series.)

VIARDOT. THE WONDERS OF SCULPTURE.

Uniform with "The Wonders of Italian Art," &c. Numerous Illustrations, square 8vo. cloth extra, gilt edges, 12s. 6d.

Volume I., 4to, cloth extra, gilt edges, 31s. 6d.

ART, PICTORIAL AND INDUSTRIAL.

An Illustrated Magazine.

This Volume contains a very large amount of matter on Art subjects by the best writers of the day, and in addition thereto upwards of 50 full-page Heliotype Pictures, thus forming a most beautiful Volume for presentation.

Handsomely bound in cloth extra, 21s.
FAVOURITE ENGLISH POEMS AND POETS.
An Entirely New and Extended Edition. With 320 Engravings on Wood, produced in the very best style of woodcut printing.

"It contains upwards of 200 examples of our sweetest singers, illustrated by above 300 engravings. Eye and sentiment are satisfied with this noble gathering of the poets of our land."—*Athenæum.* "What we most like in the Editor is that, with scarcely an exception, he selects whole poems. Extracts and beauties are often as unfair to the writer as they are misleading to the reader."—*Saturday Review.* "When we say that the list of artists includes the names of Messrs. Harrison Weir, Birket Foster, J. C. Horsley, Charles Keene, Percival Skelton, John Gilbert, Gustave Doré, and E. Duncan, and that each of these appears to have done his very best, and to have worked in harmony, we have said enough to recommend the re-issue of this volume far and wide. The poems are taken mostly from writers of the last three centuries, and the illustrations amount to upwards of 300."—*Times.*

In one volume, small 4to., choicely printed on paper specially made, with Title Vignette by Sir Noel Paton, R.S.A., Engraved on Steel by C. H. Jeens, bound cloth extra, 10s. 6d.

THE GENTLE LIFE.
Essays in Aid of the Formation of Character. By HAIN FRISWELL. The *Queen Edition*, revised and selected from the Two Series. Dedicated by express permission and desire, to Her Most Gracious Majesty the Queen.

New and cheaper edition, 5s.
CHRIST IN SONG.
Hymns of Immanuel, selected from all Ages, with Notes. By PHILIP SCHAFF, D.D. Crown 8vo., toned paper, beautifully printed at the Chiswick Press. With Initial Letters and Ornaments, and handsomely bound.

"If works of a religious character are ever seasonable as gift-books, that time certainly is Christmas. Foremost among them we have 'Christ in Song' by Dr. Philip Schaff, a complete and carefully selected 'Lyra Christologica,' embracing the choicest hymns on the person and work of our Lord from all ages, denominations, and tongues."—*Times.*

Now Publishing, in 24 Two Shilling Monthly Parts,
GUIZOT (M.) THE HISTORY OF FRANCE,
From the Earliest Times to the year 1789. Related for the Rising Generation by M. GUIZOT, Author of "The History of the Civilization of Europe," &c. Translated from the French by ROBERT BLACK, M.A. With 100 full-page Engravings, and numerous smaller ones.

Morocco, £5 5s.
THE ABBEY AND PALACE OF WESTMINSTER.
Forty Views with Letterpress Description, dedicated by permission to the Very Rev. DEAN STANLEY. Photographed by JOHN HARRINGTON.

ALPHABETICAL LIST.

ABBOTT (J. S. C.) History of Frederick the Great, with numerous Illustrations. 8vo. 1*l*. 1*s*.

About in the World, by the author of "The Gentle Life." Crown 8vo. bevelled cloth, 4th edition. 6*s*.

Adamson (Rev. T. H.) The Gospel according to St. Matthew, expounded. 8vo. 12*s*.

Adventures of a Young Naturalist. By LUCIEN BIART, with 117 beautiful Illustrations on Wood. Edited and adapted by PARKER GILLMORE, author of "All Round the World," "Gun, Rod, and Saddle," &c. Post 8vo. cloth extra, gilt edges, new edition, 7*s*. 6*d*.

Adventures on the Great Hunting Grounds of the World, translated from the French of Victor Meunier, with engravings, 2nd edition. 5*s*.

> "The book for all boys in whom the love of travel and adventure is strong. They will find here plenty to amuse them and much to instruct them besides."—*Times*.

Alcott (Miss) Old Fashioned Girl, best edition, small post 8vo. cloth extra, gilt edges, 3*s*. 6*d*.; Low's Copyright Series, 1*s*. 6*d*.; cloth, 2*s*.

―――― Camp and Fireside Stories. Fcap. 3*s*. 6*d*.

―――― Little Women. Complete in 1 vol. fcap. 3*s*. 6*d*.

―――― Little Men: Life at Plumfield with Jo's Boys. By the author of "Little Women." Small post 8vo. cloth, gilt edges, 3*s*. 6*d*.

> The *Guardian* says of "Little Women," that it is—"A bright, cheerful, healthy story—with a tinge of thoughtful gravity about it which reminds one of John Bunyan. The *Athenæum* says of "Old-Fashioned Girl"—"Let whoever wishes to read a bright, spirited, wholesome story, get the 'Old Fashioned Girl' at once."

Among the Arabs, a Narrative of Adventures in Algeria, by G. NAPHEGYI, M. D., A. M. 7*s*. 6*d*.

Andersen (Hans Christian) The Story of My Life. 8vo. 10*s*. 6*d*.

―――― Fairy Tales, with Illustrations in Colours by E. V. B. Royal 4to. cloth. 1*l*. 5*s*.

Andrews (Dr.) Latin-English Lexicon. 13th edition. Royal 8vo. pp. 1,670, cloth extra. Price 18*s*.

> The superiority of this justly-famed Lexicon is retained over all others by the fulness of its Quotations, the including in the Vocabulary Proper Names, the distinguishing whether the Derivative is classical or otherwise, the exactness of the References to the Original Authors, and by the price.
>
> "The best Latin Dictionary, whether for the scholar or advanced student."—*Spectator*.
>
> "Every page bears the impress of industry and care."—*Athenæum*.

Anecdotes of the Queen and Royal Family, collected and edited by J. G. HODGINS, with Illustrations. New edition, revised by JOHN TIMBS. 5*s*.

Angell (J. K.) A Treatise on the Law of Highways. 8vo. 1*l*. 5*s*.

Art, Pictorial and Industrial, Vol. I. 1*l*. 11*s*. 6*d*.

Audubon. A Memoir of John James Audubon, the Naturalist, edited by ROBERT BUCHANAN, with portrait. 2nd edition. 8vo. 15*s*.

Australian Tales, by the "Old Boomerang." Post 8vo. 5*s*.

ALDWIN (J. D.) Prehistoric Nations. 12mo. 4*s*. 6*d*.

Bancroft's History of America. Library edition, 8 vols. 8vo. 4*l*. 16*s*.

——— History of America, Vol. IX. 8vo. 12*s*.

Barber (E. C.) The Crack Shot. Post 8vo. 8*s*. 6*d*.

Barnes's (Rev. A.) Lectures on the Evidences of Christianity in the 19th Century. 12mo. 7*s*. 6*d*.

Barnum (P. T.) Struggles and Triumphs. Crown 8vo. Fancy boards. 2*s*. 6*d*.

THE BAYARD SERIES. Comprising Pleasure Books of Literature produced in the Choicest Style as Companionable Volumes at Home and Abroad.

Price 2s. 6d. each Volume, complete in itself, printed at the Chiswick Press, bound by Burn, flexible cloth extra, gilt leaves, with silk Headbands and Registers.

The Story of the Chevalier Bayard. By M. DE BERVILLE.

De Joinville's St. Louis, King of France.

The Essays of Abraham Cowley, including all his Prose Works.

Abdallah; or, the Four Leaves. By EDOUARD LABOULLAYE.

Table-Talk and Opinions of Napoleon Buonaparte.

Vathek: An Oriental Romance. By WILLIAM BECKFORD.

The King and the Commons: a Selection of Cavalier and Puritan Song   Edited by Prof MORLEY

Words of Wellington: Maxims and Opinions of the Great Duke

Dr. Johnson's Rasselas, Prince of Abyssinia. With Notes.

Hazlitt's Round Table. With Biographical Introduction.

The Religio Medici, Hydriotaphia, and the Letter to a Friend   By Sir THOMAS BROWNE, Knt

Ballad Poetry of the Affections. By ROBERT BUCHANAN.

Coleridge's Christabel, and other Imaginative Poems   With Preface by ALGERNON C SWINBURNE

Lord Chesterfield's Letters, Sentences and Maxims. With Introduction by the Editor, and Essay on Chesterfield by M De St Beuve, of the French Academy

Essays in Mosaic. By THOS BALLANTYNE.

My Uncle Toby, his Story and his Friends   Edited by P FITZGERALD

Reflections; or, Moral Sentences and Maxims of the Duke de la Rochefoucauld

A suitable Case containing 12 volumes, price 31s 6d ; or the Case separate, price 3s 6d

EXTRACTS FROM LITERARY NOTICES

"The present series—taking its name from the opening volume, which contained a translation of the Knight without Fear and without Reproach—will really, we think, fill a void in the shelves of all except the most complete English libraries   These little square-shaped volumes contain, in a very manageable and pretty form, a great many things not very easy of access elsewhere, and some things for the first time brought together"—*Pall Mall Gazette*   " We have here two more volumes of the series appropriately called the 'Bayard,' as they certainly are 'sans reproche' Of convenient size, with clear typography and tasteful binding, we know no other little volumes which make such good gift-books for persons of mature age "—*Examiner*   "St Louis and his companions, as described by Joinville, not only in their glistening armour, but in their every-day attire, are brought nearer to us, become intelligible to us, and teach us lessons of humanity which we can learn from men only, and not from saints and heroes   Here lies the real value of real history   It widens our minds and our hearts, and gives us that true knowledge of the world and of human nature in all its phases which but few can gain in the short span of their own life, and in the narrow sphere of their friends and enemies We can hardly imagine a better book for boys to read or for men to ponder over "—*Times*

Beecher (Henry Ward, D. D.) Life Thoughts.   Complete in 1vol   12mo   2s 6d

Beecher (Henry Ward, D.D.) Sermons Selected. 12mo. 8s. 6d.

—— Norwood, or Village Life in New England. Crown 8vo. 6s.

—— (Dr. Lyman) Life and Correspondence of. 2 vols. post 8vo. 1l. 1s.

Bees and Beekeeping. By the Times' Beemaster. Illustrated. Crown 8vo. New Edition, with additions. 2s. 6d.

Bell (Rev. C. D.) Faith in Earnest. 18mo. 1s. 6d.

—— Blanche Nevile. Fcap. 8vo. 6s.

Bellows (A. J.) The Philosophy of Eating. Post 8vo. 7s. 6d.

—— How not to be Sick, a Sequel to Philosophy of Eating. Post 8vo. 7s. 6d.

Biart (L.) Adventures of a Young Naturalist. (See *Adventures*.)

Bickersteth's Hymnal Companion to Book of Common Prayer.

The following Editions are now ready:—

		s.	d.
No. 1. A Small-type Edition, medium 32mo. cloth limp		0	6
No. 1. B ditto roan limp, red edges	..	1	0
No. 1. C ditto morocco limp, gilt edges	..	2	0
No. 2. Second-size type, super-royal 32mo. cloth limp	..	1	0
No. 2. A ditto roan limp, red edges	..	2	0
No. 2. B ditto morocco limp, gilt edges	..	3	0
No. 3. Large-type Edition, crown 8vo. cloth, red edges	..	2	6
No. 3. A ditto roan limp, red edges	..	3	6
No. 3. B ditto morocco limp, gilt edges	..	5	6
No. 4. Large-type Edition, crown 8vo. with Introduction and Notes, cloth, red edges	..	3	6
No. 4. A ditto roan limp, red edges	..	4	6
No. 4. B ditto morocco, gilt edges	..	6	6
No. 5. Crown 8vo. with accompanying Tunes to every Hymn, New Edition	..	3	0
No. 5. A ditto with Chants	..	4	0
No. 5. B The Chants separately	..	1	6

No. 6. Penny Edition.

⁂ A liberal allowance is made to Clergymen introducing the Hymnal.

☞ THE BOOK OF COMMON PRAYER, bound with THE HYMNAL COMPANION. 32mo. cloth, 9d. And in various superior bindings.

Bigelow (John) France and Hereditary Monarchy 8vo. 3s

Bishop (J L.) History of American Manufacture. 3 vols. 8vo 2l 5s

—— (J. P.) First Book of the Law. 8vo. 1l. 1s.

Blackburn (H) Art in the Mountains : the Story of the Passion Play, with upwards of Fifty Illustrations 8vo 12s

—— Artists and Arabs. With numerous Illustrations. 8vo. 7s 6d.

—— Normandy Picturesque. Numerous Illustrations. 8vo 16s

—— Travelling in Spain. With numerous Illustrations. 8vo 16s

—— Travelling in Spain. Guide Book Edition 12mo. 2s 6d

—— The Pyrenees. Summer Life at French Watering-Places 100 Illustrations by GUSTAVE DORE. Royal 8vo 18s.

Blackmore (R. D.) Lorna Doone. New edition. Crown, 8vo 6s
"The reader at times holds his breath, so graphically yet so simply does John Ridd tell his tale 'Lorna Doone' is a work of real excellence, and as such we heartily commend it to the public "—*Saturday Review*

—— Cradock Nowell. 2nd and cheaper edition. 6s
[*In the press*

—— Clara Vaughan. [*In the press.*

—— Georgics of Virgil. Small 4to. 4s. 6d

Blackwell (E.) Laws of Life. New edition. Fcp. 3s. 6d.

Boardman's Higher Christian Life. Fcp 1s. 6d.

Bonwick (J.) Last of the Tasmanians. 8vo. 16s

—— Daily Life of the Tasmanians. 8vo. 12s 6d.

—— Curious Facts of Old Colonial Days. 12mo. cloth. 5s

Book of Common Prayer with the Hymnal Companion. 32mo. cloth 8d , bound 1s And in various bindings

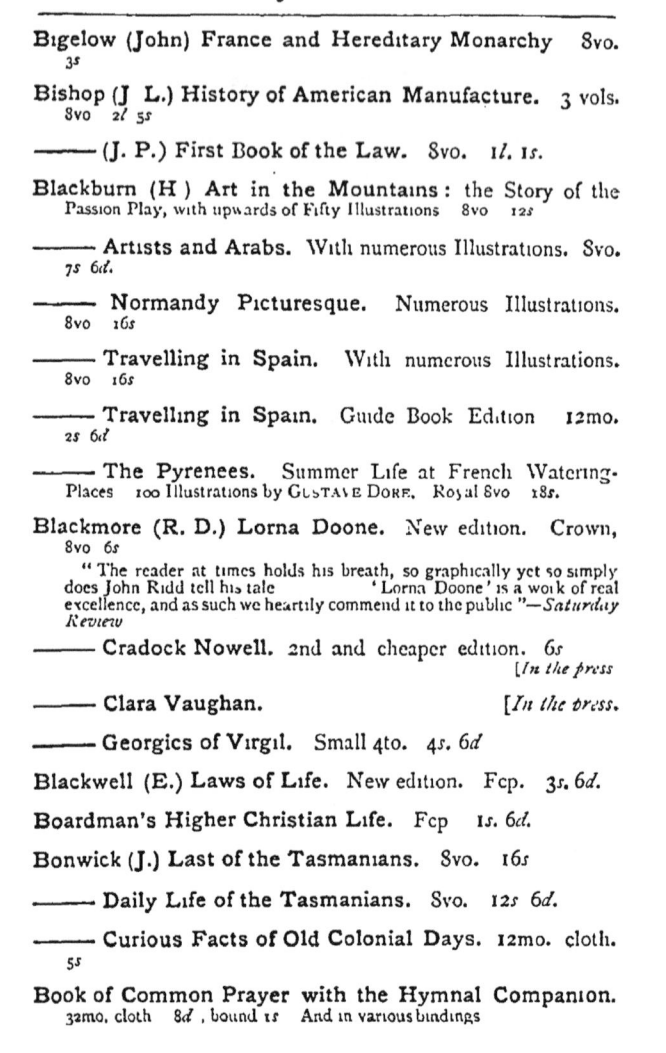

Books suitable for School Prizes and Presents. (Fuller description of each book will be found in the alphabet.)

Adventures of a Young Naturalist. 7s. 6d.
—— on Great Hunting Grounds. 5s.
Allcott's Old Fashioned Girl. 3s. 6d.
—— Little Women. 3s. 6d.
—— Little Men. 3s. 6d.
Anecdotes of the Queen. 5s.
Bayard Series (See Bayard.)
Blackmore's Lorna Doone. 6s.
Changed Cross (The). 2s. 6d.
Child's Play. 7s. 6d.
Christ in Song. 5s.
Craik (Mrs.) Little Sunshine's Holiday. 4s.
Craik (Miss) The Cousin from India. 4s.
Dana's Two Years before the Mast. 6s.
Erkman-Chatrian's, The Forest House. 3s. 6d.
Faith Gartney. 3s. 6d.; cloth boards, 1s. 6d.
Favourite English Poems. 300 Illustrations. 21s.
Franc's Emily's Choice. 5s.
—— Marian. 5s.
—— Silken Cord. 5s.
—— Vermont Vale. 5s.
—— Minnie's Mission. 4s.
Gayworthys (The). 3s. 6d.
Gentle Life, (Queen Edition). 10s. 6d.
Gentle Life Series. (*See* Alphabet).
Glover's Light of the Word. 2s. 6d.
Hayes (Dr.) Cast Away in the Cold. 6s.
Healy (Miss) The Home Theatre. 3s. 6d.
Henderson's Latin Proverbs. 10s. 6d.
Hugo's Toilers of the Sea. 10s. 6d.
,,   ,,   ,,   6s.
Kingston's Ben Burton. 3s. 6d.
Kennan's Tent Life. 6s.
Lyra Sacra Americana. 4s. 6d.
Macgregor (John) Rob Roy Books. (*See* Alphabet.)
Maury's Physical Geography of the Sea. 6s.
Parisian Family. 5s.
Phelps (Miss) The Silent Partner. 5s.
Stowe (Mrs.) Pink and White Tyranny. 3s. 6d.
—— Old Town Folks. Cloth extra 6s. and 2s. 6d.
—— Minister's Wooing. 5s.; boards, 1s. 6d.
—— Pearl of Orr's Island. 5s.

Books for School Prizes and Presents, *continued*.
    Tauchnitz's German Authors. (*See* Tauchnitz.)
    Twenty Years Ago. 4*s.*
    Under the Blue Sky. 7*s.* 6*d.*
    Whitney's (Mrs.) Books. (*See* Alphabet.)

Bowen (Francis) Principles of Political Economy. 8vo. 14*s.*

Bowles (T. G.) The Defence of Paris, narrated as it was Seen. 8vo. 14*s.*

Boynton (Charles B., D.D.) Navy of the United States, with Illustrations of the Ironclad Vessels. 8vo. 2 vols. 2*l.*

Bremer (Fredrika) Life, Letters, and Posthumous Works. Crown 8vo. 10*s.* 6*d.*

Brett (E.) Notes on Yachts. Fcp. 6*s.*

Broke (Admiral Sir B. V. P., Bart., K.C.B.) Biography of. 1*l.*

Browne (J. R. Adventures in the Apache Country. Post 8vo. 8*s.* 6*d.*

Burritt (E.) The Black Country and its Green Border Land : or, Expeditions and Explorations round Birmingham, Wolverhampton, &c. By ELIHU BURRITT. Second and cheaper edition. Post 8vo. 6*s.*

—— A Walk from London to John O'Groat's, and from London to the Land's End and Back. With Notes by the Way. By ELIHU BURRITT. Two vols. Price 6*s.* each, with Illustrations.

—— The Lectures and Speeches of Elihu Burritt. Fcp. 8vo. cloth, 6*s.*

Burroughs (John), *See* Wake Robin.

Bush (R. J.) Reindeer, Dogs, and Snow Shoes : a Journal of Siberian Travel. 8vo. 12*s.* 6*d.*

Bushnell's (Dr.) The Vicarious Sacrifice. Post 8vo. 7*s.* 6*d.*

—— Nature and the Supernatural. Post 8vo. 3*s.* 6*d.*

—— Christian Nurture. 3*s.* 6*d.*

—— Character of Jesus. 6*d.*

—— The New Life. Crown 8vo. 3*s.* 6*d.*

CHANGED Cross (The) and other Religious Poems, 2s. 6d.

Child's Play, with 16 coloured drawings by E. V. B. An entirely new edition, printed on thick paper, with tints, 7s. 6d.

Child (F. J.) English and Scotch Ballads. A new edition, revised by the editor. 8 vols. fcp. 1l. 8s.

Choice Editions of Choice Books. New Editions. Illustrated by C. W. Cope, R.A., T. Creswick, R.A., Edward Duncan, Birket Foster, J. C. Horsley, A.R.A., George Hicks, R. Redgrave, R.A., C. Stonehouse, F. Taylor, George Thomas, H. J. Townshend, E. H. Wehnert, Harrison Weir, &c. Crown 8vo. cloth, 5s. each ; mor. 10s. 6d.

Bloomfield's Farmer's Boy.	Keat's Eve of St. Agnes.
Campbell's Pleasures of Hope.	Milton's l'Allegro.
Cundall's Elizabethan Poetry.	Rogers' Pleasures of Memory.
Coleridge's Ancient Mariner.	Shakespeare's Songs and Sonnets.
Goldsmith's Deserted Village.	Tennyson's May Queen.
Goldsmith's Vicar of Wakefield.	Weir's Poetry of Nature.
Gray's Elegy in a Churchyard.	Wordsworth's Pastoral Poems.

Christ in Song. Hymns of Immanuel, selected from all Ages, with Notes. By PHILIP SCHAFF, D.D. Crown 8vo. toned paper, beautifully printed at the Chiswick Press. With Initial Letters and Ornaments and handsomely bound. New Edition. 5s.

Christabel. See Bayard Series.

Christmas Presents. See Illustrated Books.

Chronicles of Castle of Amelroy. 4to. With Photographic Illustrations. 2l. 2s.

Classified Catalogue of School, College, Technical, and General Educational Works in use in Great Britain, arranged according to subjects. In 1 vol. 8vo. 3s. 6d.

Coffin (G. C.) Our New Way Round the World. 8vo. 12s.

Coleridge (Sir J. D.) On Convents. 8vo. boards, 5s.

Commons Preservation (Prize Essays on), written in competition for Prizes offered by HENRY W. PEEK, Esq. 8vo. 14s.

Cradock Nowell. See Blackmore.

Craik (Mrs.), Little Sunshine's Holiday (forming Vol. 1. of the John Halifax Series of Girls' Books. Small post 8vo. 4s.

—— **(Georgiana M.) The Cousin from India,** forming Vol. 2. of John Halifax Series. Small post 8vo. 4s.

—— **Hero Trevelyan.** 2 Vols. Post 8vo. 21s.

Craik's American Millwright and Miller. With numerous Illustrations. 8vo. 1l. 1s.

Cronise (Titus F.) The Natural Wealth of California, comprising Early History, Geography, Climate, Commerce, Agriculture, Mines, Manufactures, Railroads, Statistics, &c. &c. Imp. 8vo. 1l. 5s.

Cummins (Maria S.) Haunted Hearts (Low's Copyright Series). 16mo. boards. 1s. 6d. ; cloth, 2s.

DALTON (J. C.) A Treatise on Physiology and Hygiene for Schools, Families, and Colleges, with numerous Illustrations. 7s. 6d.

Dana ( ) Two Years before the Mast and Twenty-four years After. New Edition, with Notes and Revisions. 12mo. 6s.

Darley (Felix O. C.) Sketches Abroad with Pen and Pencil, with 84 Illustrations on Wood. Small 4to. 7s. 6d.

Daughter (A) of Heth, by WM. BLACK. Seventh Edition. 3 vols. 1l. 11s. 6d.

Dawson (Professor) Archaia. Post 8vo. 6s.

Devonshire Hamlets; Hamlet 1603, Hamlet 1604. I Vol. 8vo. 7s. 6d.

Draper (John W.) Human Physiology. Illustrated with more than 300 Woodcuts from Photographs, &c. Royal 8vo. cloth extra. 1l. 5s.

Dream Book (The) with 12 Drawings in facsimile by E. V. B. Med. 4to. 1l. 11s. 6d.

Duplais and McKennie, Treatise on the Manufacture and Distillation of Alcoholic Liquors. With numerous Engravings. 8vo. 2l. 2s.

Duplessis (G.) Wonders of Engraving. With numerous Illustrations and Photographs. 8vo. 12s. 6d.

Dussauce (Professor H.) A New and Complete Treatise on the Art of Tanning. Royal 8vo. 1l. 10s.

———— **General Treatise on the Manufacture of Vinegar.** 8vo. 1l. 1s.

ENGLISH Catalogue (The), 1835 to 1863, Amalgamating the London and the British Catalogues. Med. 8vo. half-morocco. 2l. 5s.

———— **Supplements, 1863, 1864, 1865**, 3s. 6d. each; 1866, 1867, 1868, 5s. each.

———— **Writers**, Chapters for Self-improvement in English Literature; by the author of "The Gentle Life." 6s.

Erckmann-Chatrian, Forest House and Catherine's Lovers. Crown 8vo. 3s. 6d.

FAITH GARTNEY'S Girlhood, by the Author of "The Gayworthys." Fcap. with Coloured Frontispiece. 3s. 6d.

Favourite English Poems. New and Extended Edition, with 300 illustrations. Small 4to. 21s.

Few (A) Hints on Proving Wills. Enlarged Edition, sewed. 1s.

Fletcher (Rev. J. C.) and Kidder (Rev. D. P.) Brazil and the Brazilians. New Edition, with 150 Illustrations and supplementary matter. 8vo. 18s.

Franc (Maude Jeane) Emily's Choice, an Australian Tale. 1 vol. small post 8vo. With a Frontispiece by G. F. ANGAS. 5s.

—— Marian, or the Light of Some One's Home. Fcp. 3rd Edition, with Frontispiece. 5s.

—— Silken Cords and Iron Fetters. 5s.

—— Vermot Vale. Small post 4to., with Frontispiece. 5s.

—— Minnie's Mission. Small post 8vo., with Frontispiece. 4s.

Friswell (J. H.) Familiar Words, 2nd Edition. 6s.

—— Other People's Windows. Crown 8vo. 6s.

—— One of Two. 3 vols. 1l. 11s. 6d.

GAYWORTHYS (The), a Story of New England Life. Small post 8vo. 3s. 6d.

Gentle Life (Queen Edition). 2 vols. in 1. Small 4to. 10s. 6d.

THE GENTLE LIFE SERIES.
Printed in Elzevir, on Toned Paper, handsomely bound, forming suitable Volumes for Presents. Price 6s. each; or in calf extra, price 10s. 6d.

I.

The Gentle Life. Essays in aid of the Formation of Character of Gentlemen and Gentlewomen. Tenth Edition.

"His notion of a gentleman is of the noblest and truest order. A little compendium of cheerful philosophy."—*Daily News.*

"Deserves to be printed in letters of gold, and circulated in every house."—*Chambers' Journal.*

II.

About in the World. Essays by the Author of "The Gentle Life."

"It is not easy to open it at any page without finding some happy idea."—*Morning Post.*

III.

Like unto Christ. A New Translation of the "De Imitatione Christi" usually ascribed to Thomas à Kempis. With a Vignette from an Original Drawing by Sir Thomas Lawrence. Second Edition.

"Evinces independent scholarship, and a profound feeling for the original."—*Nonconformist.*

"Could not be presented in a more exquisite form, for a more sightly volume was never seen."—*Illustrated London News.*

IV.

Familiar Words. An Index Verborum, or Quotation Handbook. Affording an immediate Reference to Phrases and Sentences that have become embedded in the English language. Second and enlarged Edition.

"The most extensive dictionary of quotation we have met with."—*Notes and Queries.*

"Will add to the author's credit with all honest workers."—*Examiner.*

V.

Essays by Montaigne. Edited, Compared, Revised, and Annotated by the Author of "The Gentle Life." With Vignette Portrait. Second Edition.

"We should be glad if any words of ours could help to bespeak a large circulation for this handsome attractive book; and who can refuse his homage to the good-humoured industry of the editor."—*Illustrated Times.*

VI.

The Countess of Pembroke's Arcadia. Written by Sir PHILIP SIDNEY. Edited, with Notes, by the Author of "The Gentle Life." Dedicated, by permission, to the Earl of Derby. 7s. 6d.

"All the best things in the Arcadia are retained intact in Mr. Friswell's edition.—*Examiner.*

VII.

The Gentle Life. Second Series. Third Edition.

"There is not a single thought in the volume that does not contribute in some measure to the formation of a true gentleman."—*Daily News.*

VIII.

Varia: Readings from Rare Books. Reprinted, by permission, from the *Saturday Review, Spectator,* &c.

"The books discussed in this volume are no less valuable than they are rare, and the compiler is entitled to the gratitude of the public for having rendered their treasures available to the general reader."—*Observer.*

IX.

The Silent Hour: Essays, Original and Selected. By the Author of "The Gentle Life." Second Edition.

"All who possess the 'Gentle Life' should own this volume."—*Standard.*

X.

Essays on English writers, for the Self-improvement of Students in English Literature.

"The author has a distinct purpose and a proper and noble ambition to win the young to the pure and noble study of our glorious English literature. To all (both men and women) who have neglected to read and study their native literature we would certainly suggest the volume before us as a fitting introduction."—*Examiner.*

XI.

Other People's Windows. By J. HAIN FRISWELL. Second Edition.

"The chapters are so lively in themselves, so mingled with shrewd views of human nature, so full of illustrative anecdotes, that the reader cannot fail to be amused."—*Morning Post.*

German Primer; being an Introduction to First Steps in German. By M. T. PREW. 2s. 6d.

Girdlestone (C.) Christendom. 12mo. 3s.

———— **Family Prayers.** 12mo. 1s. 6d.

Glover (Rev. R.) The Light of the Word. Third Edition. 18mo. 2s. 6d.

Goethe's Faust. With Illustrations by Konewka. Small 4to. Price 10s. 6d.

Gouffé: The Royal Cookery Book. By JULES GOUFFÉ, Chef-de-Cuisine of the Paris Jockey Club; translated and adapted for English use by ALPHONSE GOUFFÉ, head pastrycook to Her Majesty the Queen. Illustrated with large plates, beautifully printed in colours, together with 161 woodcuts. 8vo. Coth extra, gilt edges. 2l. 2s.

———— Domestic Edition, half-bound. 10s. 6d.

"By far the ablest and most complete work on cookery that has ever been submitted to the gastronomical world."—*Pall Mall Gazette.*

———— **The Book of Preserves;** or, Receipts for Preparing and Preserving Meat, Fish salt and smoked, Terrines, Gelatines, Vegetables, Fruits, Confitures, Syrups, Liqueurs de Famille, Petits Fours, Bonbons, &c. &c. By JULES GOUFFE, Head Cook of the Paris Jockey Club, and translated and adapted by hi sbrother ALPHONSE GOUFFE, Head Pastrycook to her Majesty the Queen, translator and editor of "The Royal Cookery Book." 1 vol. royal 8vo., containing upwards of 500 Receipts and 34 Illustrations. 10s. 6d.

Gough (J. B.) The Autobiography and Reminiscences of John B. Gough. 8vo. Cloth, 12s.

Grant, General, Life of. 8vo. 12s.

Guizot's History of France. Translated by ROBERT BLACK. Royal 8vo. Numerous Illustrations. In Parts, 2s. each (to be completed in about twenty parts).

Guyon (Mad.) Life. By Upham. Third Edition. Crown 8vo. 7s. 6d.

—— Method of Prayer. Foolscap. 1s.

HALL (E. H.) The Great West; Handbook for Emigrants and Settlers in America. With a large Map of routes, railways, and steam communication, complete to present time. Boards, 1s.

Harrington (J.) Pictures of Saint George's Chapel, Windsor. Photographs. 4to. 63s.

Harrington's Abbey and Palace of Westminster. Photographs. 5l. 5s.

Harper's Handbook for Travellers in Europe and the East. New Edition. Post 8vo. Morocco tuck, 1l. 1s.

Hawthorne (Mrs. N.) Notes in England and Italy. Crown 8vo. 10s. 6d.

Hayes (Dr.) Cast Away in the Cold; an Old Man's Story of a Young Man's Adventures. By Dr. I. ISAAC HAYES, Author of "The Open Polar Sea." With numerous Illustrations. Gilt edges, 6s.

Hazlitt (William) The Round Table; the Best Essays of WILLIAM HAZLITT, with Biographical Introduction (Bayard Series). 2s. 6d.

Healy (M.) Shadow and Substance. A Novel. 3 Vols. 1l. 11s. 6d.

—— The Home Theatre. Small post 8vo. 3s. 6d.

Henderson (A.) Latin Proverbs and Quotations; with Translations and Parallel Passages, and a copious English Index. By ALFRED HENDERSON. Fcap. 4to., 530 pp. 10s. 6d.
   "A very handsome volume in its typographical externals, and a very useful companion to those who, when a quotation is aptly made, like to trace it to its source, to dwell on the minutiæ of its application, and to find it illustrated with choice parallel passages from English and Latin authors."—*Times*.
   "A book well worth adding to one's library."—*Saturday Review*.

Hearth Ghosts. By the Author of 'Gilbert Rugge.' 3 Vols. 1l. 11s. 6d.

Heber's (Bishop) Illustrated Edition of Hymns. With upwards of 100 Designs engraved in the first style of art under the superintendence of J. D. COOPER. Small 4to. Handsomely bound, 7s. 6d

Hitherto. By the Author of "The Gayworthys." New Edition. 6s.

Hoge—Blind Bartimæus. Popular edition. 1s.

Holmes (Oliver W.) The Guardian Angel; a Romance. 2 vols. 16s.

——— (Low's Copyright Series.) Boards, 1s. 6d.; cloth, 2s.

——— Autocrat of the Breakfast Table. 12mo. 1s.; Illustrated edition, 3s. 6d.

——— The Professor at the Breakfast Table. 3s. 6d.

——— Songs in Many Keys. Post 8vo. 7s. 6d.

——— Mechanism in Thought and Morals. 12mo. 1s. 6d.

Home Theatre (The), by MARY HEALY. Small post 8vo. 3s. 6d.

Homespun, or Twenty Five Years Ago in America, by THOMAS LACKLAND. Fcap. 8vo. 7s. 6d.

Hoppin (Jas. M.) Old Country, its Scenery, Art, and People. Post 8vo. 7s. 6d.

Howell (W. D.) Italian Journeys. 12mo. cloth. 8s. 6d.

Hugo's Toilers of the Sea. Crown 8vo. 6s.; fancy boards, 2s.; cloth, 2s. 6d.; Illustrated Edition, 10s. 6d.

Hunt (Leigh) and S. A. Lee, Elegant Sonnets, with Essay on Sonneteers. 2 vols. 8vo. 18s.

——— Day by the Fire. Fcap. 6s. 6d.

Huntington (J.D., D.D.) Christian Believing. Crown 8vo. 3s. 6d.

Hymnal Companion to Book of Common Prayer. *See* Bickersteth.

Ice, a Midsummer Night's Dream. Small Post 8vo. 3s. 6d.

ILLUSTRATED BOOKS, suitable for Christmas, Birthday, or Wedding Presents. (The full titles of which will be found in the Alphabet.)

Anderson's Fairy Tales. 25s.
Werner (Carl) Nile Sketches. 3l. 10s.
Gœthe's Faust illustrations by P. KONEWKA. 10s. 6d.

Illustrated Books, *continued*.
    Art, Pictorial and Industrial. Vol. I. 31*s*. 6*d*.
    St. George's Chapel, Windsor.
    Favourite English Poems. 21*s*.
    The Abbey and Palace of Westminster. 5*l*. 5*s*.
    Adventures of a Young Naturalist. 7*s*. 6*d*.
    Blackburn's Art in the Mountains. 12*s*.
    —— Artists and Arabs. 7*s*. 6*d*.
    —— Normandy Picturesque. 16*s*.
    —— Travelling in Spain. 16*s*.
    —— The Pyrenees. 18*s*.
    Bush's Reindeer, Dogs, &c. 12*s*. 6*d*.
    Duplessis' Wonders of Engraving. 12*s*. 6*d*.
    Viardot, Wonders of Sculpture. 12*s*. 6*d*.
    —— Wonders of Italian Art. 12*s*. 6*d*.
    —— Wonders of European Art. 12*s*. 6*d*.
    Sauzay's Wonders of Glass Making 12*s*. 6*d*.
    Fletcher and Kidder's Brazil. 18*s*.
    Gouffe's Royal Cookery Book. Coloured plates. 42*s*.
    —— Ditto.   Popular edition. 10*s*. 6*d*.
    —— Book of Preserves. 10*s*. 6*d*.
    Heber (Bishop) Hymns. Illustrated edition. 7*s*. 6*d*.
    Christian Lyrics.
    Milton's Paradise Lost. (Martin's plates). 3*l*. 13*s*. 6*d*.
    Palliser (Mrs.) History of Lace. 21*s*.
    —— Historic Devices, &c. 21*s*.
    Red Cross Knight (The). 25*s*.
    Dream Book, by E. V. B. 21*s*. 6*d*.
    Schiller's Lay of the Bell. 14*s*.
    Peaks and Valleys of the Alps. 6*l*. 6*s*.

Index to the Subjects of Books published in the United Kingdom during the last 20 years. 8vo. Half-morocco. 1*l*. 6*s*.

In the Tropics. Post 8vo. 6*s*.

JACK HAZARD, a Story of Adventure by J. T. TROWBRIDGE. Numerous illustrations, small post. 3*s*. 6*d*.

KAVANAGH'S Origin of Language. 2 vols. crown 8vo. 1*l*. 1*s*.

    Kedge Anchor, or Young Sailor's Assistant, by WM. BRADY. 8vo. 16*s*.

Kennan (G.) Tent Life in Siberia. 3rd edition. 6s.

"We strongly recommend the work as one of the most entertaining volumes of travel that has appeared of late years."—*Athenæum*.
"We hold our breath as he details some hair-breadth escape, and burst into fits of irresistible laughter over incidents full of humour.— *Spectator*.

—— **Journey through the Caucasian Mountains.** 8vo. cloth. [*In the press*.

Kent (Chancellor) Commentaries on American Law. 11th edition. 4 vols. 8vo. 4*l*. 10*s*.

Kilmeney, by WM. BLACK. 3 vols. 31*s*. 6*d*.

Kingston (W. H. G.) Ben Burton, or Born and Bred at Sea. Fcap. with Illustrations. 3*s*. 6*d*.

LANG (J. D.) The Coming Event. 8vo. 12*s*.

Lascelles (Arthur) The Coffee Grower's Guide. Post. 8vo. 2*s*. 6*d*.

Lee (G. R.) Memoirs of the American Revolutionary War. 8vo. 16*s*.

Like unto Christ. A new translation of the "De Imitatione Christi," usually ascribed to Thomas à Kempis. Second Edition. 6*s*.

Little Gerty, by the author of "The Lamplighter. Fcap. 6*d*.

Little Men. See Alcott.

Little Preacher. 32mo. 1*s*.

Little Women. See Alcott.

Little Sunshine's Holiday. *See* Craik (Mrs.)

Log of my Leisure Hours. By an Old Sailor. Cheaper Edition. 5*s*.

Longfellow (H. W.) The Poets and Poetry of Europe. New Edition. 8vo. cloth. 1*l*. 1*s*.

Loomis (Elias). Recent Progress of Astronomy. Post 8vo. 7*s*. 6*d*.

—— **Practical Astronomy.** 8vo. 8*s*.

Lorna Doone. *See* Blackmore.

Lost amid the Fogs: Sketches of Life in Newfoundland. By Lieut.-Col. R. B. McCREA. 8vo. 10*s*. 6*d*.

Low's Copyright Cheap Editions of American Authors, comprising Popular Works, reprinted by arrangement with their Authors :—

1. Haunted Hearts. By the Author of "The Lamplighter."
2. The Guardian Angel. By "The Autocrat of the Breakfast Table."
3. The Minister's Wooing. By the Author of "Uncle Tom's Cabin."
4. Views Afoot. By BAYARD TAYLOR.
5. Kathrina, Her Life and Mine. By J. G. HOLLAND.
6. Hans Brinker : or, Life in Holland. By Mrs. DODGE.
7. Men, Women, and Ghosts. By Miss PHELPS.
8. Society and Solitude. By RALPH WALDO EMERSON.
9. Hedged In. By ELIZABETH PHELPS.
10. An Old-Fashioned Girl. By LOUISA M. ALCOTT.
11. Faith Gartney.
12. Stowe's Old Town Folks. 2s. 6d.; cloth, 3s.
13. Lowell's Study Windows.
14. My Summer in a Garden. By CHARLES DUDLEY WARNER.

Each volume complete in itself, price 1s. 6d. enamelled flexible cover ; 2s. cloth.

Low's Monthly Bulletin of American and Foreign Publi-cations, forwarded regularly. Subscription 2s. 6d. per annum.

Low's Minion Series of Popular Books. 1s. each :—

The Gates Ajar. (The original English Edition.)
Who is He?
The Little Preacher.
The Boy Missionary.

Low (Sampson, Jun.) The Charities of London. A Guide to 750 Institutions. New Edition. 5s.

——— **Handbook to the Charities of London,** for the year 1867. 1s. 6d.

Ludlow (FitzHugh). The Heart of the Continent. 8vo. cloth. 14s.

Lyra Sacra Americana. Gems of American Poetry, selected and arranged, with Notes and Biographical Sketches, by C. D. CLEVE-LAND, D. D., author of the "Milton Concordance." 18mo. 4s. 6d.

MACGREGOR (John, M. A.) "Rob Roy" on the Baltic. Third Edition, small post, 8vo. 5s.

——— **A Thousand Miles in the "Rob Roy"** Canoe. Eleventh Edition. Small post, 8vo. 2s. 6d.

——— **Description of the "Rob Roy" Canoe,** with plans, &c. 1s.

Macgregor (John M. A.) The Voyage Alone in the Yawl "Rob Roy." Second Edition. Small post, 8vo. 5s.

Mackay (Dr.) Under the Blue Sky. Open-air Studies of Men and Nature. Crown 8vo. Cloth extra. 7s. 6d.

March (A.) Anglo-Saxon Reader. 8vo. 7s. 6d.

—— Comparative Grammar of the Anglo-Saxon Language. 8vo. 8s. 6d.

Marcy, (R. B.) Thirty Years of Army Life. Royal 8vo. 12s.

—— Prairie and Overland Traveller. 2s. 6d.

Marsh (George P.) Man and Nature. 8vo. 14s.

—— Origin and History of the English Language. 8vo. 16s.

—— Lectures on the English Language. 8vo. 16s.

Maury (Commander) Physical Geography of the Sea and its Meteorology. Being a Reconstruction and Enlargement of his former Work; with illustrative Charts and Diagrams. New Edition Crown 8vo. 6s.

McCrea (Col.) Lost amid the Fogs. 8vo. 10s. 6d.

Queer Things of the Service. [*In the press.*

McMullen's History of Canada. 8vo. 6s.

Mercier (Rev. L.) Outlines of the Life of the Lord Jesus Christ. 2 vols. crown 8vo. 15s.

Milton's Complete Poetical Works; with Concordance by W. D. CLEVELAND. New Edition. 8vo. 12s.; morocco 1l. 1s.

—— Paradise Lost, with the original Steel Engravings of JOHN MARTIN. Printed on large paper, royal 4to. handsomely bound. 3l. 13s. 6d.

Missionary Geography (The); a Manual of Missionary Operations in all parts of the World, with Map and Illustrations. Fcap. 3s. 6d.

Monk of Monk's Own. 3 vols. 31s. 6d.

Montaigne's Essays. *See* Gentle Life Series.

Mountain (Bishop) Life of. By his Son. 8vo. 10s. 6d.

My Summer in a Garden. See Warner.

NEW Testament. The Authorized English Version; with the various Readings from the most celebrated Manuscripts, including the Sinaitic, the Vatican, and the Alexandrian MSS., in English. With Notes by the Editor, Dr. TISCHENDORF. The whole revised and carefully collected for the Thousandth Volume of Baron Tauchnitz's Collection. Cloth flexible, gilt edges, 2s. 6d.; cheaper style, 2s.; or sewed, 1s. 6d.

Norris (T.) American Fish Culture. 6s. 6d.

Nothing to Wear, and Two Millions. By WILLIAM ALLEN BUTLER. 1s.

OLD Fashioned Girl. See Alcott.

Our Little Ones in Heaven. Edited by Rev. H. ROBBINS. With Frontispiece after Sir JOSHUA REYNOLDS. Second Edition. Fcap. 3s. 6d.

PALLISER (Mrs.) A History of Lace, from the Earliest Period. A New and Revised Edition, with upwards of 100 Illustrations and coloured Designs. 1 vol. 8vo. 1l. 1s.

"One of the most readable books of the season; permanently valuable, always interesting, often amusing, and not inferior in all the essentials of a gift book."—*Times.*

——— **Historic Devices, Badges, and War Cries.** 8vo. 1l. 1s.

Parsons (T.) A Treatise on the Law of Marine Insurance and General Average. By Hon. THEOPHILUS PARSONS. 2 vols. 8vo 3l.

Parisian Family. From the French of Madame GUIZOT DE WITT; by Author of "John Halifax." Fcap. 5s.

"The feeling of the story is so good, the characters are so clearly marked, there is such freshness and truth to nature in the simple incidents recorded, that we have been allured on from page to page without the least wish to avail ourselves of a privilege permitted sometimes to the reviewer, and to skip a portion of the narrative."—*Pall Mall Gazette.*

Parton (J.) Smoking and Drinking. 3s. 6d.

Peaks and Valleys of the Alps. From Water-Colour Drawings by ELIJAH WALTON. Chromo-lithographed by J. H. LOWES, with Descriptive Text by the Rev. T. G. BONNEY, M.A., F.G.S. Folio, half-morocco, with 21 large Plates. Original subscription, 8 guineas. A very limited edition only now issued. Price 6 guineas.

Phelps (Miss) Gates Ajar. 32mo. 1*s.*; 6*d.*; 4*d.*

——— Men, Women, and Ghosts. 12mo. Sewed, 1*s.* 6*d.* cloth, 2*s.*

——— Hedged In. 12mo. Sewed, 1*s.* 6*d.*; cloth, 2*s.*

——— Silent Partner. 5*s.*

Phillips (L.) Dictionary of Biographical Reference. 8vo. 1*l.* 11*s.* 6*d.*

Plutarch's Lives. An Entirely New and Library Edition. Edited by A. H. CLOUGH, Esq. 5 vols. 8vo. 3*l.* 3*s.*
"'Plutarch's Lives' will yet be read by thousands, and in the version of Mr. Clough."—*Quarterly Review.*
"Mr. Clough's work is worthy of all praise, and we hope that it will tend to revive the study of Plutarch."—*Times.*

——— Morals. Uniform with Clough's Edition of "Lives of Plutarch." Edited by Professor GOODWIN. 5 vols. 8vo. 3*l.* 3*s.*

Poe (E. A.) The Poetical Works of. Illustrated by eminent Artists. An entirely New Edition. Small 4to. 10*s.* 6*d.*

Poems of the Inner Life. Post 8vo. 8*s.*; morocco, 10*s.* 6*d.*

Poor (H. V.) Manual of the Railroads of the United States for 1868-9; Showing their Mileage, Stocks, Bonds, Cost, Earnings, Expenses, and Organisations, with a Sketch of their Rise, &c. 1 vol. 8vo. 16*s.*

Portraits of Celebrated Women. By C. A. ST. BEUVE. 12mo. 6*s.* 6*d.*

Publishers' Circular (The), and General Record of British and Foreign Literature; giving a transcript of the title-page of every work published in Great Britain, and every work of interest published abroad, with lists of all the publishing houses
Published regularly on the 1st and 15th of every Month, and forwarded post free to all parts of the world on payment of 8*s.* per annum.

RASSELAS, Prince of Abyssinia. By Dr. JOHNSON. With Introduction by the Rev. WILLIAM WEST, Vicar of Nairn. (Bayard Series). 2*s.* 6*d.*

Recamier (Madame) Memoirs and Correspondence of. Translated from the French, and Edited by J. M. LUYSTER. With Portrait. Crown 8vo. 7*s.* 6*d.*

Red Cross Knight (The). *See* Spenser.

Reid (W.) After the War. Crown 8vo. 10*s.* 6*d.*

Reindeer, Dogs, &c. *See* Bush

Reminiscences of America in 1869, by Two Englishmen. Crown 8vo 7s 6d

Rogers (S.) Pleasures of Memory. See " Choice Editions of Choice Books " 5s

SAUZAY, (A) Marvels of Glass Making Numerous illustrations Demy 8vo 12s 6d

Schiller's Lay of the Bell, translated by Lord Lytton With 42 illustrations after Retsch Oblong 4to 14s

School Books. *See* Classified.

School Prizes. *See* Books.

Seaman (Ezra C) Essays on the Progress of Nations in civilization, productive history, wealth, and population , illustrated by statistics. Post 8vo 10s 6d

Sedgwick, (J.) Treatise on the Measure of Damages. 8vo. 1l 18s

Shadow and Substance. 3 vols 31s 6d. *See* Healy (M).

Shakespeare's Songs and Sonnets, selected by J HOWARD STAUNTON , with 36 exquisite drawings by JOHN GILBERT See " Choice Series " 5s

Sheridan's Troopers on the Borders. Post 8vo. 7s 6d

Sidney (Sir Philip) The Countess of Pembroke's Arcadia, edited, with notes, by the author of "Gentle Life," 7s 6d Large paper edition 12s

Silent Hour (The), Essays original and selected, by the author of "The Gentle Life" Second edition. 6s

Silent Partner. *See* Phelps.

Silliman (Benjamin) Life of, by G. P. FISHER 2 vols. crown 8vo 1l 4s

Simson (W) A History of the Gipsies, with specimens of the Gipsy Language 10s 6d

Smiley (S. F.) Who is He ? 32mo. 1s.

Smith and Hamilton's French Dictionary. 2 vols. Cloth, 21s. , half roan, 22s

Snow Flakes, and what they told the Children, beautifully printed in colours. Cloth extra, bevelled boards. 5s.

Spayth (Henry) The American Draught-Player. 2nd edition. 12mo. 8s.

Spenser's Red Cross Knight, illustrated with 12 original drawings in facsimile. 4to. 1l. 5s.

Steele (Thos.) Under the Palms. A Volume of Verse. By THOMAS STEELE, translator of "An Eastern Love Story." Fcap. 8vo. Cloth, 5s.

Stewart (D.) Outlines of Moral Philosophy, by Dr. McCosh. New edition. 12mo. 3s. 6d.

Stories of the Great Prairies, from the Novels of J. F. COOPER. With numerous illustrations. 5s.

Stories of the Woods, from J. F. COOPER. 5s.

———— Sea, from J. F. COOPER. 5s.

St. George's Chapel, Windsor, or 18 Photographs with descriptive Letterpress, by JOHN HARRINGTON. Imp. 4to.

Story without an End, from the German of Carové, by the late Mrs. SARAH T. AUSTIN, crown 4to. with 15 exquisite drawings by E. V. B., printed in colours in facsimile of the original water colours, and numerous other illustrations. 12s.; morocco, 1l. 1s.

———— square, with illustrations by HARVEY. 2s. 6d.

———— of the Great March, a Diary of General Sherman's Campaign through Georgia and the Carolinas. Numerous illustrations. 12mo. cloth, 7s. 6d.

Stowe (Mrs. Beecher). Dred. Tauchnitz edition. 12mo. 3s. 6d.

———— Geography, with 60 illustrations. Square cloth, 4s. 6d.

———— House and Home Papers. 12mo. boards, 1s.; cloth extra, 2s. 6d.

———— Little Foxes. Cheap edition, 1s.; library edition, 4s. 6d.

———— Men of our Times, with portrait. 8vo. 12s. 6d.

———— Minister's Wooing. 5s.; copyright series, 1s. 6d.; cloth, 2s.

———— Old Town Folk. 2s. 6d.

"This story must make its way, as it is easy to predict it will, by its intrinsic merits."—*Times.*

"A novel of great power and beauty, and something more than a mere novel—we mean that it is worth thoughtful people's reading. . . It is a finished literary work, and will well repay the reading."—*Literary Churchman.*

Stowe (Mrs. Beecher) Pink and White Tyranny. Small post 8vo. 3*s*. 6*d*.

────── Queer Little People. 1*s*. ; cloth, 2*s*.

────── Religious Poems ; with illustrations. 3*s*. 6*d*.

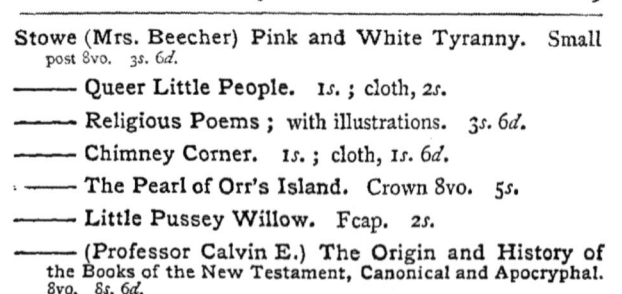

────── Chimney Corner. 1*s*. ; cloth, 1*s*. 6*d*.

────── The Pearl of Orr's Island. Crown 8vo. 5*s*.

────── Little Pussey Willow. Fcap. 2*s*.

────── (Professor Calvin E.) The Origin and History of the Books of the New Testament, Canonical and Apocryphal. 8vo. 8*s*. 6*d*.

STORY'S (JUSTICE) WORKS:

Commentaries on the Law of Agency, as a Branch of Commercial and Maritime Jurisprudence. 6th Edition. 8vo. 1*l*. 11*s*. 6*d*.

Commentaries on the Law of Bailments. 7th Edition. 8vo. 1*l*. 11*s*. 6*d*.

Commentaries on the Law of Bills of Exchange, Foreign and Inland, as administered in England and America. 4th Edition. 8vo. 1*l*. 11*s*. 6*d*.

Commentaries on the Conflict of Laws, Foreign and Domestic, in regard to Contracts, Rights, and Remedies, and especially in regard to Marriages, Divorces, Wills, Successions, and Judgments. 6th Edition. 8vo. 1*l*. 12*s*.

Commentaries on the Constitution of the United States; with a Preliminary Review of the Constitutional History of the Colonies and States before the adoption of the Constitution. 3rd Edition. 2 vols. 8vo. 2*l*. 2*s*.

Commentaries on the Law of Partnership as a branch of Commercial and Maritime Jurisprudence. 6th Edition by E. H. BENNETT. 8vo. 1*l*. 11*s*. 6*d*.

Commentaries on the Law of Promissory Notes, and Guarantees of Notes and Cheques on Banks and Bankers. 6th Edition ; by E. H. BENNETT. 8vo. 1*l*. 11*s*. 6*d*.

Treatise on the Law of Contracts. By WILLIAM W. STORY. 4th Edition, 2 vols. 8vo. 3*l*. 3*s*.

Treatise on the Law of Sales of Personal Property. 3rd Edition, edited by Hon. J. C. PERKINS. 8vo. 1*l*. 11*s*. 6*d*.

Commentaries on Equity Pleadings and the Incidents relating thereto, according to the Practice of the Courts of Equity of England and America. 7th Edition. 8vo. 1*l*. 11*s*. 6*d*.

Commentaries on Equity Jurisprudence as administered in England and America. 9th Edition. 3*l*. 3*s*.

Suburban Sketches, by the Author of "Venetian Life." Post 8vo. 6s.

Summer in Leslie Goldthwaite's Life, by the Author of "The Gayworthys," Illustrations. Fcap. 8vo. 3s. 6d.

Swiss Family Robinson, 12mo. 3s. 6d.

TAUCHNITZ'S English Editions of German Authors. Each volume cloth flexible, 2s.; or sewed, 1s. 6d. The following are now ready:—

1. On the Heights. By B. AUERBACH. 3 vols.
2. In the Year '13. By FRITZ REUTER. 1 vol.
3. Faust. By GOETHE. 1 vol.
4. Undine, and other Tales. By Fouqué. 1 vol.
5. L'Arrabiata. By PAUL HEYSE. 1 vol.
6. The Princess, and other Tales. By HEINRICH ZSCHOKKE. 1 vol.
7. Lessing's Nathan the Wise.
8. Hacklander's Behind the Counter, translated by MARY HOWITT.
9. Three Tales. By W. HAUFF.
10. Joachim v. Kamern; Diary of a Poor Young Lady. By M. NATHUSIUS.
11. Poems by Ferdinand Freiligrath. Edited by his daughter.
12. Gabriel. From the German of PAUL HEYSE. By ARTHUR MILMAN.
13. The Dead Lake, and other Tales. By P. HEYSE.
14. Through Night to Light. By GUTZKOW.
15. Flower, Fruit, and Thorn Pieces. By JEAN PAUL RICHTER.

Tauchnitz (B.) German and English Dictionary, Paper, 1s.: cloth, 1s. 6d.; roan, 2s.

——————— French and English. Paper 1s. 6d.; cloth, 2s.; roan, 2s. 6d.

——————— Italian and English. Paper, 1s. 6d.; cloth, 2s.; roan, 2s. 6d.

——————— Spanish and English. Paper, 1s. 6d.; cloth, 2s.; roan, 2s. 6d.

—————— New Testament. Cloth, 2s.; gilt, 2s. 6d. *See* New Testament.

Taylor (Bayard) The Byeways of Europe; Visits by Unfrequented Routes to Remarkable Places. By BAYARD TAYLOR, author of "Views Afoot." 2 vols. post 8vo. 16s.

—————— Story of Kennett. 2 vols. 16s.

—————— Hannah Thurston. 3 vols. 1l. 4s.

—————— Travels in Greece and Russia. Post 8vo. 7s. 6d.

—————— Northern Europe. Post 8vo. Cloth, 8s. 6d.

List of Publications. 31

Taylor (Bayard). Egypt and Central Africa.
—— A Summer in Colorado. Post 8vo 7s 6d.
—— Joseph and his Friend. Post 8vo. 10s. 6d.
—— Views Afoot. Enamelled boards, 1s. 6d ; cloth, 2s. *See* Low's Copyright Edition

Tennyson's May Queen ; choicely Illustrated from designs by the Hon Mrs Boyle Crown 8vo See "Choice Series" 5s

Thomson (W M) The Land and the Book. With 300 Illustrations 2 vols 1l 1s

Tischendorf (Dr) The New Testament. *See* New Testament

Townsend (John) A Treatise on the Wrongs called Slander and Libel, and on the remedy, by civil action, for these wrongs 8vo 1l 10s

Twenty Years Ago (Forming Volume 3 of the John Halifax Series of Girls' Books) Small post 8vo 4s

Twining (Miss) Illustrations of the Natural Orders of Plants, with Groups and Descriptions By ELIZABETH TWINING Reduced from the folio edition, splendidly illustrated in colours from nature 2 vols Royal 8vo 5l 5s

UNDER the Blue Sky. *See* Mackay.
Under the Palms *See* Steele.

VANDENHOFF'S (George), Clerical Assistant. Fcap 3s 6d
—— Ladies' Reader (The). Fcap. 5s.

Varia, Rare Readings from Scarce Books, by the author of "The Gentle Life" Reprinted by permission from the "Saturday Review," "Spectator," &c 6s

Vaux (Calvert). Villas and Cottages, a new edition, with 300 designs 8vo 15s

Viardot (L) Wonders of Italian Art, numerous photographic and other illustrations Demy 8vo 12s 6d

—— Wonders of Painting, numerous photographs and other illustrations Demy 8vo 12s 6d.

—— Wonders of Sculpture. Numerous Illustrations Demy 8vo 12s 6d

WAKE ROBIN; a Book about Birds, by JOHN BURROUGHS. Crown 8vo. 5*s.*

Warner (C. D.) My Summer in a Garden. Boards, 1*s.* 6*d.*; cloth, 2*s.* (Low's Copyright Series.)

We Girls; a Home Story, by the author of "Gayworthys." 3*s.* 6*d.*

Webster (Daniel) Life of, by GEO. T. CURTIS. 2 vols. 8vo. Cloth. 36*s.*

Werner (Carl), Nile Sketches, 6 Views, with Letterpress In Portfolio, Imperial Folio. 3*l.* 10*s.*

Wheaton (Henry) Elements of International Law, edited by DANA. New edition. Imp. 8vo. 1*l.* 10*s.*

Where is the City? 12mo. cloth. 6*s.*

White (J.) Sketches from America. 8vo. 12*s.*

White (R. G.) Memoirs of the Life of William Shakespeare. Post 8vo. Cloth. 10*s.* 6*d.*

Whitney (Mrs.), The Gayworthys. Small post 8vo. 3*s.* 6*d.*

—— **Faith Gartney.** Small post 8vo. 3*s.* 6*d.* And in Low's Cheap Series, 1*s.* 6*d.* and 2*s.*

—— **Hitherto.** Small post 8vo. 6*s.*

—— **Summer in Leslie Goldthwaite's Life.** 'Small post 8vo. 3*s.* 6*d.*

—— **We Girls.** Small post 8vo. 3*s.* 6*d.*

Whyte (J. W. H.) A Land Journey from Asia to Europe. Crown 8vo. 10*s.* 6*d.*

Wonders of Sculpture. *See* Viardot.

Worcester's (Dr.), New and Greatly Enlarged Dictionary of the English Language. Adapted for Library or College Reference, comprising 40,000 Words more than Johnson's Dictionary. 4to. cloth, 1,834 pp. Price 31*s.* 6*d.* well bound; ditto, half russia, 2*l.* 2*s.*

"The volumes before us show a vast amount of diligence; but with Webster it is diligence in combination with fancifulness,—with Worcester in combination with good sense and judgment. Worcester's is the soberer and safer book, and may be pronounced the best existing English Lexicon."—*Athenæum.*

Words of Wellington, Maxims and Opinions, Sentences and Reflections of the Great Duke, gathered from his Despatches, Letters, and Speeches (Bayard Series). 2*s.* 6*d.*

14 DAY USE
RETURN TO DESK FROM WHICH BORROWED

LOAN DEPT.

This book is due on the last date stamped below, or on the date to which renewed.
Renewed books are subject to immediate recall.

LIBRARY USE	
FEB 17 1960	
30Apr'62DC	
REC'D LD MAY 3 1962	
JUN 7 '62 A	
REC'D LD MAY 27 1962	

LD 21A-50m-4,'59
(A1724s10)476B

General Library
University of California
Berkeley

492950

UNIVERSITY OF CALIFORNIA LIBRARY

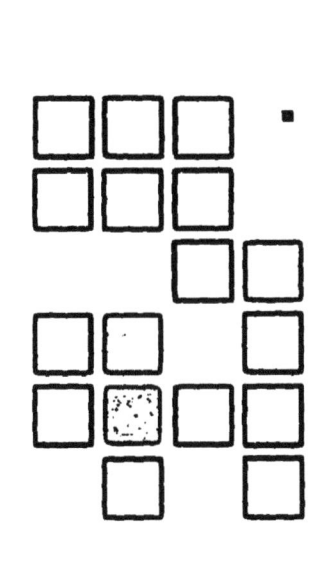

Lightning Source UK Ltd.
Milton Keynes UK
UKHW020813250221
379343UK00003B/172